Power in the Global Era

Grounding Globalization

Edited by

Theodore H. Cohn
Professor
Department of Political Science
Simon Fraser University
Burnaby
Canada

Stephen McBride
Professor
Department of Political Science
Simon Fraser University
Burnaby
Canada

and

John Wiseman
Associate Professor
School of Social Science and Planning
RMIT University
Melbourne
Australia

HD
2755.5
.P68
2000

First published in Great Britain 2000 by
MACMILLAN PRESS LTD
Houndmills, Basingstoke, Hampshire RG21 6XS and London
Companies and representatives throughout the world

A catalogue record for this book is available from the British Library.

ISBN 0–333–77884–7

First published in the United States of America 2000 by
ST. MARTIN'S PRESS, LLC,
Scholarly and Reference Division,
175 Fifth Avenue, New York, N.Y. 10010

ISBN 0–312–23562–3

Library of Congress Cataloging-in-Publication Data
Power in the global era : grounding globalization / edited by Theodore H. Cohn,
Stephen McBride, and John Wiseman.
    p.   cm.
    Includes bibliographical references and index.
    ISBN 0–312–23562–3
    1. International business enterprises—Congresses. 2. Globalization–
–Congresses. I. Cohn, Theodore H., 1940– II. McBride, Stephen, 1947– III.
Wiseman, John Richard, 1957–

    HD2755.5 .P68 2000
    338.8'8—dc21
                                                                    00–033300

This book is printed on paper suitable for recycling and made from fully managed and sustained
forest sources.

10   9   8   7   6   5   4   3   2   1
09   08   07   06   05   04   03   02   01   00

Printed and bound in Great Britain by
Antony Rowe Ltd, Chippenham, Wiltshire

Power in the Global Era

Also by Theodore H. Cohn

GLOBAL POLITICAL ECONOMY: Theory and Practice

THE INTERNATIONAL POLITICS OF AGRICULTURAL TRADE:
Canadian–American Relations in a Global Agricultural Context

CANADIAN FOOD AID: Domestic and Foreign Policy Implications

INNOVATION SYSTEMS IN A GLOBAL CONTEXT: The North American
Experience (*co-editor with R. Anderson, J. Day, M. Howlett and C. Murray*)

Also by Stephen McBride

DISMANTLING A NATION: The Transition to Corporate Rule (*with John Shields*)

TRAINING TRAP: Ideology, Training and the Labour Market (*co-editor with
T. Dunk and R. Nelsen*)

CONTINUITIES AND DISCONTINUITIES: The Political Economy of Social
Welfare and Labour Market Policy in Canada (*co-editor with A. F. Johnson and
P. J. Smith*)

NOT WORKING: State, Unemployment and Neo-conservatism in Canada

Also by John Wiseman

GLOBAL NATION: Australia and the Politics of Globalisation

ALTERNATIVES TO GLOBALISATION: An Asia-Pacific Perspective (*editor*)

MAKING SOCIAL POLICY IN AUSTRALIA: An Introduction (*with T. Dalton,
M. Draper and W. Weeks*)

Contents

Notes on Contributors

Isabella Bakker teaches Political Economy at York University, Toronto, Canada. She has written extensively on issues of gender and macro-economics, restructuring, development and neoliberalism. She is the editor of *The Strategic Silence: Gender and Economic Policy* and *Rethinking Restructuring: Gender and Change in Canada*.

David N. Balaam is professor of Politics and Government and International Political Economy at the University of Puget Sound in Tacoma, Washington, USA. He has published a book and numerous articles on food politics and hunger issues. He also co-authored with Michael Veseth, *Introduction to International Political Economy* (1996).

Steven Bernstein is an assistant professor in the Department of Political Science, University of Toronto. His forthcoming book, *The Compromise of Liberal Environmentalism*, examines the evolution of global environmental norms. He is currently working on a project on institutionalization and change in world politics.

Benjamin Cashore is Assistant Professor, forest policy and economics, in the School of Forestry at Auburn University. Dr Cashore has published widely on Canada/US sustainable forestry issues. He is currently engaged in a cross-country study that examines the international and domestic sources of forest certification (green labeling) programs.

Theodore H. Cohn is Professor in the Department of Political Science at Simon Fraser University. His books include *The International Politics of Agricultural Trade* (1990) and *Global Political Economy: Theory and Practice* (2000).

Claire Cutler is an Associate Professor in the Political Science Department at the University of Victoria, British Columbia, Canada where she teaches International Law and Organization and International Relations Theory. She is interested in developing a critical understanding of international commercial law. She has published numerous articles on this topic and co-edited *Private Authority and International Affairs* (1999).

Laurent Dobuzinskis teaches Political Science at Simon Fraser University; he specializes in policy studies, classical political economy and modern normative economics. He has published or edited books and articles on public administration and policy analysis, the role of think-tanks in policy debates, and the philosophy of the social sciences.

James Goodman has been active in a number of the campaigns discussed in his chapter. He is a post-doctoral researcher at the University of Technology, Sydney. Books include *Nationalism and Transnationalism* (1996), *Dis/Agreeing Ireland* (co-editor, 1998), *Corporate Power and Globalisation* (co-editor, 1999), and *Protest and Globalisation* (editor, 1999).

Luc Juillet teaches governance and environmental politics in the Department of Political Science and is a fellow at the Centre on Governance of the University of Ottawa. His recent publications include 'Sustainable Agriculture and Global Trade: Emerging Institutions and Mixed Incentives', with F. Scala and J. Roy, in *Society and Natural Resources* (10, no. 3, 1997).

Christopher Leo is Professor of Political Science at the University of Winnipeg and Adjunct Professor of City Planning at the University of Manitoba. Recent articles have appeared, among other publications, in the *International Journal of Urban and Regional Research, Journal of Urban Affairs, Urban Affairs Review,* and *World Transport Policy and Practice.*

Carla Lipsig-Mummé is Professor and Director of the Centre for Research on Work and Society at York University. She received her doctorate from the Université de Montréal, and has taught at Queen's University and Université Laval. She has been a union staffer in education, agriculture and garment production, and a consultant to unions in Quebec, English Canada and Australia.

Stephen McBride is Professor and Chair of Political Science at Simon Fraser University. He has published widely on comparative political economy and public policy. His books include *Not Working: State, Unemployment and Neo-conservatism in Canada*, which won the 1994 Smiley Prize, and (co-author) *Dismantling a Nation.*

Andrew Molloy is an Assistant Professor in the Department of Politics, Government and Public Administration at the University College of Cape Breton, Sydney, Nova Scotia. Areas of research and publication include labour markets, political parties, Quebec politics, environmental public policy, taxation, public sector restructuring and local and urban government and development.

Kenneth Shadlen is a Visiting Assistant Professor of Political Science and Latin American Studies at Brown University. His work appears in *Government and Opposition* and *Latin American Research Review*, and he is currently completing a book manuscript on small business politics in Latin America.

John Shields is a Professor in the Department of Politics and School of Public Administration and a Senior Researcher with the Ryerson Social Reporting Network at Ryerson Polytechnic University in Toronto, Canada. He has published widely on labour market policy, neo-liberalism and welfare state restructuring in Canada. His two most recent co-authored books are *Dismantling a Nation: the Transition to Corporate Rule in Canada* (1997) and *Shrinking the State: Globalization and Public Administration 'Reform'* (1998).

Patrick J. Smith is a Professor in, and past Chair of, the Department of Political Science, Simon Fraser University; Director, Institute of Governance Studies, Simon Fraser. He has co-authored *The Vision and the Game: Making the Canadian Constitution* (1987), *The Almanac of Canadian Politics*, 2nd edn (1995) and *Ties That Bind: Voters and Parties in Canada* (1999).

José M. Vadi is Professor of Political Science specializing in Latin America and comparative politics at the California State Polytechnic University at Pomona. His current research interest is in economic globalization, its impact on states, and the political opposition to which it gives rise. He has published a study of these issues covering Argentina in the Menem era as part of a larger work on globalization, political opposition, and the state in Latin America.

John Wiseman is Associate Professor in the School of Social Science and Planning, RMIT University, Melbourne, Australia. His most recent publication is *Global Nation? Australia and the Politics of Globalisation* (1998).

Preface

The contributions to this book were originally presented at a conference on 'Globalization and Its Discontents' held at Simon Fraser University in Vancouver in July 1998. The conference was jointly sponsored by the Department of Political Science at Simon Fraser University and the Department of Social Science and Planning at RMIT University, Melbourne. Since then the original papers have been reviewed and extensively revised. None the less, it would be remiss of us not to acknowledge their origins in a highly successful conference that was the occasion of spirited debate and discussion that will have left as much of an imprint on the revised versions as the formal review process.

Accordingly we would like to thank those who made possible the conference and an associated series of research workshops designed to facilitate international collaborative research. The Vancouver organizing and program committee consisted of Jeannette Ashe, James Busumtwi-Sam, Marjorie Griffin Cohen, Ted Cohn, Kevin Ginnell, Michael Howlett, Stephen McBride, Gerardo Otero and Russell Williams. A magnificent poster for the conference was designed by Juan Sanchez and produced by Nora Patrich. Alan Whitehorn provided enthusiastic support for the project and was especially helpful with the poster and fund-raising. Financial support was received from the Boag Foundation, the Social Science and Humanities Research Council of Canada, the Offices of the President (Jack Blaney), Vice-President Academic (David Gagan), and Dean of Arts (John Pierce) at Simon Fraser University and, specifically in connection with the research linkage workshops that were held following the conference, from the Program for International Research Linkages of the International Council of Canadian Studies. Jack Blaney, President of Simon Fraser University, was kind enough to present the opening address to the conference. Our thanks to all. But our biggest thank you should go to two staff members from Simon Fraser's Department of Political Science, Joanne Harrington and Sherry Lloyd, whose efficiency and grace under pressure made organizing and running a complex event seem effortless. In Sherry's case, we would also like to thank her for secretarial assistance in preparing this volume, and its companion, 'Globalization and Its Discontents', for publication.

Finally, we would like to thank our initial commissioning editor at Macmillan, Sunder Katwala, and his successor, Alison Howson, for their assistance.

Introduction

Theodore H. Cohn, Stephen McBride and John Wiseman

The literature on globalization has increased exponentially in the 1990s, but the concept is inadequately defined. Although most would agree that globalization involves the broadening and deepening of interactions and interdependence among societies and states throughout the world, there is considerable controversy over the causes and effects of globalization, and even over the importance of globalization in today's world. (Chapters 1 and 2 in this volume, by Dobuzinskis and Bakker, outline some of the competing perspectives on globalization.) Some analysts argue that globalization is not unique to the present-day period, and that in some respects there was a higher degree of interdependence in trade and foreign investment before the First World War. This interdependence was eroded during the interwar period, and only after the Second World War did global economic ties again begin to increase. Nevertheless, one could argue that with advances in technology, communications and transportation, globalization is more encompassing today than it was at any time in the past; the capitalist economic system for the first time covers the entire globe. The authors in this volume generally adopt this latter point of view; for example, Wiseman argues that 'it is truer than ever that local and national struggles between labour and capital are fought on a global stage.'

Some extreme globalizers claim that we are entering a 'borderless world' in which transnational corporations (TNCs) are losing their national identities, and distinct national economies are being subsumed under the global marketplace. Politically, extreme globalizers sometimes suggest that globalization is leading to some sort of world society or world government. The authors in this volume, by contrast, view globalization as leading to fragmentation and conflict as well as to unity and cooperation. Central to most of the chapters is a discussion of changing

1

power relationships between TNCs, transnational capital, the state, sub-national governments, labour, and social action groups.

A number of the chapters focus on the increased power of TNCs and transnational capital in our globalizing world. Thus, Goodman asserts that globalization reveals the full force of corporate power; and Cutler argues that TNCs are able to expand their power and influence in accordance with neo-liberal discipline and the deepening of market relations, while remaining largely 'invisible' in international law. Despite the general consensus among writers that transnational capital and TNCs benefit from today's neoliberal globalization, Shadlen makes the important point that there are sometimes cleavages among business groups. Although many larger firms devise strategies to benefit from the neo-liberal environment, a weaker segment of local capital has less access to credit and is generally more threatened. Nevertheless, the larger firms normally have the most power and influence, and they have often been able to impose neo-liberal discipline on others.

While transnational forces are eroding state autonomy in some import-ant respects, they are *not* causing the state to wither away. Thus, Balaam argues that much of the literature generalizes about the effects of global-ization on the state without differentiating between sectoral areas; and Leo contrasts the response of the state to globalization in Europe as against that of the United States. On the other hand, neo-liberal changes under globalization have sometimes occurred with the permission, or even the encouragement, of powerful states. Vadi, for example, examines the Mexican government's efforts to meet its foreign debt obligations by pauperizing further the country's poor majority; and Wiseman discusses the efforts of Australian governments to crush unionism in the name of maintaining international competitiveness.

Several of the chapters discuss the efforts of transnational capital to weaken labour unions and a wide range of social action groups in order to make production 'leaner and meaner' in a globally competitive world. For example, Molloy and Shields argue that high unemployment levels have played a key role in disciplining labour. A number of the authors, however, point out that this can be a double-edged process since the disadvantaged groups can mobilize to counter the rising power of trans-national capital. Thus, Goodman argues that globalization can raise cross-national political consciousness and political mobilization; Bernstein and Cashore, and Juillet, examine the role of environmental groups in developing alternative discourses or counter-hegemonic world-views which question neo-liberal policies; and Lipsig-Mummé and Wiseman discuss labour's efforts to establish bonds with community organizations and create new forms of social movement unionism at the local, national and transnational levels.

Finally, many writers believe that globalization is blurring the distinctions between domestic and foreign policy, and subjecting policies that were formerly considered domestic to increased international scrutiny. Most of the papers in this volume are sensitive to the domestic–international linkages that must be considered when we examine the characteristics and effects of globalization. Bernstein and Cashore in their study of the British Columbia lumber industry show how growing ecological consciousness can direct world-wide attention to local problems. Smith and Leo explicitly focus on the role of cities and other subnational governments in channelling and responding to the forces of globalization.

In summary, the contributors emphasize the fact that globalization is a complex process with variegated effects on the state, subnational governments, TNCs, transnational capital, labour, and social action groups. Below is a brief summary of the main themes of each of the papers.

The first part of this book focuses on competing perspectives on globalization. Using the literature produced by Canadian policy research organizations of various ideological persuasions, Laurent Dobuzinskis asserts that the think-tanks reflect three contending perspectives on globalization. The only major problems according to libertarian policy analysts and their business allies are the obstacles governments pose to the natural evolution toward free markets. While mainstream analysts and most business and political leaders would agree with the libertarian group that globalization is an irresistible trend, they believe that some channelling of globalization's effects may be necessary to avoid destabilization. Progressive critics of globalization, unlike the first two types, attribute current social upheavals to corporate actors that are pursuing a social agenda aimed at domination by transnational corporations and transnational capital. Isabella Bakker focuses on the gendered aspects of globalization, a subject hardly mentioned in much of the burgeoning literature on the subject. Thus, Bakker argues that the emerging research on globalization has been decidedly silent about the gendered underpinnings of the current transformation. Although transnational strategies are vital in an era of globalization, Bakker asserts that national political and economic institutions remain important focus points for equity-seeking groups and outlines the role that gender-sensitive budgetary exercises might play.

Part II focuses on the interaction of states with transnational corporations and other transnational actors in the globalization process. Drawing on Australian-based examples, James Goodman discusses the double-edged or dialectical impacts of globalization. Globalization, on the one hand, reveals the full force of corporate power and has a disempowering effect on nation-state policies. In response to these changes, however, globalization raises cross-national political consciousness and political mobilization. Thus, social movements and NGO movements develop political campaigns against transnational corporations, international institutions with a neo-liberal agenda, and the internationalizing state. Claire Cutler argues that the forces of globalization are expanding corporate power and influence in the world in accordance with neo-liberal discipline and the deepening of market relations. Neo-liberal discipline privileges transnational over local or national capital, and forces states to adjust their domestic policies and practices to increasingly competitive international markets. Thus, the 'competition state' is replacing the welfare state, both locally and globally. Despite the growing power of TNCs, they remain largely invisible in international law, and the law thus contributes to their influence and opportunities. Cutler concludes that it is therefore important to review the status of TNCs in international law.

Two of the papers in Part II, by Kenneth Shadlen and José Vadi, examine the transnational and neo-liberal challenges confronting Third World states in an age of globalization. Shadlen focuses on the effects of the increased role of foreign capital and international financial institutions on political alliances in two Latin American states, Argentina and Brazil. While many larger firms were able to devise strategies to benefit from the changing economic environment, a weaker segment of local capital had less access to credit and was generally more threatened. Thus, Shadlen points out that globalization can, under certain conditions, contribute to cleavages within the business class. Indeed, in Argentina, big business's backlash against peronist institutions resulted in a bifurcated pattern of business association in which the weak segment of local capital forged recurrent alliances with workers and populist political movements. In Brazil, by contrast, big business's enthusiasm for Vargas-era institutions produced a unified pattern of business association which remained united in opposition to organized labour. Vadi discusses the effects of globalization on the corrupt and repressive Institutional Revolutionary Party (PRI), which has dominated Mexican politics for over 60 years. In order to meet its foreign debt obligations, Mexico's government adopted economic policies that pauperized further the country's poor majority and eroded the living standards of its middle class. As a result, an intensive class struggle developed, marked by rejection of the PRI at the ballot box, massive urban demonstrations, and armed uprisings in the countryside. To maintain its substantial but degraded hegemony, the PRI has used military force and occupation in rebel areas such as Chiapas and has opened some space for alternating power selectively with political parties that it could co-opt. Vadi concludes that Mexico's hope lies in changes wrought from below by an awakened civil society of independent labour unions, neighbourhood organizations, and peasant-based organizations.

The papers in Part III focus on the impact of globalization on national, transnational and local policy-making in a variety of issue areas. David Balaam argues that much of the anti-globalization literature generalizes about the effects of globalization on the state without giving sufficient attention to differences among sectoral areas. In the agriculture and food sector, Balaam notes that the state has proved to be far more resilient and able to withstand globalization pressures than many anti-globalists would assume. Using the Uruguay round negotiations of the General Agreement on Tariffs and Trade (GATT) as a case study, Balaam describes how the negotiators agreed to liberalize trade in agriculture far less than in many other sectors. Although agriculture was no longer treated as an 'exception' as it had been in earlier GATT negotiations, the state maintained considerable control over the negotiating process. The major trading nations agreed to liberalize agricultural trade partly as a means of reforming their own domestic support policies and programs. However, the liberalization was only partial, and agriculture continues to be a highly protected sector in international trade.

Steven Bernstein and Ben Cashore discuss the importance of distinguishing between 'globalization' and 'internationalization' when exploring the external causes of domestic policy change. While globalization primarily concerns increasing economic transactions that transcend borders, internationalization concerns increased activities and influence of transnational or international actors and institutions ranging from corporations to activist groups, scientific associations and individuals. Using the influence of transnational actors on domestic eco-forest policy change as a case study, Bernstein and Cashore demonstrate two major points: First, that globalization and internationalization can have independent effects. On the one hand, British Columbia's growing dependence on the international market for its lumber exports through globalization can produce *downward* pressures on its environmental standards as a means of becoming more competitive. On the other hand, internationalization pressures from transnational environmental groups can induce BC through intense international scrutiny to *raise* its environmental standards. Second, the BC lumber case shows how growing ecological consciousness can direct world-wide attention to local problems. Due to external pressures from environmental groups, policies formerly considered to be domestic, such as BC's clearcut logging practices, have become matters of global concern.

Luc Juillet, like Bernstein and Cashore, discusses the role that environmental groups can play in affecting domestic policy-making. The Juillet chapter examines the formation of transnational coalitions among non-state (e.g., environmental) actors, subnational state actors, and domestic institutions (e.g., the US Senate) to oppose attempts to amend the US–Canada Migratory Birds Convention. The *Protocol Amending the Migratory Birds Convention between Canada and the US* aimed at altering the ban on spring hunting in the Convention by granting northern residents of both countries (especially aboriginal peoples) the right to hunt migratory game birds during the spring in order to meet their subsistence needs. Although the Canadian and US governments negotiated and signed the Protocol without consulting subnational state agencies, environmentalists, hunters and even aboriginal organizations, these groups managed to prevent ratification of the protocol in the US Senate through transnational coalition behaviour. Juillet points out that globalization has blurred the division between domestic and international politics, and that subnational groups can exert pressure on the state from above (through transnational coalitions) as well as from below. Like Bernstein and Cashore, Juillet concludes that globalization can contribute to the development of alternative discourses or counter-hegemonic world-views by citizens and non-governmental organizations such as environmental groups.

Although some of the chapters in Part III (e.g., Bernstein and Cashore, and Juillet) examine the involvement of subnational groups in transnational coalitions, those in Part IV focus more explicitly on subnational initiatives at the municipal level. Patrick Smith points out that traditional nation-state-centric assumptions of international relations overlook the important role that cities play in responding to globalization. Those who examine cities as international actors often focus on the largest and most important 'global' or 'world class' cities which serve as urban settings for global production, consumption and exchange. Smith argues, however, that cities which are not of 'world class' importance in countries like Canada and Australia can also have important roles by taking broader globalist policy stances. Referring to the Greater Vancouver region as a case study, Smith shows how Vancouver and smaller surrounding cities have gradually developed a more active and varied municipal internationalism. In addition to an economic component involving international trade and investment, this municipal internationalism also has world peace, foreign aid, ecological, social equity and cultural diversity components.

Christopher Leo points to the tendency of globalization to 'homogenize' society. By exposing people around the world to the same ideas, images and market pressures, globalization exerts pressures on societies and cultures to become more alike (and often more like the United States, with its high-rise towers and McDonald's restaurants). Nevertheless, Leo notes that there are differential responses to globalization pressures in Europe and North America; these differences result largely from the relationship between the state/region on the one hand, and its cities on the other. In Europe, there is a strong national state presence in urban politics which results in more state control and a lack of receptiveness to developers and grassroots participation in urban development decisions. In the United States by contrast, there is a more receptive environment for grassroots participation combined with a climate that enhances the power of developers. In Canada and Britain, the role of the nation-state in urban politics is somewhere in between the European and American examples. While the more powerful role of the nation-state in Europe may enhance the state's position in its bargaining with corporate interests, Leo argues that the public must be involved more actively in decision-making if urban politics is to constructively channel the forces of globalization.

Part V, focusing on labour and the challenge of globalization, provides an important contrast with Part II's discussion of transnational corporations. Andrew Molloy and John Shields argue that the polarization of work, between those with too much and those with too little or none, is contributing to significant social inequalities. These inequalities have resulted largely from global economic restructuring, with its demands for just-in-time production and a flexible workforce consisting of part-time, contract and temporary employment. The restructuring has fostered an employer strategy of utilizing an ever smaller core of workers whose work time has increased through the extensive use of overtime. To supplement the core workforce, employers have drawn on cheap pools of non-standard and disposable workers. High unemployment levels have played a key role in disciplining labour, and maintaining large numbers of skilled and educated labour for capital's flexible utilization. In view of high unemployment levels, even during periods of sustained expansion, Molloy and Shields maintain that governments should be proactive with regard to job creation, and that work-week reduction with no loss of pay should be advanced as a key political demand.

Carla Lipsig-Mummé argues that the key question facing unions in the era of globalization is: how can unions recapture representation of the new, but still domestically anchored working classes, while simultaneously transcending competition amongst unions in different countries in order to confront and contain capital internationally? She addresses the efforts made by unions in developing countries to renew their organizing strategies and to relate new domestic organizing to effective international labour action.

John Wiseman uses the 1998 Australian waterfront dispute to demonstrate the dilemmas facing unions in resisting corporate and state assaults in an age of globalization. While maritime trade has always been crucial for Australia, the globalizing strategies of both Labour and Liberal governments intensified pressure on Australian employers to maintain international competitiveness by cutting costs and increasing productivity. To further these goals, the Howard Liberal government engaged in a brutal attempt to crush unionism in Australia and shift the balance of power from labour to capital; and this set the stage for the 1998 Australian waterfront dispute. As Wiseman notes, the dispute united the Australian labour movement in an unprecedented way, and forged new labour alliances with community organizations and religious groups. The most important lessons from the 1998 waterfront dispute, according to Wiseman, relate to the fact that local and national struggles between labour and capital are now being fought on a global stage. If labour is to fare well in this struggle, Wiseman argues that it must build on its bonds with community organizations and create new forms of social movement unionism at the local, national and transnational levels.

Part I
Competing Perspectives

.

1
Global Discord: the Confusing Discourse of Think-tanks

Laurent Dobuzinskis

'Globalization' is on everybody's lips; a fad word fast turning into a shibboleth, a magic incantation, a pass-key meant to unlock the gates to all present and future mysteries. For some, 'globalization' is what we are bound to do if we wish to be happy; for others [it] is the cause of our unhappiness.[1]

The birth of a notion

National economies have become far more integrated and interdependent than they were only thirty years ago. Over the last two decades, the term 'global' began to be used in various phrases (e.g., 'the global economy' or 'the global marketplace,' and on the cultural front, Marshall MacLuhan coined the phrase 'the global village' back in the 1960s). Globalization itself became the fashionable platitude of the 1990s. Indeed, globalization is treated either as a convenient catchword alluding to a myriad of discrete changes or, as an explanatory concept, it is shorthand for a new theory of capitalistic development at the eve of the new millennium. It is either trite or mythical.

Some observers caution that economic integration is not new: 'the process of globalization has generally been longer and slower than much contemporary conceit will admit':[2] it took 60 years for the share of international trade in the Gross Domestic Product (GDP) of the world's most advanced economies to return to the level reached in 1913. The gold standard of the nineteenth century can be considered the symbol of an earlier period of globalization, while the interwar period and the early decades of the second half of this century marked the nadir of a long-term trend. Something new must be happening, however, in view of the scope of present developments: 'it is a fundamental mistake to argue that we have returned to the international economy of the nine-teenth-century.'[3] Never before has the logic of the market economy exerted its influence so profoundly on so many diverse political, social and cultural institutions around the world. Others argue that two crucial elements of the contemporary scene were absent in the pre-1913 period: the liberalization of trade (only Britain in the pre-1913 era was committed to free trade) and the diminishing role of the state.[4]

Most definitions of globalization refer to more or less the same set of factors:

> globalization . . . involves the rapid and pervasive diffusion around the globe of production, consumption and investment of goods, services, technology and capital. Developments in information processing, communications technology and transportation facilities have erased borders and shrunk distances, underpinning fundamental changes in business organization and techniques.[5]

Some definitions allude to loosely interdependent processes occurring spontaneously or, at any rate, not as the result of coordinated strategies. However, 'globalization' is more typically found in definitions that focus on the dynamic, transformative aspects of the new economic order and often imply that this new order is deliberately brought about by power-ful economic and political forces.

A definition of spontaneous globalization reads:

> It has become commonplace to talk about the globalization of busi-ness and economic relations. Much of this process takes place without the help of negotiated international rules aimed at opening up mar-kets. Instead, it relies on the impetus provided by such factors as new technologies in communication and finance or, in some countries, unilateral regulatory reform.[6]

Daniel Schwanen insists that 'Globalization was not, for the most part, created by governments. Rather, it can best be described as the result of a large number of actors in the private sector tapping new opportunities stemming from . . . technological changes.'[7]

Richard Simeon does not believe that the global economy is purely the outcome of blind, impersonal forces, yet he does not think that globalization 'represents the success of the political coalition dominated by the business class.' Rather, he suggests that, at least in Canada's case, globalization is 'arrived at by default.'[8] That is, governments at the federal and provincial levels lack the policy instruments and the resources needed to steer in any other direction.

At the other end of the spectrum, organizations like the Canadian Centre for Policy Alternatives (CCPA) or the Council of Canadians want to alert Canadians about what they see as the emergence of a new world order in which transnational corporations play the decisive role as architects. And, if not directly, then through the intermediary of pliable governments, transnational corporations also rule this new order. Tony Clarke (the director of the Polaris Institute in Canada) concedes that there is no deliberate conspiracy behind what is happening; however, it is definitely not a spontaneous occurrence or the outcome of imper- sonal technological trends. The title of his book (published and actively promoted by the CCPA), *Silent Coup: Confronting the Big Business Takeover of Canada*, says it all![9] If democratic governments in North America and Europe no longer control and plan the economy as was the case from the 1940s to the 1970s, then global corporations must be doing it. The corporate elite has its 'agenda,' part of which includes dismantlement of the welfare state and, more generally, imposition of a straitjacket on the democratic nation-state. So, for example, the Business Council on National Issues (BCNI) wants, and exercises enough power, to 'redesign the state.'[10] International agreements like NAFTA or the – now practically defunct – Multilateral Agreement on Investment (MAI) are presented as 'a bill of rights and freedoms for transnational corporations.'[11]

This interpretation is very common among progressive political activ- ists, trade unionists and members of the new social movements. Two qualifications need to be added. First, not all intellectuals on the left subscribe unreservedly to it. Leo Panitch, a prominent left-wing polit- ical scientist, for one, argues it is an exaggeration to say that capital has been able to subdue state institutions that had previously supported progressive social policies. For Panitch, the state never has been capable of controlling capital. He also downplays the extent to which state actors have pushed for, and been instrumental in bringing about, globalization.[12]

Secondly, traditional conservatives and nationalist-populist leaders have resisted globalization. For somewhat different reasons, both groups, left and right, have very negative images of capitalists and international organizations. John Gray sees globalization as having been politically engineered, albeit through more complex social forces than the inter- vention of transnational corporations.[13] Far less intellectually subtle are the diatribes of populist leaders like Ross Perot or Pat Buchanan in the United States, Jörg Haider in Austria, or Jean-Marie LePen in France.

Populist nationalists are able to tap into xenophobic fears and popular mistrust of faceless international bureaucrats abroad and recent immigrants at home. The rise of such xenophobic political forces is indeed one of the risks that Gray expects will afflict the world being fashioned by the advocates of global markets. The Asian crisis also has led some observers who situate themselves closer to the fuzzy middle ground between the progressive left and the conservative right to raise questions about 'the dark side of globalization.'[14]

Three perspectives on globalization

One can place some order on these competing discourses by reading them as if they originated in three different worlds. World I is inhabited by libertarians and their allies or fellow travellers in certain strata of the business and professional classes. It is one in which all economic and social systems naturally converge toward global free markets. This is so because *Homo Economicus* is the most effective model for policy-making. And all this is as it should be, given the moral theories prevalent among residents of World I. They believe that opposition to market outcomes based on appeals to social justice has corrosive effects on individual freedoms and the responsibilities that go with them.

Globalization is not a concern for the denizens of World I; it is not even occurring. They see no extraordinary set of circumstances at work to transform the meaning and implications of economic laws. Global markets were bound to evolve, and are doing so spontaneously. Indeed, were it not for the misguided policies pursued between the 1930s and the 1970s, global markets would have been in existence earlier. Markets are global almost by definition. From a World I standpoint, this is not an issue that needs to be discussed; rather what needs constantly to be denounced are the protectionist measures by which governments attempt to circumvent the logic of the market.

World I policy research organizations – like the Fraser Institute in Canada, the Cato Institute in the United States or the Adam Smith Institute in the United Kingdom – have very little to say about globalization *per se*. One can detect traces of scepticism among those within World I toward globalization initiatives undertaken by government or international institutions sympathetic to a market-oriented approach. The International Monetary Fund (IMF) and the World Bank are often targets of their barbs.[15] On government intervention in general they have a lot to say, and they devote most of their resources to describing government failures of all kinds. The Fraser Institute, for example, continuously attacks government regulation; this is a staple of its research agenda. The accumulated rigidities and inefficiencies caused by governments since the 1930s offered World I opinion leaders plenty of ammunition for their defence of free markets, and afforded them significant recognition and influence over the last two decades. Now, if they persist in their refusal to acknowledge the profound transformations that are taking place and widespread fears about the effects of these changes on social cohesion and cultural stability, they risk being pushed back to the margin of public debates.

Residents of World II include most economists, the leaders of mainstream political parties including some social democratic parties such as Tony Blair's New Labour; international trade and monetary organizations bureaucrats; most members of the business class; their allies in the media, and a sizable following among professionals. There is both a (moderate) left-wing and a conservative wing within World II, but this reflects the fact that over the last two decades most social democrats have moved closer to the proverbial centre on economic issues, abandoning more or less explicitly the tenets of Keynesianism and protectionist industrial policy goals.

From a World II standpoint, globalization is indeed something rather new, and momentous, but inevitable. On the left fringes of World II, it is argued that one must make the best of it. On the right fringes, there is more optimism, albeit often muted because, while inevitable, the course of globalization is believed to be somewhat unpredictable. However, it is not a single phenomenon but the conjunction of many interdependent trends. The driving force behind these trends is technological innovation and the acceleration of technological change in some key areas like information and telecommunications, transportation and biotechnologies.

Richard Lipsey has analysed these trends in a nuanced academic style[16] and provides the theoretical foundation for the more detailed analyses of international trade and investment carried out by the C.D. Howe Institute. In the United States, the Brookings Institution and the American Enterprise Institute (AEI), are equivalents; in the United Kingdom, the Royal Institute of International Affairs (RIIA) or the National Institute of Economic and Social Research (NIESR) join institutes situated somewhat left of centre like Demos or the Institute for Public Policy Research (IPPR) as exemplars. An interesting characteristic of these British think-tanks is that they display a rather unenthusiastic attitude toward globalization, which they treat more as a fact of life, as it were, than as a golden opportunity; Demos, in particular, has tried to stake out a 'third way' that would reap the benefits of the new economy (i.e., the globalized knowledge economy) without blindly acquiescing to all its costs.[17] On the international scene, the International Monetary Fund (IMF) and the World Bank belong to World II, as does the OECD.

Lipsey argues that economic prosperity depends almost entirely on an economy's ability to take advantage of technological progress. As leading technologies change, so should the policy responses from governments and the strategic decisions by investors, entrepreneurs and managers. In the present context, the internationalization of industrial production and services, accompanied by the deregulation of the labour market, the removal of obstacles to international competition and investment, and trade liberalization, are the appropriate responses from private and public decision-makers.

World I and World II overlap to some degree (the OECD sometimes appears to have a foot in both camps). The essential difference between the two is that economic success in World II is more chancy. There are no convincing alternatives to free markets but market outcomes are not always entirely benign; difficult adjustments continually have to be undertaken. The Schumpeterian process of creative destruction is not a safe road to economic prosperity. Laissez-faire is not exactly what is needed. Policy-makers have an active role to play and if they, or private sector managers, take the wrong turn, they could end up in an impasse while technological progress leaves them behind. Thus, globalization is something that they should actively contribute to, but their choices are severely constrained by the logic of competitive markets. The role of government is to facilitate and accompany the inexorable but capricious course of technological progress. Its role is also to retool the welfare state in a manner that renders social programs more adaptive to changing circumstances, more oriented toward 'active' measures such as retraining as opposed to passive income support, less bureaucratic and more reliant on partnership agreements with the voluntary and not-for-profit sector. Above all, government must be more cost-effective.[18]

The citizens of World III form a more heterogeneous group. Some traditional conservatives and nationalist populists have ventured into World III, but most inhabitants are situated ideologically toward the left. They include a sizeable fraction of social scientists, leaders and followers of some social democratic parties (e.g., the federal NDP in Canada; minority fractions within European socialists and communist parties in France, Italy or Russia); members of various new social movements, mainstream churches (Catholics and non-evangelical Protestants); trade unionists, especially in the public sector, and the strongly protectionist wing of the US Democratic Party, led by Dick Gephart. Policy research organizations like the CCPA, or the Canadian Council on Social Development (CCSD), and the Council of Canadians; in the United States, the Center for Policy Alternatives (CPA) and the Economic Policy Institute (EPI), as well as public interest groups like Global Trade Watch (a division of Ralph Nader's Public Citizen) also fall into World III.

Globalization is one of the most pressing – if not the most pressing – issue in World III. Very few things happen spontaneously in World III. Strong determining forces rule out all sorts of options and push social actors in foreseeable directions. But the actions they undertake and the decisions they make must be understood in relation to a structure of unequal power. Whatever happens can ultimately be explained in terms of the strategic advantages that thereby accrue to the most powerful class-based social groups. These groups have power and they exercise it. Less powerful groups can mobilize large numbers of ordinary citizens, and gain sufficient countervailing power to derail occasionally the plans of the dominant class.

A discourse of discontent

From left to right, most observers consider that the emerging global economic system causes many economic and social disuptions. The management of most firms, other than transnationals, enter this new world with some apprehension. And even some transnationals can fail badly, as have giant Japanese banks. But in its most persistently critical form, the discourse on globalization is clearly an expression of profound discontent. Whenever globalization is not used merely as a shortcut for increased competition but as a concept endowed with a complex meaning of its own, it typically finds its place in a discourse that purports to explain how and why the lives of most people on this planet are getting worse.

At the root of the radical critique of globalization is the conviction that political economy is essentially about how economic and social goals can be achieved through political means. Different interests seek different goals, and obviously the most powerful interests find it easier to achieve their goals; but the assumption common to World III analysts is that political will can control social and economic forces. If inequalities are increasing, if environmental degradation is accelerating, it is because the political will to correct these problems is lacking or is being thwarted by corporate interests. Therefore, their discontent is not a lament about our tragic fate but an expression of dissent premised on the idea that participatory democracy holds the key to these problems.

The most common criticism of globalization is that it results in a severe worsening of inequalities, both domestically and internationally. Social and economic justice are threatened. For World III critics, this has serious consequences for unionized labour, women and economically disadvantaged groups.

This results from the combination of two processes. On the one hand, there is a classical process of exploitation as evidenced in the movement of some industries from high wage countries or regions toward low wage countries or regions. This is not an altogether new development; the qualitative difference between the old international division of labour and the new is that today, as a result of technological change, even industries producing highly sophisticated products or even services that until recently could only be provided domestically by middle-ranking white collars (e.g., bookkeeping) can now be moved to Newly Industrialized Countries (NICs) in Asia or Latin America.

On the other hand, a new kind of inequality is also emerging. A process of marginalization renders numbers of individuals more or less permanently unemployable in the richest countries and leaves entire economies largely outside of the new global markets, thereby accentuating already serious disparities between rich and poor countries. Indeed marginalization is a phenomenon that radical critics of globalization and advocates of global free trade tend to worry about. 'Downsizing' has contributed to the marginalization not only of unskilled workers but also of a fraction of the middle class which today puts pressure on centrist and right-of-centre political parties to pay more attention to job creation and income distribution. This is evident in a recent declaration by Canada's Finance Minister, Paul Martin, who expresses concern about globalization 'eating away' the middle class.[19]

For World III critics, however, the effects of globalization are not limited to the worsening of income disparities. They claim that globalization makes life harder for most workers by creating incentives to lower safety standards and, generally, to eliminate government regulations in a number of areas (e.g., environmental protection, product safety, etc.). They also point out that globalization threatens the whole ecological balance of the planet; in their view, the global market economy is not sustainable.

Moreover, there are effects that go beyond these specific problems and have an impact on the whole social fabric of globalized societies. The boundaries between the private and public sectors are shifting. There is widespread agreement that the powers of the nation-state are being eroded. Critics in the social democratic camp stress that transnational

corporations and the private sector in general benefit from this realign-
ment and have been instrumental in bringing it about. A few traditional
conservatives and extreme right politicians, on the other hand, are
more inclined to blame international bureaucrats, immigrants and the
willingness of mainstream parties to seek their support, or some more
or less sinister forces controlled by anti-patriotic cosmopolitan financial
elites and speculators, or a decline in moral standards. However, conservative critics draw relatively few practical conclusions from these observations, other than to decry the loss of national sovereignty as a serious
threat in itself. Leftist critics have more to say on the subject.

The most serious threat that globalization poses for the discontents is
that the democratic state will cease to be an effective agent of social
change. It is not state sovereignty *per se* that they are worried about as
much as the weakening of the state in its relations with corporations.
Many gains have been achieved during the last four decades: state institutions are now open to inputs from a wide variety of public interest
groups and are moderately responsive to social and environmental
concerns. However, the trend seems to be going in the other direction
because of pressures coming from the private sector and because of the
limits on state capacities imposed by recent international trade and
investment agreements (e.g., NAFTA) – agreements that are not worked
out in open democratic forums.[20] World III critics fear that, ultimately,
democracy itself is threatened.[21]

Critics of globalization point out that this is happening already.
Defenders of a universal and comprehensive public health insurance
system, for example, fear that the gates will soon be opened to private
clinics and, more ominously, large US-based corporations. Similar criticisms have focused on the educational system where the influence of
the corporate sector through the use of new multimedia technologies is
already felt, from primary school to universities.

From a World III standpoint, however, power relations never remain
static. Economic and technological transformation also create new political dynamics that eventually bring about revolutionary changes. While
critics of globalization come from many different ideological camps,
they often reproduce the Hegelian/Marxist 'ruse of reason/history' sche-
mata. Thus we hear that new social movements will be able to mobilize
resistance to the neo-conservative agenda, that the state will be able to
regain control over global market forces in countries where a social democratic tradition exists, and that globalization could actually usher in a
new era of radical democratic politics. In other words, globalization seems
to be constructed by some of the most radical critics as a necessary stage

in the *Aufhebung* of capitalism. As they see it, globalization must be resisted but also used in a strategic way to galvanize political forces that could demand and succeed in achieving a redrawing of the boundaries between the private and public sectors. A more decentralized, participatory state will emerge from these struggles, supported by a renewed and more progressive nationalism and/or by a new internationalism. And is not the new global order falling apart already as a result of the worsening crisis in Asia?

Neo-Schumpeterian analyses

Discontent, of course, is not universal. But defenders of economic liberalism rarely sing the praise of globalization. Libertarians simply go on arguing that the state exercises far too much control on economic matters and that this, rather than any possible downfall of globalization, is the real problem (the publications list of the Fraser Institute is a case in point). Global markets help their cause but their emergence is not problematic, by definition. Therefore, they pay minimal attention to it.

Most mainstream defenders of economic liberalism attempt to convince the public that things are not quite as bad as the critics say they are. Some, like the economist and columnist William Watson in his latest book *Globalization and the Meaning of Canadian Life*, do it with more bravado than others, but even this usually rather pugnacious polemicist is content to assert that, contrary to what World III critics pretend, 'We Canadians . . . remain free, for the most part, to choose what sized government we should have.'[22] World II pundits concede that the Schumpeterian processes of creative destruction that are at work in both the private and public sectors pose new problems.[23] However, they also argue that new opportunities have opened up and that judicious policy-makers will seek and find a new balance between these challenges (one of their favorite words!) and opportunities. These ambiguities are present, for example, in the writings of an archetypical World II analyst like Tom Courchene.

Courchene prefers to speak about 'glocalization' rather than globalization.[24] Not all trends go in the same direction. The internationalization of the economy has complex implications for domestic policy-making. On the one hand, the federal government faces new constraints and has less room to manoeuvre. On the other hand, new opportunities arise at the provincial level; as the economic goals and social needs of regions become increasingly divergent, determined as they are more and more by linkages with external markets rather than by interprovincial links,

Canadians have an opportunity to redesign their institutions on the basis of the principle of subsidiarity.

This principle is seen as both pragmatically efficient and morally just. It states that in a system where the sovereignty of the state is divided, as in a federal system, or in emerging supranational communities (e.g., the European Union), government responsibilities should be assigned to the level that is closest to the people it is capable of serving; inversely, of course, those responsibilities that cannot be fulfilled at the local or regional level ought to be assigned to the national, or possibly supranational, level. Since for Courchene, and many mainstream economists and classical liberals, a decentralized and competitive federal system is both more efficient and normatively desirable, globalization could usher in precisely the kinds of reforms that Canadians would benefit from.[25] The recent agreement on Canada's 'social union,' which provides a structure for the management of social programs in a more decentralized federal system, goes some way toward that goal.

Conclusion

For some, globalization is shorthand for the mysterious forces of technological advancement and economic growth. For others, it sits at the top of the 'agenda' relentlessly pursued by the privileged few. The contrast is clear: World II analysts see globalization as an important but exogenous and uncontrollable process of economic change that also creates opportunities for political and social reforms; for World III analysts, it is a politically driven process and a symptom of everything that is wrong with existing economic and political structures.

Constructed representations of politics make sense of the confusing whirlwind of events they subsume in two ways. On the one hand, they provide a coherent picture of complex and, therefore, at least partly incomprehensible phenomena; they point to structural connections that bring these phenomena in focus. On the other hand, they also serve as tools that societal actors can use in pursuing their own individual or collective strategies. The rationale for and internal coherence of a social construction can be derived from a knowledge of the political goals pursued by those who use it in their discourse. Thus 'globalization' often stands in an instrumental relation to the political objectives of those who most explicitly convey their discontent about current economic and political dynamics. Inversely, individuals and groups who see in these processes more good than harm have no need for the rhetorical power packed into the term globalization. Not surprisingly therefore, they live in a world where either no such thing is happening, or is happening in more benign ways for which they often use a panoply of terms other than globalization itself.

Under these conditions, there is little hope that a meaningful debate can ever take place on the causes and effects of globalization. The quality of democratic politics in this country could, however, benefit from a refocusing of the attention of political parties, think-tanks and social movements on an issue that almost everyone admits needs to be addressed and, more importantly, can be conceptualized in roughly similar ways across a wide range of ideological differences: the terms and conditions of the implicit social contract that sustains civil society and political institutions. There is little doubt that the new social contract will be less collectivist than the one that emerged in the post-war years, in spite of the recent revival of communitarian values. But it might be possible for reasonable participants in Worlds II and III to agree on a re-balancing of values, a new synthesis of entrepreneurship and responsibility, on the one hand, and egalitarian concerns for a fair distribution of resources and a renewed commitment to the ideals of citizenship and reciprocity, on the other. Justice remains a goal that residents of the mythical 'global village' care about.

Notes

1 Z. Bauman, *Globalization: the Human Consequences* (Cambridge: Polity Press, 1998), p. 1.
2 V. Cable, 'The Diminished Nation-State: A Study in the Loss of Economic Power,' *Daedalus* 124 (1995), no. 2, p. 24.
3 J. Gray, *False Dawn: the Delusions of Global Capitalism* (London: Granta Books, 1998), p. 61.
4 P. Baroch and R. Kozul-Wright, 'Globalization Myths: Some Historical Reflections on Integration, Industrialization and Growth in the World Economy,' in R. Kozul-Wright and R. Rowthorn, eds, *Transnational Corporations and the Global Economy* (London: Macmillan, 1998), p. 63.
5 M. Hart, *What's Next: Canada, the Global Economy and the New Trade Policy* (Ottawa: Centre for Trade Policy and Law, 1994), p. 1.
6 T. Kierans, 'Foreword,' in P. Sauvé and D. Schwanen, eds, *Investment Rules for the Global Economy*, Policy Study 28 (Toronto: C.D. Howe Institute, 1996), p. vii.
7 D. Schwanen, 'Trading Up: the Impact of Increased Continental Integration on Trade, Investment, and Jobs in Canada,' *Commentary* 89 (Toronto: C.D. Howe Institute, 1997), p. 3.
8 R. Simeon, 'Canadian Responses to Globalization,' in K. Brownsey, ed., *Canada–Japan: Views on Globalization* (Halifax: Institute for Research on Public Policy, 1989), pp. 23–4.

9 T. Clarke, *Silent Coup: Confronting the Big Business Takeover of Canada* (Ottawa/ Toronto: CCPA/Lorimer, 1997), p. 106. For a non-Canadian perspective, see D. Korten, *When Corporations Rule the World* (West Hartford, Conn.: Kumarian Press, 1995).

10 Clarke, *Silent Coup*, p. 37.

11 T. Clarke, 'MAI-DAY! The Corporate Rule Treaty,' http://www.policyaltern-atives.ca/mai.html, p. 1. For its part, the Council of Canadians proclaims that the MAI is 'a constitution for the largest corporations to rule the world' ('MAI and our Sovereignty,' http://www.canadians.org/sovernm.html, p. 1).

12 L. Panitch, 'Globalization, State, and Left Strategies,' *Social Justice* 1–2 (1996): 79–91.

13 See J. Gray, *False Dawn* and 'Globalization – The Dark Side,' *New Statesman* 11, no. 495 (13 March 1998), pp. 32–4.

14 Charles E. Morrison, 'Overview,' in C.E. Morrison and H. Soesastro, eds, *Domestic Adjustments to Globalization* (Tokyo: Japan Center for International Exchange, 1998), p. 11.

15 See, for example, B.T. Johnson and J.P. Sweeney, *Down the Drain: Why the IMF Bailout in Asia Won't Work*, Backgrounder 1150 (Washington, DC: Heritage Foundation, 1997).

16 See R.G. Lipsey, *Economic Growth, Technological Change, and Canadian Economic Policy* (Toronto: C.D. Howe Institute, 1996).

17 See *Tomorrow's Politics: The Third Way and Beyond*, eds I. Hargreaves and I. Christie (London: Demos, 1998).

18 See, for example, the series of studies recently published by the C.D. Howe Institute under the collection title 'The Social Policy Challenge.'

19 Cited in G. Gherson, 'Paul Martin Makes His Global Pitch,' *National Post* (27 February 1999), p. B1.

20 See *Canada Under Free Trade*, eds D. Cameron and M. Watkins (Toronto: Lorimer, 1993).

21 See J. McMurtry, *Unequal Freedoms: the Global Market as an Ethical System* (Toronto: Garamond Press, 1998); the CCPA has advertised this book by publishing portions of it before its completion.

22 W. Watson, *Globalization and the Meaning of Canadian Life* (Toronto: University of Toronto Press, 1998), p. x.

23 On the international scene, the World Bank plays an active role in this regard.

24 T.J. Courchene, 'CHASTE and Chastened: Canada's New Social Contract,' in *The Welfare State in Canada: Past, Present and Future*, eds R.B. Blake, P.E. Bryden, J.F. Strain (Concord, Ont.: Irwing Publishing, 1997), pp. 10–11.

25 Courchene has argued recently that the logic of international competitiveness will place severe constraints on the renegotiation of the equalization formula (i.e., the method for redistributing fiscal resources from the richer to the poorer provinces); there are some gains to be made here, as this could be an opportunity to improve the flexibility of the Canadian federal system, but this adjustment is expected to be a delicate balancing act. See T. Courchene, 'Renegotiating Equalization: National Policy, Federal State, International Economy,' *C.D. Howe Commentary* 113 (1998).

2
Restructuring Discourse and its Gendered Underpinnings: Toward a Macro-analytical Framework

Isabella Bakker

Introduction

There is a vigorous debate within political economy about whether modern nation-states have lost power and, in Bob Jessop's terms, have been 'hollowed out', or whether state power is in fact being redeployed in some new ways.[1]

A strong case can be made for the latter that the redeployment of state energies toward international markets and investments is the primary tendency of OECD economies, the hollowing out of states' policy capacities a result. This has in turn enabled a much more aggressive class politics. It has also signalled a massive off-loading to the sphere of reproduction (the 'care' economy) which acts as an effective shock absorber or may signal an ultimate crisis in social reproduction.[2] Certainly the dilemmas of Western European welfare states are inextricably linked to changes in women's labour force participation and declining fertility rates which have implications for pension schemes and the future viability of these welfare states.[3] However, the gender-based nature of this broader process of globalization is largely invisible in most of the restructuring discourse. This 'conceptual silence' obscures the very social foundations upon which market relations rest as well as their gendered and racial underpinnings. In response, feminist scholars and activists have begun to focus on the macro-analytical frameworks of political economy. One such thrust has been the political campaigns around gender-sensitive national budgets. Such exercises offer the possibility of exposing the impositional claims of neo-liberal restructuring and also challenge the further disembedding of economies, especially the money economy, from the social realm of public scrutiny.

The processes of globalization which are intensifying social exclusion and marginalization of large parts of populations around the globe are being met with resistances aimed at opening up spaces for democratic participation and alternatives to dominant forms of development and knowledge.[4] Feminist attempts to introduce social reproduction into questions of redistributive efficiency, accountability and well-being, are described in the second part of this chapter. I begin in the first section with the linkages between disciplinary neo-liberalism and social reproduction.

Disciplinary neo-liberalism and social reproduction

States are increasingly being disciplined to behave as if they were private markets operating in a global territory. Stephen Gill refers to the emerging system of global economic governance as 'disciplinary neo-liberalism': it relies on the market, especially the capital market, to discipline economic agents, and privileges investors who are seen as central to the process of economic growth.[5] This 'new constitutionalism' whereby transnational capital creates a 'quasiconstitutional framework for the reconstitution of the legal rights, prerogatives, and freedom of movement for capital on a world scale', locks in political reforms, thereby insulating dominant economic forces from democratic accountability.[6] Gill identifies several components of the new constitutionalism, two of which are directly relevant to a discussion of gender, namely: strategies for reconfiguring state apparatuses so that governments themselves become the facilitators of market values and discipline; and measures to construct markets through legal and political structures which both redefine and internationally guarantee private property rights (e.g., the World Trade Organization).

First, reconfiguring state apparatuses involves deregulation and the reduction of government, in other words, a dramatic shift in commitment from securing the welfare of citizens to facilitating the flow of global capital. This has often been accomplished through a depoliticizing, technical discourse of deficits, competitiveness and balanced budgets, and an aura of technocratic neutrality. The whole idea of public goods is being severely tested through such policies as privatization and the introduction of user fees.

Second, the emerging Global Political Economy is characterized by the growth in power of institutional processes outside the formal boundaries of the state. For governments, credibility with the financial markets and the multilateral development banks is becoming perhaps more important than credibility with the voters. Saskia Sassen suggests that these markets do exercise the accountability functions associated with citizenship: they can vote government economic policies down or up, they can force governments to take certain measures over others.

For example, with deregulation of interest rates central banks can now only rely on changes in interest rate levels to influence the level of demand in the economy; they can no longer use interest rate ceilings.[7] The power of governments to influence interest and foreign exchange rates and fiscal policy can also be severely reduced, if not neutralized, by the foreign exchange and bond markets even in hegemonic centres such as the USA. Bond raters are important because of their link to state budgets and the debt question. Governments so far have failed to develop policies to control these markets, partly because it will require a coordinated effort, partly because key branches of government have been captured by neo-liberal forces. This has meant pathologizing those ministries of the state aligned with social welfare and validating others such as finance, trade and the police.

On the revenue side of fiscal policies, before the current period of transition, taxes were used to redistribute incomes within societies with particular social consequences. Now falling tax revenues in the North are increasingly curtailing the scope for government welfare and public spending projects. Corporation taxes have been falling in Europe for twenty years. Tax revenues are also going down due to high unemployment: the casualization of labour and policy decisions around tax cuts and balanced budgets. Moves to enshrine balanced budgeting or capping deficits through legal measures have underscored fiscal conservatism by demarcating caps on spending and taxation. Such measures discourage proactive policies to promote equality because of the perceived political costs now attached to spending initiatives.[8] In the South, states have literally been hollowed out through successive rounds of privatization and huge pressures of debt refinancing and balance of payments demands.[9]

This raises a bigger issue. The presumption that everyone can now meet their needs through the market rests on the belief that earnings from jobs are sufficient and that all able adults engage in the labour market. For far too many, the changing global order and the increased influence of markets signals an intensification of inequalities not just in the West but globally between the winners and losers of the race to get on the fast-moving train of globalization. For example, the poorest 20 per cent of the world's people have benefitted little from globalization, sharing only 1 per cent of world trade. Three-quarters of the people of the world live in developing countries yet they enjoy only 16 per cent of the world's income while the richest 20 per cent have 85 per cent of global income. There has, of course, been tremendous progress in human development in life expectancy, in nutrition, in infant mortality.

Nevertheless, despite this progress, considerable human deprivation is a fact in both the developing and the industrial world. 1.3 billion people continue to survive on less than the equivalent of $1 per day. Nearly 1 billion people are illiterate and some 840 million face food insecurity.[10]

For feminist economists, this paradox between production and consumption is highlighted by women's position at the crossroads of production and reproduction. This vantage point leads to many views of markets, ranging from support to ambivalence to deep suspicion. Feminist critical economics, which offers a home to a number of heterodox approaches to economics, questions whether markets are a reliable means of mobilizing resources for production and an effective means of meeting needs.

For one, markets as social institutions are inevitably structured asymmetrically to the advantage of some participants over others. The UNDP's Gender Development Index (GDI) 1 is one important statistical indicator which shows the difference between capabilities and opportunities for women in societies around the globe. Second, while markets entail opportunities they also involve risks such as unemployment and changes in demand for certain goods. So in order to counteract market insecurity, non-market safety nets (kin, community, state provisions) are seen as necessary.[11] This insight highlights one of the limits of a purely production-oriented approach to political and economic globalization. Non-market relations are key to gauging the nature and depth of the globalization process as it plays itself out in the daily lives of real people, of women and men.

So there is a sense that markets cannot just be viewed in the one-dimensional aspect of competition and exchange. Rather, markets must also be analysed in terms of two other dimensions: command, that is, economic relationships in which power plays a predominant role such as those between employers and employees; and change, which refers to the way in which the operation of the economic system changes over time. The time dimension of markets forces us to remember that each economic system works differently at different points in time, and that the people who make up a system also develop over time.[12]

How do these insights inform notions of globalization? Feminist economists in concert with other transformative scholarship and progressive social movements, raise a number of very important concerns about how markets allocate resources and determine welfare, how social solidarities can be built and maintained as they were through welfare states, and how growth can take place from the perspective of people. Like all forms of knowledge, economics reflects and helps produce pervasive social beliefs about men and women and their social positions. The most general critique levelled against mainstream economic accounts of global restructuring is that they tend to subsume all experiences under a universal rubric of 'human' that is in fact an expression of the masculine experience.[13] A fundamental consequence of this way of thinking is that need and production are not situated within an analysis of systemic reproduction that includes human reproduction, sustenance and the biosphere.

A further important critique from writers in the South has been the tendency to view economic, political and social change through Western concepts which leave little room for the mutual recognition of distinct traditions of civilization. Chandra Mohanty criticizes white, Western feminists for their universalizing tendencies ('sisterhood is global') and their process of 'Othering' third world women (Eurocentrism).[14]

Mohanty and other third world writers have been particularly critical of the victimology in Western feminist accounts of global restructuring. For example, discussion of international restructuring of manufacturing industries and the rise of Export Processing Zones frequently sees third world women as the passive victims of multinational capital. Newer approaches originating from writers outside of the Western framework examine the interaction of constraining structures and women's varied responses to changing material incentives. Naila Kabeer, for instance, has demonstrated how women garment workers in Bangladesh have taken the new insecurities and opportunities of the government's active encouragement of garment industries and reconstituted purdah norms and customary practices toward a new, more participatory definition of women's roles.[15] Such an approach has meant that scholars and practitioners have had to reevaluate their notions of agency, especially poor women's agency and resistance, and has opened the door to new voices in the policy process.

Challenging impositional claims through gender-sensitive budgets

Several trends discussed in the previous section have contributed to a shift in how feminist policy communities articulate gender issues in institutional settings. As was discussed, the trend towards the de-nation-alization of the state has meant a continuous shift in state power upwards (to multilateral agencies such as the IMF and agreements such as NAFTA or the European Union), downwards (to subnational and local levels of government) and sideways (to different government departments, such as the shift toward ministries of finance). Second, there has been a trend towards the de-statization of the political system, what some observers refer to as the shift from government to governance; the latter emphasizes partnerships between governmental, para-governmental and non-governmental organizations in which the state apparatus is not sovereign but seen as a first among equals.[16] Third, is the trend towards the internationalization of policy regimes, that is, extra-territorial or transnational factors and processes, especially neo-liberalism, have become more important for shaping domestic state action. These three trends have changed both the substance and the sites of how and where gender issues are articulated.

In this sense, the shifting context for state policy is paralleled by a shift in feminist policy communities. Earlier initiatives to engender 'neutral' aggregates in order to expose inequalities, along with efforts to make visible the triple load of women, are now being linked to attempts to develop a macro-analytical framework which, as Antonella Picchio notes, starts 'from the work and the needs of reproduction, bring[s] out the links between poverty and the structural insecurity of labour markets'.[17]

In mainstream discourse about restructuring and crisis, women are largely invisible. The national budget reflects a country's values about whose work it values and who it rewards, and is generally assumed to affect men and women within the same class equally. The process of preparing budgets is also assumed to be a highly technical exercise best left to the 'experts' in government, international agencies and certain professional segments of the private sector such as accountants and tax lawyers. As a response to these two forces, alternative gender-sensitive budget processes have been launched in a number of countries.

The technical discourse of neo-liberal fiscal policy has increasingly circumscribed the possibilities of political practice in both the North and the South. Technical discourses like those related to deficits and balanced budgets derive a good deal of their power from scientific rationality, removing issues from the realm of public debate by lim-iting discussion to those who master the required technical language of economics. Those labelled as non-technical advocates like labour, women's groups and environmental actors are quickly dismissed as special interests in contrast to tax lawyers, accountants and financial experts who are portrayed as representing the general interest of a good business climate.[18] Power in this sense resides in consent and representation.[19]

In North America, fiscal policies bracket the political struggles over modes of governance and the challenges to Fordist welfare states. The social wage, for instance, which is a product of fiscal policies like taxation and social spending, sustained and valued a public sphere that claimed a certain share of economic production for collective purposes including aspects of reproduction and human development. In restructuring discourse, this iteration of the public sphere has been pathologized, shrunken or devolved to subnational levels of government which do not have the financial means to deal with entitlements, redistribution and effective regulation over capital.[20]

Restructuring discourse tends to emphasize certain macroeconomic indicators of governmental performance including deficit reduction and interest rate stability. This is presented as advancing a common good and economic progress. Yet this prescription rests on certain assumptions about the actors who comprise the economy. The individual who underwrites this discursive economy is relatively autonomous and able to participate in markets, is mobile between sectors and regions, and can access a limitless supply of social reproductive services in the family when they are withdrawn from the state.[21] This 'conceptual silence' obscures the social foundations of market relations and their embeddedness including their gendered and racial underpinnings.[22]

In response, feminist scholars and activists in the North (Canada, Australia, Switzerland, the UK) and the South (Barbados, Mozambique, Namibia, Tanzania, Sri Lanka, South Africa, Uganda) have begun to concentrate on 'engendering' the main economic debates of the day.[23] This means making visible the gendered underpinnings of the new welfare thinking and traditional macroeconomic policies; making an argument for social investment and showing that not all burdens can be transferred to the unpaid economy without resulting human and economic costs.

Gender-sensitive budgets represent a transition from advocacy to accountability: they audit government budgets for their impact on women and girls, men and boys. Some are conducted from within government (Australia, for example) and some are outside government or a combination of the two, as is the case in South Africa where The Women's Budget Initiative (WBI) started in 1995 as a joint effort of parliamentarians and non-governmental organizations.

Engendering economic models

Substantive equality rights require a recognition that budgetary decisions (about the allocation of resources, the distribution of income and
wealth, and stabilization of the economy) affect the lives of men and
women differently given pre-existing gender inequalities grounded in
both the division of labour and gender differentiated social rights and
obligations. These gender-based differences are generally structured in
such a way as to leave women in an unequal position in relation to the
men in their community, with less economic, social and political power
but greater responsibilities for caring for those who need the care of
others such as children and the elderly. The neo-liberal thrust in the
fiscal arena is contributing to this fundamental shift in dominant understandings of government and citizenship. Brodie refers to this process as
the 'meso narrative' of changing state forms, which she defines in the
following way: 'Meso narratives are an historical consensus (a.k.a.
philosophy of governing, societal paradigm or impositional claims)
about what is understood to be rational, progress, emancipation, justice
and so on. As such, they act as historically defined templates which
underlie a policy field, shaping the content and delivery of public
goods, and allowing for a certain measure of coherence to state activities, identity formation and kinds of political contestation.'[24]

Existing conceptual frameworks and statistics used to create budget
scenarios rest on specific notions of economic and political citizenship.
From the perspective of gender, they fail to recognize that: 'Women's
contribution to the macroeconomy is underestimated because of absent
and biased markets as well as incomplete statistics; there is an unpaid
economy (which has been variously labelled 'domestic,' 'social reproduction,' 'reproductive' or the 'care' economy) in which women do
most of the work of maintaining the labour force and keeping the social
framework in good order, both vital services for the paid economy; the
parameters of aggregate production, saving, investment, imports and
exports in the paid economy may be sensitive to different patterns of
gender relations and gender distribution of resources.'[25]

Women's alternative budgets are based on the argument that the
creation of wealth in a country depends on the output of three sectors:
the private sector commodity economy, the public service economy
and the household and community care economy.[26] Sometimes it is
assumed that the wealth creating sector is the private commodity economy while the public service economy and the household and community care economy spend what the private commodity economy has

produced. This mistaken view results from considering the circular flow of national income in isolation from the circular flow of national output. The three domains of the economy are in reality interdependent. The private commodity economy would be unable to create wealth for use by the government and families and communities if the government and families and communities did not in turn create wealth for use by the private sector. The wealth of a country consists not only of the commodities produced by the private sector, but also the public services provided by the government (law and order, communication networks, health and education) and the care economy (human capacities, social cohesion). As Budlender et al. note: 'Government budgets and policies that do not account for transfers in resource use between the market oriented, paid productive sector, and the unpaid reproductive sector cannot be guaranteed to be efficient. Instead, they are more likely to transfer costs than minimize costs. They are in danger of being a false economy. This can have feedback effects on other sectors in the economy.'[27]

A gender-sensitive budget analysis helps ensure that Efficiency in the use of resources is more broadly defined to include shifts in the unpaid care economy. Mobilization of new resources takes account of the fact that women's labour is not an underutilized resource, but an overutilized resource, in limited supply; and that households are internally differentiated and tend not to pool all their resources. Reorganization of the pattern of expenditures takes account of the fact that some externalities are gender specific. Given the existing division of labour, women's work in the care economy produces services with benefits far beyond families, raising productivity in the private commodity economy and the public service economy. The issue of sustainability is understood very broadly, going beyond financial sustainability to encompass the sustainability of the social framework, and of the economy of care that is so important to maintaining it.

Such insights would change how the effectiveness of fiscal policy is evaluated. A key issue of aggregate budgetary policy, for example, is the extent to which a budget deficit is sustainable.[28] This is conventionally judged in terms of whether it will tend to lead to financial problems, such as accelerating inflation; balance of payments crises; and an increasing and unsustainable debt burden.

Inflation and balance of payments problems are likely if the public and private sectors are already fully utilizing their capacity; labour is fully employed and the government keeps increasing the money supply to finance a growing deficit. If the deficit is instead financed by borrowing, this will be less inflationary, but may tend to drive up interest rates especially if financial markets have been deregulated. This in turn means that more and more future tax revenue will be pre-empted to service the debt. It may also deter private investment, 'crowding out' private investors because they cannot afford the high interest rates. The sustainability of a budget surplus is not conventionally judged to be a problem because a surplus does not tend to lead to financial problems. But it may lead to unemployment, low levels of capacity utilization, and an overburdening of the care economy, with consequent social and economic problems, and a breakdown in social cohesion.

One of the factors that is usually assumed to be constant is the social framework of norms, rules and values (what some economists call the 'social capital'). For instance to work well an economy needs a fund of goodwill, trust, and acceptance of and obedience to the law; plus some institutions that provide social stability and security, even though the economy is changing; institutions that can cushion individuals against shocks and see them through times of transition and restructuring. Family and community institutions in the care economy are important pillars of the social framework, generating and maintaining it. However, the social framework is not static and does interact with macroeconomic policy. High and rising deficits that generate hyperinflation may tend to lead the social framework to crumble; but so also will severely deflationary policies in which the deficit is cut rapidly and extensively, creating widespread unemployment and idle capacity. Some economists are now starting to pay attention to the interrelation between macroeconomic policies and the social framework and to ask whether in some circumstances too a rapid an inflation runs down to dangerous levels the fund of goodwill and acceptance of social norms that is needed for economies to function well. They do not, however, connect the maintenance of the social framework to women's unpaid work in the care economy.

Several policy areas illustrate these connections. First, tax cuts. The clamour for tax cuts is part of an ideology of privatization which sees a diminished role for governments. Several assumptions underpin tax cuts: a great deal of faith is placed in market forces and their ability to generate and distribute wealth in an adequate manner through the consumption and investment decisions of individual persons and firms. It signals, as Lisa Philipps suggests, a downgrading of the traditional post-war emphasis on distributive equity within tax policy.[29] Given fiscal pressures such as deficit reduction, it also undermines the state's ability to provide minimum levels of social security for those faring badly in the market or those who work in the care economy. It remains at best unclear, given gender-based economic disadvantages, to what extent women will benefit from the increased consumption power supposedly generated by tax cuts.

A second significant policy area is the de-universalization of benefits. Since the late 1980s, successive national governments in Canada have undermined the principle of universal entitlement to social welfare benefits. Both Family Allowance and the Old Age Security Program were shifted to being targeted programs. There are two ways in which these policy shifts represent a form of privatization with particular implications for women. First, the trend to de-universalize benefits suggests that poverty or low incomes are an exceptional circumstance in a person's life rather than a systemic problem that society has a stake in resolving. Women's lower incomes and wealth are factors suggesting they will be particularly vulnerable to the shrinking social safety net and the narrowing of support for social programs through targeting.[30] Second, measuring need according to joint spousal income overlooks a good deal of economic and sociological literature which demonstrates that income within households is not necessarily shared on an equal basis.

Both of these examples highlight how budgetary measures and related discursive strategies are transforming key components of the gender order. Yet there are contradictions to this neo-liberal project of privatization and contraction of the state. The privatization project is simultaneously placing greater demands on women as care-givers in the family and community and as workers in the labour market.[31] Reprivatizing the costs of social reproduction are intensifying women's labour in the provision of needs and individualizing the risks of lifetime income streams through private savings and pension funds. Yet at the same time the material conditions of the traditional family are being eroded as more and more women are providing a vital contribution to the living standard of their family through waged income. In this double movement, reprivatization is intensifying the material and discursive claims made on the family while undermining the very material and discursive conditions that could support these claims. Greater responsibility for care-giving and women's financial contribution through labour force activity is assumed, yet dependency, whether on the family or the state, is pathologized.

Gender-sensitive budget exercises such as those conducted in South Africa for the last three years offer the possibility for revealing the contradictions of such impositional claims in a concrete manner. It is through direct engagement with neo-liberal forces at the national (Departments of Finance) and international (IMF, WTO) levels that the new impositional claims of the new gender neutral, self-reliant citizen and atomistic market player are being challenged, and potentially transformed.

Alternative budgets (including local government initiatives and environmental accounting), also challenge the further disembedding of economies, especially the money economy, from the social realm of public scrutiny.[32] In this sense, they offer one strategy for challenging hegemonic ideas and representations of the art of the possible.

Notes

1 B. Jessop, 'Capitalism and Its Future: Remarks on Regulation, Government and Governance', in *Review of International Political Economy*, 4, no. 3 (1997), p. 573.
2 D. Elson, 'Macro, Meso and Micro: Gender and Economic Analysis in the Context of Policy Reform', in I. Bakker, ed., *The Strategic Silence: Gender and Economic Policy* (London: Zed Press/North South Institute, 1994) and L. McDowell, 'Life Without Father and Ford: the New Gender Order of Post-Fordism', in *Transactions of the Institute of British Geography*, 16 (1991).
3 G. Esping-Andersen, 'Welfare States at the End of the Century: the Impact of Labour Market, Family and Demographic Change', in *Social Policy Studies 21: Family, Market and Community: Equity and Efficiency in Social Policy* (Paris: OECD, 1997).
4 B. DeSousa Santos, 'Participatory Budgeting in Porto Alegre: Toward a Redistributive Democracy', in *Politics and Society*, 26, no. 4 (Dec. 1998).
5 S. Gill, 'New Constitutionalism, Democratisation and Global Political Economy', *Pacifica Review*, 10, no. 1 (1998), p. 25.
6 Ibid., p. 12.
7 S. Sassen, *Losing Control? Sovereignty in an Age of Globalization* (New York: Columbia University Press, 1996), pp. 45–46.
8 L. Philipps, 'The Rise of Balanced Budget Laws in Canada: Fiscal (Ir)Responsibility', *Osgoode Hall Law Journal*, 34, no. 4 (Winter, 1996).
9 EURODAD/WIDE, *World Bank Structural Adjustment Policies and Gender Policies* (Brussels, Sept. 1994).
10 UNDP, *Human Development Report* (Oxford: Oxford University Press, 1997 and 1998).
11 S. Razavi and C. Miller, 'Conceptual Frameworks for Gender Analysis within the Development Context', Paper Prepared for InterAgency Review Meeting, SocioEconomic and Gender Analysis, Pearl River, New York, March 69, 1997, p. 30.
12 S. Bowles and R. Edwards, *Understanding Capitalism* (New York: Collins, 1993).
13 I. Bakker, 'Identity, Interests and Ideology: the Gendered Terrain of Global Restructuring', in S. Gill, ed., *Globalization, Democratisation and Multilateralism* (Tokyo, New York: Macmillan/United Nations University Press, 1997)

and V. Spike Peterson, 'Transgressing Boundaries: Theories of Knowledge, Gender and International Relations', *Millennium*, 21, no. 2 (1992).

14   C. Mohanty, 'Under Western Eyes: Feminist Scholarship and Colonial Discourses', *Feminist Review*, 30 (Autumn, 1988).

15   N. Kabeer, 'Cultural Dopes or Rational Fools? Women and Labour Supply in the Bangladesh Garment Industry', *The European Journal of Development Research*, Nov. 1989.

16   Jessop, p. 575.

17   A. Picchio, 'The Analytical and Political Visibility of the Work of Social Reproduction', Background Papers, *Human Development Report* 1995 (New York: UNDP, 1995), p. 100.

18   See Philipps.

19   A. Gramsci, *Selections from the Prison Notebooks of Antonio Gramsci* (New York: International Publishers, 1971) and M. Foucault, *The Archaeology of Knowledge* (London: Tavistock, 1972).

20   See Philipps.

21   Ibid.

22   I. Bakker, *The Strategic Silence: Gender and Economic Policy* (London: Zed Books and the NorthSouth Institute, 1994).

23   D. Budlender and R. Sharpe, with K. Allen, *How to Do a GenderSensitive Budget Analysis: Contemporary Research and Practices* (London: Commonwealth Secretariat, 1998); S. Himmelweit, 'The Need for Gender Impact Analysis', in S. Robinson, ed., *The Purse or the Wallet? Proceedings of the Women's Budget Group Seminar, Westminster London, Feb. 12* (London: Fawcett Society, 1998); R. Sharp and R. Broomhill, 'International Policy Developments in Engendering Government Budgets', in E. Shannon, ed., *Australian Women's Policy Structures* (Hobart: Centre for Public Management and Policy, University of Tasmania, 1998); D. Budlender, ed., *The Third Women's Budget* (Cape Town: Institute for Democracy in South Africa, 1998); D. Elson, 'Gender Neutral, Gender Blind or Gender Sensitive Budgets?', Preparatory Commission to Integrate Gender into National Budgetary Policies and Procedures, London: Commonwealth Secretariat, 1997; D. Elson, 'Gender and Macroeconomic Policy', *Link in to Gender and Development*, 2 (Summer, 1997); and D. Elson, 'Integrating Gender Issues into National Budgetary Policies and Procedures within the Context of Economic Reform: Some Policy Options', Preparatory Country Mission to Integrate Gender Into National Budgetary Policies and Procedures, London: Commonwealth Secretariat, 1997.

24   J. Brodie, 'MesoDiscourses, State Forms and the Gendering of Liberal Democratic Citizenship', *Citizenship Studies*, 1, no. 2 (1997).

25   I. Bakker and D. Elson, 'Toward Engendering Budgets in Canada', *Alternative Federal Budget 1998*. Ottawa: Canadian Centre for Policy Alternatives, 1998.

26   Ibid.

27   Budlender, p. 24.

28   See Bakker and Elson.

29   See Philipps.

30   Ibid.

31   I. Bakker, ed., *Rethinking Restructuring: Gender and Change in Canada* (Toronto: University of Toronto Press, 1996).

32   See DeSousa Santos.

Part II

States, Corporations and the Potential for Transnational Politics

3
Transnational Contestation: Social Movements Beyond the State

James Goodman

Neo-liberal 'globalization' serves dominant interests and sharpens social divides, but is not a monolith.[1] The transnational integration that results from globalized neo-liberalism has double-edged or dialectical impacts. While having disempowering effects, especially on national states, it also highlights and politicizes previously obscured realms of social life.

First, it reveals the full force of corporate power, which previously dwelt in the relatively depoliticized harbour of 'domestic' civil society. The myth that business interests are national interests becomes increasingly unconvincing, and national corporate 'champions' are revealed as powerful transnational political actors. Second, neo-liberal 'globalization' exposes the logic of intergovernmentalism, previously defined as foreign or 'external' relations. To stabilize cross-border flows, dominant states construct powerful cross-national regulations; the resulting regimes are distanced from formal democracy, yet increasingly shape 'domestic' policy. Third, it disrupts national identity and forces political consciousness out of the national 'container'. National identities are increasingly constituted by a range of transnational contexts – not least by cultures of consumerism and by the political rhetoric of 'globalization'.

The result, in terms of campaigning, is three-fold. First, movements target transnational corporations (TNCs). With the shift out of national economies, corporate power greatly exceeds corporate legitimacy, opening a gap to be exploited by popular movements. Second, movements work together to mirror the scope of interstate agreements, arguing for the democratization of transnational relations, whether through national or international mechanisms. These demands receive limited recognition, as states seek to reground their legitimacy at the international level, for instance, through some re-regulation of the environment, human rights or women's rights. Third, there is a sharpening contest to establish transnational political identities, breaking the containment of national consciousness. The hierarchical state system divides political identification into local, national and global levels, taken for granted as elements of a fixed spatial scale, with the local 'contained' in the national and the national set against the global. With heightened transnational integration there is less insulation or containment, and all 'levels' operate simultaneously to constitute political cultures. In response, movements attempt to align commitments and affiliations across 'levels', and construct political identities that do not set one 'level' against another. Often these identities centre on communities of conscience, drawing on traditions of celebration and commemoration, and engaging in highly personalized forms of collective action.

The first section below, 'Transnational frameworks', draws on international political economy theory to contextualize the emerging channels for movement politics. It argues that an increasingly transnational capitalism is undermining the ideological hegemony of the states system, and that the capitalist world system has begun to engulf the states system on which it depends. The resulting contradictions open up legitimacy deficits, which are exploited by movements that define widening dimensions of transnational contestation. The second section, 'Transnational channels', discusses these movement strategies, using international and Australian examples. These fall into three fields: strategies that exploit the illegitimacy of transnational corporate power; strategies that seek to democratize intergovernmentalism; and strategies that define transnational political identities as a basis for collective action. These strategies create sharp tactical dilemmas over how to challenge neo-liberal 'globalization', and the conclusions debate ways of superseding these dilemmas.

Transnational frameworks

Global politics is conventionally analysed as encompassing interstate and non-state relations, with social movements falling into the 'non-state' category. Debates about whether state power should be accorded priority have dominated international political theory, with the 'realist' tradition according priority to state actors, while liberal internationalists emphasize non-state actors. Neo-marxists, such as Meiskins Wood and Justin Rosenberg, have argued that these debates miss the significance of the state versus non-state separation. The distinction between the political realm of the state and the depoliticized realm of society is seen as central – and unique – to capitalist society; the resulting distinctions between 'politics' and 'economics' are the 'defining characteristic of capitalism as a political terrain'.[2] In the international sphere states are defined as independent and formal equals precisely because they are bound together in a world capitalist system. Sovereignty is central to this as it 'involves the idea of the state being outside, over against civil society, autonomous, "purely political"'.[3] While questions of citizenship and jurisdiction are focused on the state, 'any aspects of social life which are mediated by relations of exchange in principle no longer receive a political definition'.[4] This separates the 'public political aspect' of global politics – formal equality within the states system – from the 'private political aspect', which involves exploitation and subordination on an unprecedented scale. The result is 'non-political' imperialism legitimated by 'political' sovereign equality – nothing less than the emergence of an 'empire of civil society'.

Formal equality – in the states system – is contradicted by substantive inequality. According to the power-political script, sovereign states are independent, isolated and constantly ready for conflict with each other. But 'their' societies are at the same time unified into a common empire of capitalist relations. This contradiction creates sharp ideological tensions, and these constantly threaten to disrupt systems of national legitimation. The tensions are intensified by neo-liberal 'globalization' as the national state is increasingly downgraded as a political agent. Ostensibly non-political institutions of the world system, such as transnational corporations, are politicized, and become vulnerable to challenges from what Wallerstein would characterize as 'anti-systemic movements'.[5]

The depoliticized realm of global politics encompasses social, economic and cultural relations, which are defined as 'normal' and outside formal politics. For world system theorists, the capitalist 'market' affects all aspects of civil society, imposing a systemic logic – the pursuit of ever-increasing rates of extracted surplus – that is constantly prone to destabilizing crises. To offset these crises, in effect to prevent the rate of profit from falling, the frontiers of surplus extraction have to be constantly expanded. This leads, by definition, to higher levels of inequality and higher rates of 'dumping', both through social oppression and environmental destruction.

The various forms of dumping impose legitimation, co-optation and other 'mop-up' requirements, including repression, that historically have been met by the state. But increasingly the state is unable to perform this role. As the private 'non-political' realm of commodification expands, both within and beyond state borders, and as the cost of that expansion rises, in terms of lost legitimacy and in terms of socio-environmental degradation, states are caught in a pincer movement. The capacity of the state system to meet capitalism's 'political' costs is undermined at just the time when the costs of accumulation are soaring. The national state can no longer pretend to contain the costs, which increasingly spill across state borders, and movements respond by sharpening the resulting legitimacy deficits.

In this way, the emergence of a relatively coherent transnational capitalist class, promoting the ideology of neo-liberal 'globalization', pulls the ground from under national social democracy.[6] Globalized neo-liberalism removes 'the national social contracts produced though centuries of social struggle without providing any significant replacement on either a global or regional scale'.[7] The neo-liberal state form is globalized, and to contain the resulting legitimacy deficits, takes on a more authoritarian role in maintaining social control and in shaping social reproduction; movement of people across borders for instance is more heavily controlled, as are social relations in the informal and household sectors.[8] Responsibility for economic regulation is increasingly handed over to interstate bodies lacking in political legitimacy and wedded to neo-liberal ideology. Internationalized dominant states govern the rest through a series of interstate bodies, leading to a form of global apartheid, with sharper exclusions within the first world, as well as between the 'first' and 'the rest'.

If state structures do indeed underpin the global extraction of surplus value, then a diminished role for the state would imply a destablization of the extraction process. If interstate competition is a key factor in constructing capitalist hegemony and is the motor force of capitalist transformation, then what happens when that motor is superseded?[9] Arrighi suggests that sharpened transnational integration both prevents the emergence of a new state-sponsored hegemony and compresses the economic cycle, simultaneously removing the spatial and temporal room for systemic stability. The result is a strengthening of interstate organizations that 'look more and more like . . . committee[s] for managing the common affairs of the world bourgeoisie'.[10]

The transfer of power to such committees undermines the non-political/political divide on which system legitimation rests; myths of state sovereignty are punctured and new realms of political contestation open up. With the emergence of interstate regimes to manage collective transnational interests, national legitimation is increasingly supplemented, and supported by legitimation at the supranational level. Challenged by movements that highlight the failure of the states system to respond to increasingly salient 'non-political' issues, states construct international regimes – generally more rhetorical than substantive – to re-ground their political legitimacy. Supranational neo-liberalism requires supranational legitimation: in the European Union for instance, a deregulated Economic and Monetary Union is paired with social, regional and citizenship policies.[11] In global fora the legitimacy gulf is for instance papered over with initiatives on the environment, population, civil rights, women's rights and indigenous peoples' rights (tellingly, not on labour rights).

Neo-liberal 'globalization', then, reveals the full scope of corporate power and fractures the mythic catch-all image of the sovereign state. Movements exploit these legitimacy deficits to wedge open a transnational ideological space, and forge new transnational linkages allowing the emergence of broad orientations bridging issues of class, gender, culture and the environment.[12] This points towards political movements that are not enclosed in the either–or choice of nationalism versus internationalism, but work through and beyond it, balancing 'levels' of identification rather than setting one against the other. In this way, transnational integration perhaps can allow 'the intermeshing extensions of locality, nationality and globality...to qualify and enhance each other rather than, as the prophets of globalism would have it, be subsumed under the latest wave of rationalising, commodifying, information-charged development'.[13]

Three ideological cleavages may be emerging, centred on modes of corporate power, institutional domination and political consciousness. In each, there are intense contradictions between national legitimation and transnational integration, and each constitutes a potential or actual realm of transnational contestation. The following section explores how these are being exploited by social movements.

Transnational channels

Three channels for movement politics have been identified – campaigns that challenge transnational corporations, contest intergovernmentalism, and define transnational consciousness. These may be combined in a single movement; but here, to highlight their contrasting logic, they are dealt with separately.

First, movements increasingly target transnationals as the primary source of social or environmental problems, exploiting gaps between corporate rhetoric and social reality. Corporate power has become increasingly internationalized as companies dodge state jurisdictions and gain greater influence over national economies. The economic power of most national states pales into insignificance in the face of global corporations. States are often unwilling or unable to impose regulations on capital, and compete in a downward spiral of deregulation. TNC priorities are increasingly set against popular priorities and movements are able to exploit corporate vulnerability.

With increased TNC exposure, the opinions of leading social movement organizations become part of the corporate 'risk profile', with reputation and profitability hinging on the ability to successfully manage NGO opinion.[14] In response, companies and industry councils produce codes of conduct, and invest much time and capital in creating consultative structures, with some moving to 'independent' evaluation and auditing of their paper commitments. For corporations there are clear dangers in this process: as the British-based *Financial Times* noted in June 1998, 'the risk of this sort of *rapprochement* is that it gives favoured NGOs greater bargaining power, which may rebound on the companies'; significantly, though, this is a 'risk worth taking... NGOs, after all, face a similar risk. Closer ties with them should help companies shape policy and operations in a way less likely to cause offence'.[15]

For many movement organizations this creates unprecedented opportunities, and some have gained significant influence over company decision-making, forcing companies to match reality with rhetoric and helping them to become socially and environmentally 'responsible'. These demands are often focused on shareholders, in what has become a genre of NGO campaigning. Many of these campaigns aim to widen the range of corporate 'stakeholders', to include those who have a 'stake', for instance in the land that corporations use, the environment they create, or the labour conditions they implement.

For example, the international campaign against Rio Tinto encompasses a wide range of movement organizations and has produced a 'stakeholders' report challenging the company's version of its corporate responsibilities. The Report focuses on three main categories of 'stakeholder': the company shareholders affected by unsustainable profit rates, poor management, high returns to senior executives and risky investments; indigenous peoples and company employees affected by violations of human rights, including land rights and rights to freedom of association; and local communities affected by the company's environmental impacts, and by its health and safety infringements.[16]

While primary industry – in this case mining – lends a particular logic to campaigning, there are similar experiences in other sectors.

NikeWatch, for instance, is a consumer boycott campaign that works on the disjuncture between marketing and lifestyle claims targeted at 'Western' consumers on the one hand and the conditions of production faced by mostly 'Third World' workers on the other. It inverts the company's advertising slogan 'Just do it' into 'Just don't do it', and focuses on the company profits, of close to $US800 million in 1996, to argue that 'if anyone can afford to provide basic rights to the workers that make its products, Nike can'.[17]

Second, movements target intergovernmental institutions. As globalizing pressures intensify, states have constructed a range of intergovernmental regimes designed to manage cross-border economic relations. These intergovernmental trade and finance regimes have involved realms of policy not conventionally seen as 'international', or even 'economic'. Agreements are seen to have wide political implications, to the extent of imposing strict across-the-board limits on legislative capacity. Powerful movements have emerged to challenge the resulting de-democratization.

The International Confederation of Free Trade Unions (ICFTU), for instance, has targeted the World Trade Organization (WTO), set up in 1994 to take over from the less institutionalized General Agreement on Tariffs and Trade (GATT). The ICFTU argues the WTO should enforce labour rights, not simply trade rights, suggesting 'the WTO's credibility is undermined when it ensures that Mickey Mouse has more rights than the workers who make toys, because it covers trade marks but not labour standards'.[18]

Reflecting the weak legitimacy of this unaccountable and yet far-reaching institution, the ICFTU campaign has gained some ground, especially at the WTO ministerials held in 1996 and in 1998, in contrast with consistent failure under the relatively uninstitutionalized GATT regime. Optimistically, the ICFTU argues this signals the start of a democratization process at the international level – 'After fifty years, in which international trade policy was dominated by a small elite of specialists, the WTO is obliged to build a broader basis of support for further liberalization and that means finding answers to the concerns of working men and women.'[19]

A more broad-based campaign has focused on the 'Asia-Pacific Economic Cooperation' (APEC), an intergovernmental forum which is wholly committed to neo-liberal modes of regulation and closed-off from popular pressure, with privileged access granted to 'peak' business organizations. Unsurprisingly, APEC has attracted widespread opposition from campaigning organizations in the Asia-Pacific and its yearly

Heads of State meetings are besieged by protests as NGOs meet in a parallel 'peoples forum'.[20]

Similar sets of alliances emerged out of campaigns against the Multilateral Agreement on Investment (MAI), an intergovernmental agreement negotiated under the Organization for Economic Cooperation and Development (OECD). In October 1997 sixty international campaign organizations that had been lobbying the OECD on the MAI, withdrew from dialogue with negotiators and signed a 'Joint Statement on the MAI'. Within a few months the statement had been signed by over 600 NGOs, providing a basis for common action that eventually defeated the measure while it was still on the drawing board.[21] Revealingly, the *Financial Times* argued that 'the central lesson is that the growing demands for greater openness and accountability that many governments face at home are spilling over into the international arena. That makes it harder for negotiators to do deals behind closed doors and submit them for rubber-stamping by parliaments. Instead, they face pressure to gain wider popular legitimacy for their actions by explaining and defending them in public.'[22]

Partly because of such pressures, states have been forced to act at the international level, for instance to address social or environmental crises, or to confer individual or collective rights. In these and other areas, states have permitted the emergence of an intergovernmental process of goal formation which has in many respects defined the terms for developing joint work between campaign organizations. Examples include indigenous groups drawing on the UN's Draft Declaration on the Rights of Indigenous Peoples, tabled in 1995; women's organizations referring to the UN Platform for Action signed by governments at the 1995 UN women's conference; and environmental organizations focusing on the process established under the 1992 UN Climate Change Convention. Organizations highlight government failures to abide by agreed policies, and challenge the adequacy of the intergovernmental agreements; at the same time, movements work across borders, realizing collective consciousness and enhancing political leverage.

As Mick Dodson, former Aboriginal Social Justice Commissioner in Australia, stated in 1998, 'The feeling that we are not alone has transformed the way many of us approach the whole struggle. We now see that it is a global struggle, not just between a single indigenous people and a government, but between the world's indigenous peoples and the world's colonial governments.'[23]

Third – and finally – movements develop transnational linkages and solidarities, offering a potential basis for transnational political identities.

In many respects, political action to challenge neo-liberal 'globalization' implies the necessity for transnational consciousness. Such identities may emerge out of campaigns that consciously construct alternative forms of social organization. These can be obscured as they do not generally employ the standard political channels, but when they become visible they can present a profound challenge to dominant assumptions of political culture.

Indigenous movements offer particularly fundamental examples of such campaigns, especially where they involve assertions of community ownership against colonial domination, to challenge national cultural hierarchies. One legacy of cultural colonialism is the presence of indigenous cultural objects and human remains in the museums and graveyards of former colonizers; demands that these be returned highlight the injustice of their removal, and challenge the present-day cultural assumptions held by the authorities which may prevent their return.

One example from Australia is the Tambo Repatriation Committee, which was set up to secure the return of Jimmy Tambo's remains, found in a Cleveland funeral home in 1993, to the Muinanjali people of Palm Island, Northern Australia. He had been one of nine indigenous Australians removed from Palm Island in 1883 and employed in Barnum's touring circus in the US. After his death in 1884 his body was put on show in a Cleveland museum, and in 1994 two of Tambo's descendants made the journey to Cleveland to repatriate their ancestor's remains. This story of capture, performance, death, display and eventual return has deep resonances with ongoing disputes about how to recognize the atrocities and injustices of colonial occupation.[24]

A similar process of asserting alternative political identities occurs within environmental campaigns, especially at the 'grassroots' level, as in campaigns to prevent the destruction of old-growth forests. These often take the form of direct action to protect trees, orientated around conservation values and concerns for the wider environment, including biodiversity and climate change. These campaigners forge powerful communities of resistance, explicitly defined as offering non-hierarchical social alternatives for the participants.

Western Australia's Giblett Forest blockade, for instance, was mounted in April 1997 by activists who built and occupied a platform 30 metres above the ground in an old Karri tree. For the next seven months a camp of between 50 and 200 people was maintained at the foot of the tree, as an alternative community. In December 1997 the campaign won a temporary (six-month) moratorium for the Giblett forest and agreed to dismantle the camp. The manager of the Department of Conservation and Land Management was required to make a symbolic visit to the forest camp, to make clear his public commitment, and the protest ended amid celebrations that attracted the full blaze of media publicity.

Urban environmentalists construct similar transnational identities, often defined against dominant consumer culture. Critical Mass, for instance, began as an 'organized coincidence' in San Francisco in 1992, where cyclists began joining together in a celebration of non-car transport. By 1998 rides were being held every month, in at least 70 cities mostly in the US and the UK, but also in Australia, in Israel, Brazil and Japan. Critical Mass riders have a wide range of motivations, but upper-most is the celebratory dimension, of strength and safety in numbers. This is expressed, for instance, in periodic bike-lifts, where riders dismount and lift their bikes to the sky in an expression of defiance and collective identity. The defiance is in some respects territorial, as cyclists reclaim public space from private cars, in the name of public responsibilities.

These themes of direct action and celebration are also well-established in movements for sexual liberation, which define spheres of identification distinct from dominant heterosexual identities. The resulting communities of consciousness are invariably marginalized by dominant culture, but find strength in the assertion of transnational identities, within a lineage of international lesbian and gay consciousness. These are expressed in traditions of celebrating sexual liberation, and in asserting personal and collective pride; in Australia, for instance, the first Sydney Gay Pride was held in 1978 to commemorate the Stonewall police riot in New York; it ended in a similar police action, and itself has become an event to be commemorated, through the Gay and Lesbian Mardi Gras.[25] While the event is as much a carrier for consumerist individualism as for collective action, it has played a key role in legitimizing non-heterosexual identities in Australia.

Embedded in each of these examples is a powerful emotional appeal, often involving commemoration and celebration. The appeal is aimed directly at personal identity and at forging communities of resistance that cross or challenge national borders, to transform consciousness and create alternatives. These affiliations, from 'within' the national state, can become a powerful foundation for collective action, and for transnational communities of consciousness.

Dilemmas, prospects and conclusions

The ideological stability of global politics is disrupted by the emergence of transnational corporate power, by the strengthening of intergovernmental institutions, and by social divisions that emerge out of the pursuit of transnational class interests. The transnational movements and campaigns emerge to focus on the resulting ideological disjunctures – between corporate power and popular priorities, between claims to popular sovereignty and increasing disempowerment of state structures, and between assertions of a hegemonic 'national' identity and the emergence of wider class affiliations. These campaigns and movements offer alternatives to neo-liberal 'globalization': they have the potential to re-socialize corporate power, to democratize transnational relations, and to constitute cross-national 'communities of conscience'. In this, they perhaps point the way to forms of participatory democracy that flow through and beyond the state – to match the transnational constituencies that are emerging from neo-liberal 'globalization'.

These lines of political contestation rest upon the ability to construct concerted campaigns across movement 'sectors' and across national borders. The strategies confront movements with intense dilemmas between confrontation and engagement, creating divisions which can be – and are – exploited to maintain the status quo. TNCs, for instance, may respond to movement challenges by attempting to co-opt NGOs as 'advisers' in the drawing up and implementation of 'codes of conduct'. NGOs are recruited to legitimate corporate power and to forestall demands for that power to be regulated; ideologies of corporate responsibility are invoked, with self-regulation as the explicit objective. Similarly, states may seek to 'reform' intergovernmental organizations, and recruit NGOs, for instance through 'side agreements' and 'clauses' which may be incorporated into existing institutions or agreements. Here, ideologies of accountability – for instance, through 'transparency' agreements, or through 'consultative' structures – may be invoked. Again, the primary objective may be to legitimize and to stabilize, not to change institutional practices. A similar set of issues arises in relation to transnational consciousness, which can be submerged into wider and in some ways more powerful forms of transnational consumerism and global elitism. Here, the process of invoking cosmopolitan principles may simply serve dominant interests – and be defined either as entirely consistent with modes of imperialist intervention or, alternatively, be successfully marginalized as anti-national.

In each of these fields, an ability to work across the engagement–confrontation divide may be crucial. Clearly, some NGOs judge that the costs of engagement, particularly in terms of lost legitimacy for their campaigns, are outweighed by the benefits, in terms of increased influence. Others come to different conclusions. Here, perhaps the key to any continued leverage for campaigning is solidarity between those that take the 'inside' track and those remaining on the 'outside'. Failures and frustrations, on one or the other side of the engagement–confrontation divide, can then shape the overall direction of campaigns. In this way, perhaps the tensions and conflicts between NGOs on the question of engagement – whether with TNCs, with interstate institutions, or with globalist identities – can become productive rather than destructive. Failure of engagement may lead to sharper confrontation, and vice versa; failure of both, as appears to have happened with the WTO debate, may lead to the search for genuine new alternatives.

More generally, transnational strategies are directed at political struggles beyond the state, and may be unintentionally complicit with a neo-liberal anti-statism. Reliance on abstract globalism and a 'global civil society' to achieve political ends is not only naive but can work to delegitimize local and national mobilization. But as illustrated here, transnational contestation need not involve a leap into globalism, nor its opposite, namely a retreat into local or national enclaves. Instead it is possible to align local, national and international actions, so that they become mutually reinforcing. The task of re-orientating state structures and national affiliations may then be prioritized, not rejected.

This relatively optimistic picture may read like an attempt to snatch victory from the jaws of defeat, and in some respects that is what it has to be. The wave of neo-liberal 'globalization', much like earlier waves of capitalist restructuring, is directed at overcoming obstacles to accumulation, and in the present era the main obstacle and target of neo-liberal restructuring has been the interventionist state. But the very success of this ideology creates new contradictions and instabilities, and in some ways these are more intense than those they replace, and may have greater potential of opening up possibilities for social and political transformation. In this double-sided contradictory way, neo-liberal 'globalization' contains within it the seeds of its own destruction. The seeds have to be planted and nourished, and transnational agency has a key role to play in this.

Notes

1   I would like to thank the Research Committee of the University of Technology, Sydney, Australia, for research funding.
2   E. Meiskins Wood, *Democracy against Capitalism* (Cambridge: Cambridge University Press, 1991), p. 14.
3   J. Rosenberg, *The Empire of Civil Society* (London: Verso, 1994), p. 27.
4   Ibid., p. 129.

5 I. Wallerstein, *The Capitalist World-economy* (Cambridge: Cambridge University Press, 1979).
6 K. Van Der Pijl, *Transnational Classes and International Relations* (London: Routledge, 1998) and L. Sklair, *Sociology of the Global System* (London: Harvester Wheatsheaf, 1995).
7 S. Amin, 'The Challenge of Globalisation', *Review of International Political Economy*, 3, no. 2 (1996), p. 253.
8 P. Hirst and G. Thompson, *Globalisation in Question* (Cambridge: Polity, 1996) and J. Petman, *Worlding Women* (Sydney: Allen and Unwin, 1996).
9 G. Arrighi, *The Long Twentieth Century* (London: Verso, 1994).
10 Ibid., p. 331.
11 J. Goodman, *Nationalisms and Transnationalism: the National Conflict in Ireland and European Union Integration* (Aldershot: Avebury Press, 1996) and J. Goodman, 'The European Union: Reconstituting Democracy Beyond the Nation-state', in A. McGrew, ed., *The Transformation Of Democracy? Globalisation and Territorial Democracy* (Cambridge: Polity Press, 1997).
12 J. Hirsch, 'Nation-state, International Regulation and the Question of Democracy', *Review of International Political Economy*, 2 no. 2 (1995), pp. 267–84; J. Hirsch, 'Globalisation, Class and the Question of Democracy', in L. Panitch and C. Leys, eds, *Socialist Register 1999: Global Capitalism versus Democracy* (London: Merlin Press, 1999), pp. 278–93; Y. Sakamoto, ed., *Global Transformation: Challenges to the State System* (Tokyo: United Nations University, 1994).
13 P. James, *Nation Formation: a Theory of Abstract Community* (London: Sage, 1996), pp. 196–8.
14 *No Hiding Place: Business and the Politics of Pressure*, Control Risks Group, London, July 1997. See *Drillbits & Tailings*, Aug. 1997, Project Underground, San Francisco.
15 *Financial Times*, 15 June 1998.
16 See *Rio Tinto: the Tainted Titan, the Stakeholders Report 1997*, International confederation of Chemical, Energy, Mine and General Workers' Unions, 1998, ICEM: Sydney. See ICEM website, http://www.icem.org.
17 In Australia the campaign has produced a report outlining labour conditions at factories producing Nike products in Indonesia: see *Sweating for Nike, A Report on Labour Conditions in the Sport Shoe Industry*, Community Aid Abroad Briefing Paper, 16 Nov. 1996, Melbourne.
18 ICFTU Press Release on labour standards and Trade, 'A Significant Step Forward in a Continuing Debate', 12 Dec. 1996.
19 'Geneva WTO Meeting Marks Further Step Forward in Core Labour Standards Campaign', Stephen Pursey, ICFTU, at: http://www.icftu.org
20 *Confronting Globalization: Reasserting Peoples' Rights*, Resolution of the Asia-Pacific Peoples' Assembly, 10–15 Nov. 1998, Kuala Lumpur, Malaysia; see also J. Goodman, 'Go Tell It on Smokey Mountain', *Arena Magazine*, Nov. 1996.
21 Joint NGO Statement on the MAI, Paris, 7 Oct. 1997.
22 'Network Guerrillas', *Financial Times*, 30 April 1998.
23 Cited in S. Pritchard, ed., *Indigenous Peoples, the United Nations and Human Rights* (Sydney: Zed Books and Federation Press, 1998).
24 The Australian National Library hosted an exhibition based on the Tambo story in 1997, at which the curator stated: 'what is at stake is not only the

reclamation of personal Aboriginal histories, but also the acknowledgement of the history of dispossession, destruction and removal of indigenous Australians within the narrative of the nation'. See National Library of Australia, *Captive Lives: Looking for Tambo and his Companions*, exhibition notes and background information kit, 1997.

25   See *It Was a Riot: Sydney's First Gay and Lesbian Mardi Gras*, 78ers Festival Events Group, SGLMG, 1998.

4

Globalization, Law and Transnational Corporations: a Deepening of Market Discipline

Claire Cutler

Introduction: globalization and transnational corporations

'Globalization' is surely one of the most used and contested concepts of the moment in many fields of study.[1] For example, the imaginations of eminent scholars in both politics and law have been captured by the issue of the retreat or decline of the state wrought by forces of globalization.[2] It is most curious, however, that transnational corporations, which are regarded by students of political economy as major participants in globalization processes, are given scant attention in international law. A brief review of the reasoning attending the concern of students of politics with the significance of transnational corporations will assist in setting the stage for an examination of this curiosity of law.

Political economists describe transnational corporations as the 'central organizers', the 'engines of growth' and the 'driving force' of the world economy.[3] They are the 'main actors' and 'most significant economic players in the world economy';[4] the 'linchpins', 'prime agents' of the global political economy,[5] and 'the most important economic institutions of our time.'[6] For many of these analysts, transnational corporations are regarded as central elements in contemporary transformations in the global political economy. Indeed, there is a sense that we are in the midst of qualitative transformations of the global political economy that are only intelligible by shifting our focus away from states to other actors and agents, like markets and firms.[7] Susan Strange is well-known for her efforts to focus attention on the political significance of firms as part of a more general shift from a politics based on states to that based on markets and triangular diplomacy between states, between states and firms, and between firms.[8] She argues that 'the progressive integration of the world economy, through international production, has shifted the balance of power away from states and toward world markets. That shift has led to the transfer of some power in relation to civil society from territorial states to nonterritorial TNCs'; it has 'actually made political players of the TNCs.'[9] Strange argues that transnational corporations are 'exercising a parallel authority alongside governments in matters of economic management affecting the location of industry and investment, the direction of technological innovation, the management of labour relations and the fiscal extraction of surplus value.'[10]

Others too emphasize that changes in productive relations associated more generally with forces of globalization are central to the enhanced significance of transnational corporations. Stephen Kobrin argues that the contemporary world economy differs significantly from that of the previous century in that it is broader in terms of the number of economies involved and it is deeper in terms of the density and velocity of trade and investment transactions.[11] Moreover, he argues that it is insufficient to shift focus from states to markets. Rather, the shift is from trade markets and markets for portfolio investment to the internationalization of production through multinational corporations. In addition, the transnational fusion of national markets, due to size inadequacy of even the largest markets, and the proliferation of corporate strategic alliances reflect movement to a networked global economy which Kobrin argues is transforming the 'mode of organization of international economic transactions from hierarchically structured MNEs to networks.'[12] What is significant in this analysis is the idea of a fusion of national markets. Kobrin is not arguing that national markets are linked (i.e., internationalized), but that they are fused transnationally as part of corporate strategy to adjust to the changing terms of competition generated by technological imperatives.

Many associate contemporary transformations in the world economy with the increasing adoption of transnational strategies and collaborative efforts between and among corporations.[13] Indeed, Charles-Albert Michalet differentiates multinational corporate strategies of the past from emerging global strategies and structures.[14] Global strategies involve investment initiatives to expand world market shares, while multinational strategy is focused more on local and national markets. Transnational corporations, as the main agents in the transformation from a multinational to a global political economy, are driven by a distinctive logic. This logic ties 'outward FDI, the delocation of manufacturing or services activities, mergers and acquisitions' to 'strengthening a firm's competitiveness in the world market', and regards local national inhibitory regulation as unacceptable.[15] This strategy involves government provision of an 'enabling environment' in which firms' transaction costs are reduced as much as possible and 'market forces are not constrained or distorted'.[16] In a word, the logic dictates a regulatory environment consistent with what Stephen Gill refers to as 'disciplinary neo-liberalism' and a 'new constitutionalism'.[17] Disciplinary neo-liberalism expands the opportunities for the expansion of transnational capital by disciplining societies into the acceptance of neo-liberal principles that privilege the sphere of private accumulation and set limits to possibilities for democratic challenges to corporate activities.[18] Disciplinary neo-liberalism deepens globalized market relations through the disembedding of productive processes from national political economies and is thus an integral aspect of globalization.[19] Interestingly, and here we return to our earlier legal curiosity, the globalization of law is an integral part of enabling and facilitating global corporate initiatives and strategies.[20] Law, both domestic and international, deepens economic integration and neo-liberal discipline by removing or harmonizing barriers to trade, investment and taxation,[21] thus contributing to the denationalization of relations of production, exchange and capital accumulation. However, the agents of legal globalization remain obscure. Indeed, transnational corporations are rendered 'invisible' by international legal theory which posits their incapacity to function as 'subjects' of law. There is thus an interesting and curious disjuncture between the legal status and the practical significance of transnational corporations. This paper will examine this phenomenon and suggest that there are political and ideological reasons for the disengagement of law and fact. Moreover, this disengagement parallels and reproduces a growing disengagement of law and society.

The next section examines the doctrine of international legal personality and the invisible legal status of transnational corporations. The following section then problematizes this state of affairs by examining ways in which the law does recognize the significance of transnational corporations, but treats them as exceptional deviations from the norm of invisibility. The paper then concludes with the implications of corporations using their personality strategically to advance the disengagement of law and society and to further deepen private processes of transnational capital accumulation.

The International Legal Personality of Transnational Corporations[22]

Under international law, transnational corporations are 'invisible' as 'subjects' of the law; they exists as 'objects'.[23] This requires some explanation and an excursion into legal theory, for the legal status of transnational corporations flows directly from the dominant mode of theorizing in Anglo-American law. The dominant legal theory, in turn, is influenced by the history of corporations and of their associations with states.[24]

Very basically, the dominant legal theory is legal positivism, which identifies international law with positive acts of state consent.[25] According to legal positivism, states are the only official 'subjects' or 'persons' of international law since they are the entities that have the 'capacity to enter into legal relations and to have legal rights and duties'.[26] Indeed, for legal positivists, states are the only entities with full, original and universal legal personality;[27] states are the only proper actors bound by international law.[28] In so far as non-state entities, like individuals, corporations and international organizations, are capable of asserting legal personality, it is only derivative of and conditional upon state personality and state consent. This predominant ideology originated in the nineteenth century when 'legal positivism [took] the eighteenth century law of nations, a law common to individuals and states,' and transformed it into public and private international law. The former was deemed to apply to states, the latter to individuals.'[29] Henceforth, only states would enjoy full international legal personality, which can be defined as 'the capacity to bring claims arising from the violation of international law, to conclude valid international agreements, and to enjoy privileges and immunities from national jurisdictions.'[30]

Positivist definitions of international law have had a great impact on modern conceptions of the international legal status of corporations. Corporate legal personality is analogized with the personality of individuals as objects and not as subjects of the law. As objects, corporations may be granted benefits under the law, but the grant is ultimately derivative of state authority. While there appears to be some softening of the state-centricity of international law, it is important to recognize that the law remains a subject-based order wherein the state remains the subject and other entities acquire as much personality as states confer upon them as 'objects' of the law.[31] Thus states remain the main actors and other actors like individuals and corporations exist as 'objects' with derivative personality in that they cannot make laws and they can only initiate legal claims or enjoy privileges and immunities through the instrumentality of the state.

While corporations and individuals have some international legal personality and rights under special treaties, this is explained by positivists as exceptional, rare and ultimately derivative of state authority.[32] Typically, the transnational corporation's role in international law will be defined by reference to its ties to a particular state through the laws governing nationality and state responsibility. The international legal personality of corporations was first confirmed in the *Barcelona Traction, Light and Power* case as resembling that of individuals as nationals of a state.[33] A corporation is thus regarded as having the nationality of the state in which it is incorporated and in whose territory it has its registered office. Nationality, once established, would entitle a corporation to diplomatic protection under international law. However, this case held that it is within the sole discretion of the state to determine whether it will proceed with such a claim on behalf of a corporation. Moreover, if a state refuses to take action on behalf of a corporation, the corporation is left to pursue its remedies under domestic law.

The association of corporations with individuals has been a powerful influence and can be traced to the more general theorization of corporate personality in Anglo-American domestic law. In the Anglo-American world, the doctrines governing corporate legal personality developed alongside the emergence of market society and capitalist productive relations.[34] In England, these doctrines were formulated on the basis of Roman law conceptions and were evident as early as the fifteenth century in the chartering by the Crown of craft guilds and trading companies.[35] Corporations came over time to be regarded as business entities and 'artificial persons' endowed with certain 'inherent legal attributes' analogous to those of human persons (i.e., rights to sue and be sued, to contract, to acquire and dispose of property, etc.).[36]

In addition, 'in early seventeenth century England, as in early nineteenth century Canada, the chartering of a corporation was seen as a way of choosing entrepreneurs to initiate, develop and profit from a special project thought to be for the general good.'[37] In England, the early corporation was regarded as an entrustment by the King to accomplish public purposes. So it was that foreign trading corporations were granted certain economic privileges in the seventeenth century. In the eighteenth century, both in England and in the United States, the purpose of the business corporation was still perceived as the accomplishment of some public function.[38] Domestic corporate laws developed to encourage these enterprises and to protect investors through, for example, rules limiting the liability of shareholders.

Paradoxically, the analogy between corporations and individuals works in domestic law to expand corporate legal personality, whilst under international law it produces the opposite result. International corporate persons, like individuals, enjoy only a very limited personality under international law. In theory, corporations cannot sue nor be sued under international law, save for through the state under the laws governing nationality of claims and the doctrine of state responsibility. Moreover, notions of corporate personality were developed at a time when corporate activities were limited and localized in operation. Arguably, establishing the nationality of an eighteenth- or nineteenth-century corporation was not problematic. Today however, corporations span many national jurisdictions and in some cases defy easy determination of nationality.[39] As Phillip Blumberg notes:

> Multinational corporations are challenging traditional concepts of corporation law and international law. Legal concepts fashioned to serve the needs of the largely agrarian society of yesterday, in which the role of business enterprise was both limited and local, have become archaic in a world where business is conducted worldwide by giant corporate groups composed of affiliated companies in dozens of countries.[40]

The implications are particularly acute when trying to establish corporate liability and responsibility. Under international law corporate liability must be founded through the laws governing state responsibility and nationality. When nationality is difficult to determine, the imposition of liability on a corporation for its actions or those of its subsidiaries is unlikely. Moreover, establishing corporate responsibility is made even more elusive when domestic legal doctrines (shareholder limited liability and entity theory) shield a parent corporation from domestic legal liability for the actions of its subsidiaries.[41] The implications for diminishing state authority over the activities of transnational corporations and their affiliates are significant. Moreover, corporate theory no longer rests upon presumptions of public purposes and public goods. Indeed, who is the 'public' for corporations operating in multiple national jurisdictions under multiple legal systems? Other theoretical foundations for the corporation emphasizing its private nature are being advanced, as too are growing claims to corporate constitutional rights.[42] Corporations have gained rights through precedent-setting cases in North America and Europe where the Canadian Charter of Rights and Freedoms, the American Bill of Rights, and European Union Law are being used to advance corporate rights.[43] The domestic expansion of corporate rights is not being met with a corresponding expansion of state regulation. In fact, most states are curtailing their corporate control functions in line with the adoption of more laissez-faire and permissive rules encouraging corporate investment activities.[44] Indeed, the pattern amongst many developed states appears to be competitive deregulation and a 'race to the bottom' in terms of corporate regulation.[45] Nor has there been much success in developing multilateral regulations under the auspices of the United Nations or the Organization for Economic Cooperation and Development (OECD) of any but the most permissive sort.[46]

Clearly, both domestic and international legal theories are inadequate in capturing the nature and structure of the contemporary transnational corporation. Doctrines of legal personality, when combined with the domestic expansion of corporate rights, render transnational corporations increasingly more 'invisible' and, consequently, potentially unaccountable in the public domain. Moreover, the globalization of law, through the harmonization of domestic corporate law, the global unification of transnational legal standards, and the activities of a transnational *mercatocracy* comprised of both governmental and non-governmental actors, advances the invisibility and potential unaccountability of the transnational corporation.[47] As one author observes about the growing transnationalization of corporate law, '[g]lobalization may therefore impede the goal of accountability and openness normally associated with "rule of law" jurisdictions.'[48]

The inadequacy of legal corporate theory has not been lost on all analysts. As William Twining observes '[t]he concept of legal personality, an old favorite of Austinian analytical jurisprudence, may be ripe for a revival in a global context.'[49] Others make the case for an expansion of corporate legal responsibility under international law.[50] Twining argues that the increasing globalization of law and the creation of a transnational legal order reflect a more general disengagement of law and state. However, the disengagement is better viewed as operating between law and society because states are deeply implicated in advancing and deepening neo-liberal discipline. Competition states are contributing to an expansion of corporate power and thus are assisting in driving a wedge between law and the institutions and processes of democratic society.[51] This is working what Robert Cox refers to as a 'decomposition of civil society', as a gap widens between society and its political leaders.[52] The next section will examine some instances of the expansion of private corporate power.

Theory versus practice: the practical significance of transnational corporations

Thus far we have considered the theoretical aspects of the legal personality of transnational corporations. We have also alluded to the growing practical significance of transnational corporations, both domestically and globally. However, what remains to be addressed is the growing disjuncture between legal theory and state practice as regards the legal personality of transnational corporations. While international legal theory persists in positing the invisibility of transnational corporations as subjects, states are busy endowing such corporations with powers normally exercised by subjects alone. As discussed earlier, one of the major attributes of legal subjects is the ability to sue and to be sued. We also noted above that under international law, corporations do not have the right to sue or be sued. Thus, article 34 of the Statute of the International Court of Justice provides that only states may be parties to contentious proceedings before the Court. However, there are exceptions to this rule and the exceptions appear to be proliferating.[53] We will here consider the most notable exceptions involving the legal staus of corporations in proceedings governed by the International Center for the Settlement of Investment Disputes (ICSID), the Canada–US Free Trade Agreement (FTA), the North American Free Trade Agreement (NAFTA), and the failed OECD initiative for a Multilateral Investment Agreement (MAI).

In an effort to promote foreign investment in developing countries and to protect foreign investors, the World Bank (International Bank for Reconstruction and Development) created the International Center for the Settlement of Investment Disputes (ICSID) to deal with investment disputes between states and foreign corporations.[54] It was felt that significant obstacles posed by the limited international legal personality of corporations would be overcome by giving foreign investors a legal right to make a direct claim against a host state.[55] The ability for corporations to take direct actions against host states and the 'delocalized' nature of the dispute settlement proceedings[56] have contributed greatly to investor confidence and there has been a steady increase in ICSID's case load.[57]

The Canada–US Free Trade Agreement (FTA) also provides corporations as private parties access to binational binding dispute settlement panels in cases involving investment, anti-dumping and countervailing measures.[58] Once again, corporations are provided direct access to dispute settlement in a de-localized setting. A similar procedure has been adopted in the North American Free Trade Agreement (NAFTA).[59] In contrast, 'proposals to grant private parties ... access to the GATT [General Agreement on Tariffs and Trade] dispute settlement system, in order to relieve them from the discretion of their home governments to take up the complaint, have not been included in the reform of the dispute settlement mechanism under the WTO [World Trade Organization] arrangements.'[60] This has been significant, according to Lorraine Eden, in the considerable weakness of WTO discipline when compared to NAFTA discipline.[61]

Finally, it appears that the now stalled OECD initiative for the creation of a Multilateral Investment Agreement (MAI) would have contained binding dispute settlement procedures for foreign corporations to make claims against host states.[62]

These developments are significant aspects of the expansion of corporate legal personality.[63] They sit uneasily with conventional legal theory and suggest that state practice and legal theory are out of step. The disjuncture between theory and practice is instructive politically and ideologically. It is noteworthy that in each case of expanded corporate legal personality corporations receive the benefits of the greater enforceability of their claims and the enhanced security of their investments, but are not subject to the accretion of their corporate responsibilities or public accountability. Moreover, when read in the broader context of the commitment of the trade and investment regimes to the liberalization, increased transparency and enforceability of investment practices, enhanced corporate protections complement neo-liberal discipline rather nicely. In providing enhanced protection for corporate capital accumulation the legal exceptions assist in the transnational expansion of capital. Developing states hungry for foreign capital and the access to markets that transnational corporations provide are not about to quibble with enhanced corporate protections. Indeed, there has been a major attitudinal change as regards the attractiveness of foreign investment that Strange analyses as part of the shift in power from states to markets more generally.[64]

The move to expanded corporate personality is consistent with the more general expansion of corporate power and authority in the world. It is an important move in determining 'who gets what, when and how', illustrating the political and distributional dimensions of legal personality. Relatedly, the asymmetry between legal theory and state practice is also instructive in terms of the ideological functions of law. In addition to identifying winners and losers, the law transmits imagery, ideology and mythology about the world.[65] Today the law privileges private ordering, exalting market-based regulation as the model best suited to achieving efficiency and security in a globalizing world. But the rhetoric of legal globalization obscures the distributional impact of neo-liberal discipline and market-based legal solutions. As David Kennedy notes, '[s]aying that "things are getting more and more international" is a way of not talking about who is getting what.'[66] We need to start talking about who is getting what through a critical examination of the theory and practice of corporate legal personality. Moreover, this examination must ensure that the expansion of corporate rights is accompanied by a commensurate expansion of corporate duties.

Notes

1   A review of the increasingly vast literature on 'globalization' is well beyond the scope of this essay. However, some of the more interesting analyses include A. Giddens, *The Consequences of Modernity* (Cambridge: Polity Press, 1990); D. Held, *Democracy and Global Order: From the Modern State to Cosmopolitan Governance* (Stanford: Stanford University Press, 1995); P. Hirst and G. Thompson, *Globalization in Question* (Cambridge: Cambridge University Press, 1996); J. Rogers Hollingsworth and R. Boyer, eds, *Contemporary Capitalism: the Embeddedness of Institutions* (Cambridge: Cambridge University Press, 1997); F. Jameson, *Postmodernism, or The Cultural Logic of Late Capitalism* (Durham: Duke University Press, 1991); R. Robertson, *Globalization: Social Theory and Global Culture* (London and Thousand Oaks, Calif.: Sage, 1992).

2   S. Strange, *The Retreat of the State: the Diffusion of Power in the World Economy* (Cambridge: Cambridge University Press, 1996); Oscar Schachter, 'The Decline of the Nation-State and its Implications for International Law', *Columbia Journal of Transnational Law*, 36 (7) (1997), pp. 7–23.

3   Strange, *The Retreat of the State*, p. 45, citing the *World Investment Report* (1992), pp. 1, 6.

4   C.-A. Michalet, 'Transnational Corporations and the Changing International Economic System', *Transnational Corporations*, 3 (1) (Feb. 1994), pp. 14, 17.

5   D. Held and A. McGrew, 'The End of the Old Order? Globalization and the Prospects for World Order', *Review of International Studies*, 24 (Dec. 1998), p. 231.

6   R. Sally, 'Multinational Enterprises, Political Economy and Institutional Theory: Domestic Embeddedness in the Context of Internationalization', *Review of International Political Economy*, 1 (1) (Spring 1994), p. 168.

7   For the expansion of corporate power and authority in the world see A.C. Cutler, 'Locating "Authority" in the Global Political Economy', *International Studies Quarterly*, 43 (1999), pp. 59–81.

8   *The Retreat of the State; States and Markets: an Introduction to International Political Economy* (Oxford: Blackwell, 1989); and with J. Stopford, *Rival States, Rival*

Firms: Competition for World Market Shares (Cambridge: Cambridge University Press, 1991).

9   *The Retreat of the State*, pp. 46 and 45.

10   *The Retreat of the State*, p. 65.

11   'The Architecture of Globalization: State Sovereignty in a Networked Global Economy', in *Governments, Globalization and International Business*, ed. J.H. Dunning (Oxford and New York: Oxford University Press, 1997), p. 147.

12   'The Architecture of Globalization', p. 151.

13   See A.C. Cutler, V. Haufler and T. Porter, eds, *Private Authority and International Affairs* (New York: SUNY Press, 1999) for historic and contemporary strategies and institutional structures devised by private actors to regulate corporate and state behaviour.

14   'Transnational Corporations and the Changing International Economic System'.

15   Ibid., pp. 18–19.

16   Ibid., p. 20.

17   'Globalization, Market Civilization, and Disciplinary Neoliberalism', *Millennium: Journal of International Studies*, 24 (1995), pp. 399–423.

18   A.C. Cutler, 'Global Capitalism and Liberal Myths: Dispute Settlement in Private International Trade Relations', *Millennium: Journal of International Studies*, 24 (1995), pp. 377–97.

19   On the deepening of the impact of global forces on national and local communities see J. McGrew, 'The State in Advanced Capitalist Societies', in J.P. Allen, P. Braham and P. Lewis, eds, *Political and Economic Forms of Modernity* (Cambridge: Polity Press, 1992), p. 107.

20   See A.C. Cutler, 'Public Meets Private: the International Unification and Harmonisation of Private International Trade Law', *Global Society: Journal of Interdisciplinary International Relations*, 13 (1) (Jan. 1999), pp. 25–48.

21   See L. Eden, 'The Emerging North American Investment Regime', *Transnational Corporations*, 5 (3) (Dec. 1996), pp. 61–98, for the deep integration of these areas according to neo-liberal principles resulting from the bilateral Canada–United States Free Trade Agreement (FTA), the trilateral North American Free Trade Agreement (NAFTA), and the multilateral General Agreement on Tariffs and Trade (GATT) and the World Trade Organization (WTO). For a discussion of the European situation, see C. Ball, 'The Making of a Transnational Capitalist Society: the Court of Justice, Social Policy, and Individual Rights Under the European Community's Legal Order', *Harvard International Law Journal*, 37 (2) (Spring 1996), pp. 307–88.

22   There is considerable variation in the definitions given to the terms multinational and transnational corporation. The United Nations, for example, distinguishes between multinational corporations (those owned and controlled by entities or persons from more than one country) and transnational corporations (those owned and controlled by nationals of one country, but which operate across national borders). This paper uses the term transnational corporation for both types of enterprise. See P.T. Muchlinski in *Multinational Enterprises and the Law* (Oxford: Blackwell, 1995), pp. 12–13.

23   F. Johns, 'The Invisibility of the Transnational Corporation: An Analysis of International Law and Legal Theory', *Melbourne University Law Review*, 19 (1994), pp. 893–923. R. Higgins, in 'Conceptual Thinking about the

Individual Under International Law', in R. Falk, F. Kratochwil and
S. Mendolvitz, eds, *International Law: a Contemporary Perspective* (Boulder,
Colo.: Westview Press, 1985), p. 478, defines a subject as an entity 'bearing
rights and responsibilities' without the intervention of a state, whereas
objects do not bear rights and responsibilities.
24 Muchlinski, *Multinational Enterprises and the Law; Akehurst's Modern Introduction to International Law*, 7th rev. edn by Peter Malanczuk (London and New
York: Routledge, 1997), ch. 6; P.I. Blumberg, *The Multinational Challenge to
Corporation Law: The Search for a New Corporate Personality* (New York and
Oxford: Oxford University Press, 1993).
25 For legal positivism see R.J. Beck, A. Clark Arend and R.D. Vander Lugt, *International Rules: Approaches for International Law and International Relations*
(New York and Oxford: Oxford University Press, 1993), ch. 3.
26 *Akehurst's Modern Introduction to International Law*, p. 91.
27 Ibid., p. 91.
28 Higgins, 'Conceptual Thinking About the Individual Under International
Law', p. 477.
29 M.W. Janis, 'Individuals as Subjects of International Law', *Cornell International Law Journal*, 17 (1984), p. 63. For the differentiation of public and
private international law in the context of the historical development of the
European state system and modern capitalism see A.C. Cutler, 'Artifice, Ideology and Paradox: the Public/Private Distinction in International Law',
Review of International Political Economy, 4 (2) (1997), pp. 261–85.
30 *Akehurst's Modern Introduction to International Law*, p. 91.
31 See *Akehurst's Modern Introduction to International Law*, ch. 6, for the limited
legal personality conferred by states upon international organizations, individuals and corporations; and see Janis, 'Individuals as Subjects of International Law' for critical analysis of the subject-based approach.
32 For a comparative analysis of individual and corporate legal personality see
A.C. Cutler, 'Westphalian Conceptions of International Law and Organization: a Crisis of Legitimacy?' unpublished manuscript.
33 *Belgium* v. *Spain*, Judgment (Second Phase), *International Court of Justice
Reports* 1970, 3–357.
34 For a classic analysis of the emergence of market civilization see Karl Polanyi,
The Great Transformation: the Political and Economic Origins of Our Time (Boston:
Beacon Press, 1944).
35 See Blumberg, *The Multinational Challenge to Corporation Law* for the early
history of corporate legal theory. He notes at p. 3 that notions of corporate
personality can be traced even earlier.
36 Ibid., p. 4.
37 B. Welling, *Corporate Law in Canada: the Governing Principles* (Toronto:
Butterworths, 1991), p. 86.
38 See Blumberg, *The Multinational Challenge to Corporation Law*, ch. 1. Typically
businesses were granted incorporation to build bridges, canals, turnpikes,
and for water companies. Blumberg notes that banks and insurance companies followed.
39 See Strange, 'Global Government and Global Opposition', in *Politics in an
Interdependent World: Essays Presented to Ghita Ionescu* (Aldershot, England:
Edward Elgar, 1994), p. 26.

40 Blumberg, *The Multinational Challenge to Corporation Law*, p. vii.

41 See ibid., chs 1–4 for the doctrine of limited liability and for entity theory.

42 For different theoretical rationales for corporations in Anglo-American theory see C. Tollefson, 'Corporate Constitutional Rights and the Supreme Court of Canada', *Queen's Law Journal*, 19 (1993), pp. 309–49.

43 C.J. Mayer, 'Personalizing the Impersonal: Corporations and the Bill of Rights', *The Hastings Law Journal*, 41 (March 1990), pp. 577–667, and Tollefson, 'Corporate Constitutional Rights'.

44 Muchlinski, *Multinational Enterprises and the Law*, pp. 9–11.

45 See T. Blackburn, 'The Unification of Corporate Laws: the United States, the European Community and the Race to Laxity', *George Mason Independent Law Review*, 3 (1) (1994), pp. 1–95, and D. Charney, 'Competition among Jurisdictions in Formulating Corporate Law Rules: an American Perspective on the "Race to the Bottom" in the European Communities', *Harvard International Law Journal*, 32 (2) (Spring 1991), pp. 423–56.

46 See generally Muchlinski, *Multinational Enterprises and the Law*.

47 I derive the term *mercatocracy* from the medieval *lex mercatoria* or law merchant, which was a private transnational legal order regulating the activities of private merchants engaged in long-distance trade.

48 C. Jones, 'Capitalism, Globalization and the Rule of Law: An Alternative Trajectory of Legal Change in China', *Social and Legal Studies*, 3 (1994), p. 202.

49 'Globalization and Legal Theory: Some Local Implications', *Current Legal Problems*, 49 (1996), p. 6. John Austin was a famous nineteenth-century legal positivist.

50 See A.C. Cutler, 'Private Authority in International Trade Relations: the Case of Maritime Transport', in Cutler, Haufler and Porter, eds, *Private Authority and International Affairs*, pp. 281–327, and Johns, 'The Invisibility of the Transnational Corporation'.

51 Cutler, 'Public meets Private'.

52 'A Perspective on Globalization', in J.H. Mittelman, ed., *Globalization: Critical Reflections* (Boulder, Colo.: Lynne Rienner, 1996), pp. 21–30.

53 See generally Muchlinski, *Multinational Enterprises and the Law* and *Akehurst's Modern Introduction to International Law*, ch. 6.

54 Space does not permit addressing the history of ICSID. However, it must be noted that its creation was in part a reaction to the acrimonious legal battles being fought between the North and South over the legal standards and consequences of the growing trend in the 1950s and 1960s in developing countries to nationalize and expropriate the assets of foreign corporations. These battles were fought in the legal context of the rules governing state responsibility for injury to aliens, which corporations found to be totally inadequate. ICSID was designed to both protect investors and encourage investment in developing countries. See Muchlinski, *Multinational Enterprises and the Law*, p. 542.

55 Muchlinski, *Multinational Enterprises and the Law*, pp. 534–5.

56 Ibid., p. 541. Dispute settlement proceeds independently of national legal systems in that domestic courts may not intervene in proceedings and are limited to the recognition and enforcement of awards.

57 Interview conducted with an official of ICSID, Washington DC, Aug. 1997.

58 See J.G. Castel, 'The Settlement of Disputes under the 1988 Canada–United States Free Trade Agreement', *American Journal of International Law*, 83

(1989), pp. 118–28, and Eden, 'The Emerging North American Investment Regime'.

59   *Akehurst's Modern Introduction to International Law*, p. 101.

60   Ibid.

61   'The Emerging North American Investment Regime', p. 89.

62   F. Engering, 'The Multilateral Investment Agreement', *Transnational Corporations*, 5 (3) (Dec. 1996), pp. 156–7.

63   There are additional exceptions to the legal invisibility of transnational corporations, including the Iran–United States Claims Tribunal, where individuals and corporations have legal standing; the United Nations Compensation Commission was set up after the defeat of Iraq to hear complaints of individuals and corporations; and the Permanent Court of Arbitration, which modified its procedures to apply to non-state parties. See *Akehurst's Modern Introduction to International Law*, pp. 101, 294, 296 and 398.

64   Strange, *Retreat of the State*, ch. 1.

65   See generally D. Kairys, *The Politics of Law: a Progressive Critique* (New York: Pantheon Books, 1982) and Cutler, 'Global Capitalism and Liberal Myths'.

66   'Receiving the International', *Connecticut Journal of International Law*, 10 (1) (Fall 1994), p. 26.

5

Industrialization and Business Cleavages: Organizational Resources and the Institutional Roots of Business Alliances in Post-war Argentina and Brazil (1950s–1970s)

Kenneth C. Shadlen

In the decades after the Second World War, the inflow of foreign investment into manufacturing changed the role of Latin America in the global economy. Moreover, the distinct challenges presented to various social groups by industrialization via internationalization fundamentally changed the role of the international economy in Latin America. This chapter analyses how these changes affected business alliance patterns in Argentina and Brazil.

Increased economic integration accentuated conflict among local capital: some firms could better position themselves to take advantage of tighter links to the global economy, while others were more threatened. The intra-business cleavages that developed during this period allow us to conceptualize local business in terms of two segments. One segment, referred to as 'big business', consists of large, generally capital-intensive firms, including both subsidiaries of foreign firms and local conglomerates closely tied to and associated with foreign capital. Another segment, 'small business', consists of national, less capital-intensive, firms.[1]

How business was organized, however, affected patterns of political alliances. Only where each of these distinct segments of business had organizational resources to defend its interests did intra-class cleavages become manifested in inter-class political alliances. To understand the development of organizational resources, this chapter focuses on the ways that state institutions designed to regulate associational behavior affect patterns of business organization.[2] In Argentina, a segment of business forged recurrent alliances with labour organizations. This business–worker alliance placed significant obstacles to successive Argentine governments' initiatives to further a strategy of industrialization via internationalization, and it ultimately formed the backbone of support for a resurgent populist political movement in the early 1970s. In Brazil, organized business remained united in opposition to organized labour, rejected calls for multi-class alliances, and actively opposed a labour-based political movement that gained power in the early 1960s.

Industrialization via internationalization and intra-business cleavages

This section shows how economic change in the decades after the Second World War in Latin America, referred to as industrialization via internationalization, accentuated intra-business cleavages. The critical characteristic of industrialization in this period was the increased importance of foreign capital. Prior to the late-1940s, with minimal technological and capital requirements creating low barriers to entry, industrialization generally remained a local affair: small, domestically owned enterprises proliferated, and foreign capital remained concentrated principally in the extractive industries and infrastructure. In the aftermath of the Second World War, however, policy-makers throughout the region became increasingly active in directing industrial development, deploying various promotional instruments to channel investment into more sophisticated industrial branches (e.g., automobiles, autoparts, machinery, petrochemicals and pharmaceuticals).[3] As these sectors had significantly higher technological and capital requirements, investment in manufacturing became increasingly attractive for international firms. Whereas previous direct foreign investment (DFI) tended to be directed towards raw material extraction and infrastructure, postwar DFI went increasingly towards the manufacturing sector. As a per cent of all US DFI in Latin America, manufacturing DFI increased from 17.3 per cent in 1946 to 44.9 per cent in 1967.[4] These foreign firms, which were entering into areas of activity where local firms had already been operating, came to account for increasing shares of the Latin American countries' total industrial production.[5]

The prominence of foreign capital in manufacturing presented new sets of opportunities and challenges for local capital. Larger firms, in general, were better prepared to take advantage of the new environment by associating with foreign firms. Association was direct, in the form of joint ventures, and indirect, in the form of integrating into MNC-led production chains.[6] To be sure, foreign firms' presence in the most dynamic sectors of the economy presented challenges to large firms, potentially eroding market shares. Rarely did local capital call for laissez-faire economic policies – industrial leaders throughout Latin America opposed open-door policies towards foreign investment, regularly warned of the risks of 'denationalization', and pressured the state to implement policies that would provide local investors with equal conditions and opportunities. Yet foreign investment presented an unmistakable array of opportunities as well, in the form of access to new technologies and external sources of credit. Thus, adopting a perspective that Kathryn Sikkink keenly labeled 'cosmopolitan developmentalism',[7] larger firms generally developed an interest in attracting DFI and keeping foreign enterprises in the country, as they had the political and economic resources to benefit from increased economic integration. In this regard, it is important to underscore that even 'indigenization' strategies, which attempted to limit the extent of foreign ownership to 49 per cent, tended to concentrate benefits upon the largest local firms that could raise enough capital to enter into joint ventures with foreign investors. These were not policies designed to keep foreign capital out, so much as to induce foreign investors to enter into joint ventures with large, local conglomerates.

In contrast to large firms' 'cosmopolitan developmentalism', a weaker, less competitive segment of local capital generally favoured stricter regulations on foreign investment. As indicated, prior to the late 1940s, locally owned firms proliferated, even in the most rapidly growing branches of industry. The prominence of foreign capital, however, transformed the requisites for participation in more dynamic industrial sectors, and those local firms with limited access to credit and technology, particularly smaller firms, were less able to benefit from the presence of MNCs. The strategies typically available to larger firms – joint-ventures or integration into MNC-led production chains – were less feasible for many local enterprises.

The differential implications of increased foreign investment have been illustrated by Peter Evans' study of post-war Brazilian industrialization.[8] Evans documents how the balance of challenges and opportunities that foreign firms presented to local capital varied by sector of economic activity: large, local firms' capacity to adjust to and benefit from the presence of MNCs differed according to sector. Yet a common thread that runs through each of his sectoral studies is the weakness of small firms. Even in the best cases of local adaptation, only an elite group of large firms could position themselves to benefit directly from the internationalization of domestic production.

A second policy issue that divided local business was macroeconomic stabilization. The anti-export bias of import-substituting industrialization (largely a function of exchange rates that underwent significant real appreciation) combined with extensive public investment and consumption subsidies, tended to generate external payments imbalances and recurrent inflation throughout the region. How to deal with macroeconomic and external disequilibria were contested issues.[9]

Stabilization packages negotiated with the International Monetary Fund (IMF), typically based on demand reduction and featuring currency devaluation along with restrictive monetary and fiscal policies, further accentuated intra-business cleavages. Larger firms, with more extensive ties to the global economy and desires to retain access to credit, had a greater stake in stable relations with international financial institutions. In addition, to the extent that they were integrated into transnational production chains and produced expensive non-durable consumer goods oriented towards wealthy consumers, they were less sensitive to declines in mass purchasing power produced by IMF-style stabilization policies. Indeed, greater access to credit enabled larger firms to better withstand the recessive effects of such policies; and industrial concentration tended to increase during periods of national economic contraction, as large firms expanded by taking over struggling small firms.[10] In contrast, smaller firms had greater difficulties obtaining credit; and as their production was typically oriented towards the mass, consumer goods market, they were generally more concerned with maintaining adequate levels of local demand. As a result, they were more likely to oppose tight monetary policy, fiscal contraction and currency devaluation that improved the countries' international financial position at the expense of domestic purchasing power.

To summarize, the post-Second World War strategy of industrialization via internationalization increased Latin America's integration into the global economy. This integration, particularly the increased presence of foreign capital and the heightened role of international financial institutions, amplified intra-business cleavages.

From cleavage to conflict: institutions and business alliances in Argentina and Brazil

Though smaller firms were threatened by industrialization via internationalization, they did not disappear. Indeed, the simultaneous growth and marginalization of such firms is part and parcel of capitalist development.[11] In Latin America, some individual firms were forced into bankruptcy, others survived by idling more of their existing productive capacity, and some new firms continued to emerge. Thus, independently owned, national firms remained the predominant form of business establishment throughout Latin America, even as they were pushed into less dynamic and slower-growing sectors of the economy.

The political consequence of small business's collective perseverance was that a weak segment of local capital continued to exist. And with its weakness revealed, smaller firms might be expected to seek alliances with non-business actors that were also threatened by the post-war economic changes. The extent to which they did so is related to how the business sector was organized – the extent to which the weak segment of local capital possessed the necessary organizational resources to form multi-class alliances. To illustrate this point, the remainder of this chapter looks at the distinct ways that political institutions affected patterns of business association in Argentina and Brazil.

Argentina

In Argentina, the pattern of business association reflected the same intra-business cleavages accentuated by post-war industrialization. To understand this, we need to examine both the political strategies of Juan Perón (1943–55) and the anti-peronist backlash that followed his rule.[12]

Seeking the collaboration of a comprehensive business organization, to complement the alliance established with the peak General Workers' Confederation (CGT), Perón made overtures to Argentina's largest business organization, the Argentine Industrial Union (UIA).[13] However, the UIA, dominated by the country's most important industrial firms, rejected Perón's overtures, and relations with the representatives of Argentine big business grew increasingly acrimonious. The UIA became an active and outspoken foe of the general's political ambitions and the political movement he was cultivating: the UIA assailed Perón's leadership and social welfare policies and contributed to the unsuccessful campaign of Perón's chief rival in the 1946 election. Upon winning the election, not surprisingly, Perón struck back, dissolving the UIA's executive board and eventually declaring it legally 'non-existent'.

With the UIA suppressed, Perón labored throughout the late 1940s and early 1950s to consolidate business support, and he encouraged the creation of various business organizations led by industrialists who were more favorably disposed to his policies.[14] Perón's project to organize business supporters coincided with a project from within the business community, in which smaller industrialists, mainly from the interior of the country, formed a series of organizations to increase their representation in national politics. In the early 1950s, under Perón's tutelage, the various organizations merged, creating the General Economic Confederation (CGE).[15]

The CGE staked its ties to peronism, and it appealed for support by pitting itself against Perón's nemesis, the UIA. The CGE, its misleading name notwithstanding, was controlled by smaller, domestic-oriented manufacturers. These firms, lacking access to the Buenos Aires financial system, were concerned with preserving the industrialization model prevalent during the early years of peronism, when the state made credit available and expanded the internal market by supporting rising levels of domestic purchasing power. The following passage, from the CGE's November 1952 petition for state recognition, illustrates the nature of this group's perspective on peronism and industrialization strategies:

> We are the same industrialists who signed the petition of 6 August 1946 [for the UIA intervention], the ones who aided in the unprecedented growth of industry brought about by His Excellency, General Perón, in his few years of service; the ones who responded to all his calls; the ones who, believing in justicialist premises, put our utmost efforts voluntarily at his service. We are the ones, in brief, who embody the tradition of the industrialist class that was formed under the protection of a monitoring influence which plans for the generations to come.[16]

Perón quickly rewarded the CGE. Stressing the importance of 'authentic representative business associations which can work parallel with workers organizations', he revised the Law of Professional Associations (LAP) to establish a hierarchical and rigid structure of business organizations, to which membership was compulsory.[17] Only one organization was allowed per industrial sector, and state recognition was a prerequisite for negotiating with labour and participating on government commissions and policy-making boards. The LAP converted the CGE into Argentina's most important organization, perched at the top of the official hierarchy. As a result, it was the CGE that was officially designated to represent business in formal tripartite settings.

An anti-peronist backlash following the September 1955 military coup would have important and lasting effects on the organization of business interests in post-war Argentina. The military regime that ruled from 1955–8 banned Perón's political party from national politics and repressed the CGE on the grounds that it was 'a creation of deposed totalitarian [peronist] regime'.[18] So tightly did the military junta identify the CGE with peronism that a further decree in April 1956 declared that any individuals who had held executive positions in the CGE prior to September 1955 would be prohibited from holding office in any Argentine business organizations. At the same time, under considerable pressure from the legalized UIA, the LAP was revised to eliminate compulsory business membership.[19] The return to semi-competitive, civilian politics in 1958 precipitated a rebirth of the CGE, as President Arturo Frondizi re-legalized the CGE in June 1958.[20] Yet while the CGE itself was reinstated, other aspects of the corporative framework that existed in the early 1950s remained suppressed. Organizations could no longer count on compulsory membership, and no institutional framework provided any particular organization with regularized access to the state.

This institutional vacuum must be considered as a product of the backlash against peronism and the incipient state–CGE alliance. Perón had imposed the LAP as a means to consolidate the new and supportive organization's domination of business politics – to strengthen the weaker segment of capital at the UIA's expense. As a result, the UIA not only rejected peronism and the CGE, but, critically, it also rejected the same state institutions that nourished the CGE and facilitated the menacing alliance in the first place.

In this open and unconstrained organizational setting, post-peronist Argentina came to feature a distinct, bifurcated pattern of business association, in which rival organizations came to represent distinct segments of business and distinct projects of economic development. In the same economic sectors, larger firms joined UIA-linked organizations, and smaller firms joined CGE-linked organizations. Though both organizations had members from virtually all sectors, UIA's leaders tended to be from the largest firms in any given sector, while the CGE's leaders tended to be from smaller firms.[21]

That the intra-class cleavages accentuated by industrialization were reflected in the patterns of business association had important effects on the nature of political alliances in post-war Argentina. As the UIA represented firms that were more tightly linked to the global economy, the organization lent support to post-peronist governments' strategies to attract foreign investment and, in response to balance-of-payments difficulties, contractionary stabilization initiatives. In contrast, the CGE advocated policies that would improve small firms' access to credit and retain adequate levels of domestic demand.[22] From its 1958 re-legalization until being repressed again in 1976, the CGE regularly allied with organized labour to protest precisely the same economic policies that the UIA tended to advocate (and vice versa). Under both civilian governments (Frondizi, 1958–62 and Illía, 1963–6) and military governments (1962–3 and 1966–73), the CGE and CGT allied in opposition to state initiatives to increase foreign investment, and they stridently resisted the implementation of stabilization policies that would depress local demand.

The multi-class, small business–worker alliances contributed to Argentina's polarized policy arena, one in which policy-makers, civilian and military, were unable to form stable coalitions in support of development strategies.[23] Industrialization via further international integration prompted fierce small business–worker resistance; yet more redistributive strategies were confounded by internal contradictions of the small business–worker alliance, and by the strength of economic elites in industry, finance and agriculture.[24] Indeed, in seeking to establish the conditions for stable capitalist development, one of the objectives of the extraordinarily repressive 1976–83 military regime was to dismantle this alliance.[25]

Brazil

Contrasting Argentina with Brazil highlights the important effects that patterns of business organization have on alliance formation. In Brazil, patterns of business organization did not reflect the intra-business cleavages accentuated by post-war industrialization. Instead, the proponents of industrialization via international integration controlled the principal instruments of business interest articulation, depriving the potential opponents of independent means of expression. As a result, multi-class alliances, so salient in Argentina, did not materialize in Brazil. Again, the analysis focuses on how state institutions propelled particular trajectories of business association.

Business association in Brazil occurred within the framework that emerged during the rule of Getulio Vargas (1930–45).[26] The hierarchical network outlined by the Consolidation of Labor Laws (CLT) included local, sectorally-defined *sindicatos*, to which membership was compulsory, state-level federations, and national, sectoral confederations. Within industry, the National Industrial Confederation (CNI) was formally at the peak of the hierarchy. Because of the importance of São Paulo industry, the Industrial Federation of São Paolo (FIESP) became the most important actor in the CNI and the principal representative of

Brazilian capital. FIESP, like the UIA in Argentina, was dominated by big business.

As industrialization produced greater differentiation within the business community, especially during the heavy industrialization drive of President Kubitschek (1956–61), larger firms in the more dynamic sectors of the economy began to establish separate, voluntary associations. Unencumbered by the CLT's restrictions, these associations offered Brazilian business elites greater flexibility in dealing with the state.[27] Importantly, the new, voluntary associations co-existed with and complemented the official, CLT-governed organizations.[28]

Big business's strategy of remaining within the official organizations while simultaneously creating alternative forms of representation was driven by both political and institutional features of the CLT. Because associational regulations were introduced with the principal objective of containing a growing labour movement, they were non-threatening from the perspective of big business. In fact, the details of the CLT emerged out of negotiations between the Vargas government and leading business organizations, such as FIESP.[29] The roots of such regulations provide a crucial contrast with the Argentinean case, where corporative regulations first consolidated the state's alliance with labour, and then were extended to business as an instrument to empower the weaker segment of capital, represented by the CGE. In Brazil, business elites regarded the CLT as part of a favourable project to control labour. They were not threatened by these state institutions, which they helped design; and even after the *Estado Novo* ended in 1945, leading sectors of Brazilian capital continued to benefit from and appreciate the CLT.[30]

While the political roots of the CLT provided Brazilian industrial elites with little incentive to abolish it, a distinct institutional feature encouraged them to retain control of the official organizations. The CLT, unlike the LAP in Argentina, contained the regulatory frameworks for both employers and employees. It formed the cornerstone of the Brazilian system of industrial relations, endowing the official organizations with some irreplaceable functions. For all their 'flexibility', there were some activities that the voluntary associations could not take care of. Certain issues had to go through the official organizations, as most important issues of employer–employee relations were resolved through the CLT.[31] Thus, even when large firms formed their own voluntary associations, they did not abandon the official organizations. Rather, they retained control over the most important bodies, such as the FIESP. In fact, the two types of organization usually had the same leadership.[32]

That patterns of Brazilian business association *failed* to reflect the cleavages accentuated by post-war industrialization had distinct effects on alliance possibilities. In particular, the domination of business organizations by big business meant that the weaker segment of Brazilian capital lacked the organizational resources that were available to its counterpart in Argentina. As one scholar of Brazilian small business concluded, 'passage to positions of leadership was limited, if not blocked altogether.'[33] The absence of an organization to articulate the interests of local capital's weaker segment meant that efforts in the late 1950s and 1960s to attract potentially sympathetic sectors of business into nationalist-populist movements failed.[34] Indeed, when the labour-based government of João Goulart came to power in 1961, it received virtually no collective business support. Here an important contrast is to be made with the case of Argentina, where the CGE collaborated extensively with Perón in 1973. One study of Brazilian business highlights significant tensions within FIESP regarding Goulart. A current within the organization wanted to cooperate with the new president, but these voices were drowned by the dominant current that controlled the organization.[35] Thus, the appeals of Goulart and his popular sector supporters to build multi-class coalitions received no positive response from any sector of business. Those that were potential supporters lacked organizational resources to put their interests into action; those that had such resources remained steadfastly opposed to Goulart.

Conclusion

Exposure to the international economy generates domestic social conflict. Focusing on domestic business, this chapter has shown how institutional frameworks regulating business association can affect the extent to which social conflicts are manifested in the realm of political alliances. In Argentina, big business's backlash against peronist institutions facilitated a bifurcated pattern of business association, thus allowing the weak segment of local capital to develop organizational resources to pursue multi-class alliances. In Brazil, big business's enthusiasm for Vargas-era institutions produced a unified pattern of business association, which deprived the weaker segment of organizational resources.

Though the cases analysed were drawn from an earlier period of Latin American development, it is worthwhile to note some of the key similarities between industrialization after the Second World War and the 'neo-liberal' period of the 1980s to 1990s. Analysis of Latin American political economy prior to neo-liberalism too frequently understates the extent of the region's integration into the global economy. Though formal openness (e.g., trade's share of GDP) was lower in the decades immediately following the Second World War, direct and portfolio foreign investors nevertheless played prominent roles in the post-war strategy of industrialization via internationalization. In both periods, integration into the global economy generated intra-business cleavages, as larger firms' greater access to credit and capacity to enter into joint ventures with foreign capital better positioned them to take advantage of the changing economic environments.

In light of these material continuities, what can institutional changes tell us about the sorts of alliance patterns in the current period? The analysis in this chapter points us in the direction of understanding the factors that explain business alliances. In Argentina, outright repression under the 1976–83 military government, combined with prolonged contraction of the domestic market, seriously undermined the CGE. At the same time, new patterns of high-level government–business inter-action have allowed business elites to dominate most channels of private sector representation. In Brazil, the 1964–85 military regime intensified the strategy of industrialization, further accentuating intra-class cleavages. Yet the process of democratization has created a new institutional environment: a new constitution modified important aspects of the CLT, new organizations representing small business have emerged, and increasingly they are establishing ties with popular move-ments and political parties. Thus, in terms of business organization and alliances, Argentina in the current period has important characteristics attributed to Brazil in the post-war decades, and, likewise, Brazil has many of the characteristics associated with an earlier era of Argentine political economy.

Notes

1 This distinction corresponds to that made by G. O'Donnell, 'State and Alli-ances in Argentina, 1956–1976', *The Journal of Development Studies*, 15 (1978), p. 28, no. 4, between the 'large (urban) bourgeoisie ... formed by the branches of transnational corporations and by the domestic bourgeoisie's oligopolistic faction ... and the "local" – or simply "weak" – bourgeoisie ... made up of capi-talists controlling non-ologopolistic firms, smaller and usually less capital-intensive than the large bourgeoisie's.'

2 These institutions are often referred to as 'corporative' or 'corporatist'.

3 G. Gereffi and D.L. Wyman, eds, *Manufacturing Miracles: Paths of Industrializa-tion in Latin America and East Asia* (Princeton: Princeton University Press, 1990); J. Sheahan, *Patterns of Development in Latin America* (Princeton: Prince-ton University Press, 1987), ch. 4.

4 G. Gereffi and P. Evans, 'Transnational Corporations, Dependent Development, and State Policy in the Semiperiphery: a Comparison of Brazil and Mexico', *Latin American Research Review*, 16 (Fall 1981), pp. 36–7, table 1. For a provocative analysis that documents US diplomatic pressure to encourage developing-world allies to provide American producers with privileged market access, see S. Maxfield and J. Nolt, 'Protectionism and the Internationalization of Capital: US Sponsorship of Import Substitution Industrialization in the Philippines, Turkey and Argentina', *International Studies Quarterly*, 34 (1990).

5 R. Newfarmer and W. Mueller, *Multinational Corporations in Brazil and Mexico: Structural Sources of Economic and Noneconomic Power*, Report to the Subcommittee on Multinational Corporations of the Committee on Foreign Relations (Washington, DC: United States Senate, 1975); Gereffi and Evans, 'Transnational Corporations'.

6 P. Evans, *Dependent Development: the Alliance of Multinational, State, and Local Capital in Brazil* (Princeton: Princeton University Press, 1979), ch. 3; G. O'Donnell and D. Linck, *Dependencia y autonomía: Formas de dependencia y estragias de liberación* (Buenos Aires: Amorrortu Editores, 1973).

7 K. Sikkink, *Ideas and Institutions: Developmentalism in Brazil and Argentina* (Ithaca: Cornell University Press, 1991).

8 Evans, *Dependent Development*.

9 T. Skidmore, 'The Politics of Economic Stabilization in Postwar Latin America', in J. Malloy, ed., *Authoritarianism and Corporatism in Latin America* (Pittsburgh: University of Pittsburgh Press, 1977); Sheahan, *Patterns of Development*, ch. 5.

10 P. Skupch, 'Concentración industrial en la Argentina (1956–66)', *Desarrollo Economico*, 11 (April–June 1971); O'Donnell and Linck, *Dependencia y autonomía*; H. Rattner, ed., *Pequeña empresa: O comportamiento empresarial na acumulacao e na luta pela sobrevivencia* (Sao Paulo: Brasiliense, 1985).

11 S. Berger and M. Piore, *Dualism and Discontinuity in Industrial Societies* (New York: Cambridge University Press, 1981).

12 For discussion of Perón's larger political strategy, featuring penetration and capturing control over the Argentine labour movement, see R.B. Collier and D. Collier, *Shaping the Political Arena: Critical Junctures, the Labor Movement, and Regime Dynamics in Latin America* (Princeton: Princeton University Press, 1991), pp. 331–44.

13 For discussions of Perón's interactions with the UIA, see D. Cuneo, *Comportamiento y crisis de la clase empresaria* (Buenos Aires: Editorial Pleamar, 1967); J. Freels, *Industrial Trade Associations in Argentine Politics* (Ph.D. dissertation, University of California, Riverside, 1968); E. Kenworthy, 'Did the "New Industrialists" Play a Significant Role in the Formation of Perón's Coalition, 1943–1946?', in A. Ciria et al., ed., *New Perspectives on Modern Argentina* (Bloomington, Ind.: Latin American Studies, Indiana University, 1972); P. Lewis, *The Crisis of Argentine Capitalism* (Chapel Hill: University of North Carolina Press, 1990); S. Mainwairing, 'The State and the Industrial Bourgeoisie in Perón's Argentina, 1945–1955', *Studies in Comparative International Development*, 21 (Fall 1986); L. Manzetti, *Institutions, Parties, and Coalitions in Argentine Politics* (Pittsburgh: University of Pittsburgh Press, 1993); J. Teichman, 'Interest Conflict and Entrepreneurial Support for Perón', *Latin American Research Review*, 16 (1981).

14 Lewis, *The Crisis*; Manzetti, *Institutions, Parties, and Coalitions*.

15 Cuneo, *Comportamiento y crisis.*

16 Lewis, *The Crisis*, p. 173. 'Justicialism' was the label that Perón gave his movement and, eventually, the political party that he would lead.

17 The quotation is from Perón's address to the Chamber of Deputies (Freels, *Industrial Trade Associations*, p. 55).

18 Decree No. 916, cited by Jorge Niosi, *Los empresarios y el estado argentino, 1955–1969* (Buenos Aires: Siglo XXI Argentina Editores, 1974), pp. 39–40.

19 Cuneo, *Comportamiento y crisis*, pp. 230–1.

20 The agreement to re-legalize the CGE was one element of a secretive pact between Frondizi and Perón, which included promises to legalize the peronist party and return its assets, along with reinstatement of many CGT labour leaders.

21 R. Caggiano, *Notas sobre el desarrollo de la burguesía nacional: La Confederación General de la Industria y la Unión Industrial en el período 1957–1973* (Buenos Aires: Centro de Estudios Urbanos y Regionales, Instituto Torcuato di Tella, 1975), ch. 1.

22 For contrasts between the CGE's and UIA's positions, see Caggiano, *Notas sobre el desarrollo*; Cuneo, *Comportamiento y crisis*; Freels, *Industrial Trade Associations*; Niosi, *Los empresarios*; O'Donnell, 'State and Alliances'.

23 O'Donnell, 'State and Alliances'; W. Smith, *Authoritarianism and the Crisis of the Argentine Political Economy* (Stanford: Stanford University Press, 1991).

24 For analysis of the failure of the 'social pact' in 1973–4, when Perón again was president, see R. Ayres, 'The "Social Pact" as Anti-inflationary Policy: the Argentine Experience Since 1973', *World Politics*, 28 (1976).

25 Smith, *Authoritarianism and the Crisis*, ch. 9; J. Villareal, 'Changes in Argentine Society: the Heritage of Dictatorship', in M. Peralta Ramos and C. Waisman, eds, *From Military Rule to Liberal Democracy in Argentina* (Boulder, Colo.: Westview Press, 1987).

26 See P. Schmitter, *Interest Conflict and Political Change in Brazil* (Stanford: Stanford University Press, 1971), ch. 2; M. Leopoldi, *Industrial Associations and Politics in Contemporary Brazil: the Associations of Industrialists, Economic Policy-Making and the State, with special reference to the period 1930–1961* (Ph.D. dissertation, St Antony's College, Oxford, UK, 1984), ch. 2; K. Erickson, *The Brazilian Corporative State and Working-Class Politics* (Berkeley and Los Angeles: University of California Press, 1977), chs 2–3. The CLT remained in place after the 1937–45 *Estado Novo*, though many controls were relaxed during the period of civilian rule that began in 1946.

27 E. Diniz, 'The Post-1930 Industrial Elite', in M. Conniff and F. McCann, eds, *Modern Brazil: Elites and Masses in Historical Perspective* (Lincoln: University of Nebraska Press, 1989); Leopoldi, *Industrial Associations.*

28 R. Boschi, *National Industrial Elites and the State in Post-1964 Brazil: Institutional Mediations and Political Change* (Ph.D. dissertation, University of Michigan, 1978). E. Diniz and R. Boschi, *Empresariado nacional e estado no Brasil* (Rio de Janeiro: Forense-Universit·ria, 1978), pp. 39–40, describe the relationship between the two types of organizations as 'mutual strengthening'. Leopoldi, *Industrial Associations*, refers to this as a 'combined corporatist' arrangement.

29 Leopoldi, *Industrial Associations*, ch. 2; Schmitter, *Interest Conflict*, p. 182; A.M. de Castro Gomes, 'O empresário industrial e a implantaçao de legislaçao

trabalhista', in E. Diniz and R. Boschi, ed., *Empresário nacional e estado no Brasil* (Rio de Janeiro: IUPERJ, 1976).

30   Boschi, *National Industrial Elites*, pp. 129–131.

31   E. Diniz and R. Boschi, *Empresário nacional: ideologia e atuaçao política nos anos 70* (Rio de Janeiro: IUPERJ), p. 40; K. Mericle, *Conflict Regulation in the Brazilian Industrial Relations System* (Ph.D. dissertation, University of Wisconsin, 1974), also emphasizes the key role of the official organizations.

32   Diniz and Boschi, *Empresariado nacional*, pp. 175–8; W. Nylen, *Small Business Owners Fight Back: Non-elite Capital Activism in 'Democratizing Brazil' (1978–1990)* (Ph.D. dissertation, Columbia University, 1992), pp. 111–14. In addition to shared executives, K. Mericle, *Conflict Regulation*, p. 78, notes that the official and voluntary organizations also tended to share office space and administrative personnel.

33   Nylen, *Small Business Owners*, p. 113.

34   These initiatives came not just from workers, but also from a group of prominent intellectuals in the Higher Institute of Brazilian Studies (ISEB), which FIESP eventually came to regard as a 'communist' advocacy group. Boschi, *National Industrial Elites*, p. 171.

35   Leopoldi, *Industrial Associations*, pp. 314–19.

6

A Fractured State: Globalization and Mexican Politics

José Vadi

Primarily to meet debt obligations, Mexico's government has adopted economic policies that pauperize further the country's poor majority and erode the standard of living of Mexico's middle class. To end sixty years of corruption and repression by the Partido Revolucionario Institucíonal (Institutional Revolutionary Party or PRI), an intensified class struggle is now in progress, marked by rejection of the PRI at the ballot box, massive and constant urban demonstrations, and armed uprisings in the countryside of Chiapas and Guerrero. Social movements and political parties organize under varying and, at times, competing banners of democracy as they attempt to engrave their axioms on a social order that has removed from its poor a cushion under them as they fall from the column of misery to the column of absolute disaster. No longer as able to provide patronage to maintain discipline among its local bosses, the PRI exercises a degraded hegemony signalled by a growing feudalization of power from within and a growing class struggle from without. To maintain its substantial, albeit degraded, hegemony, the PRI employs military force and occupation in Chiapas and Guerrero and alternates power selectively in a few states, mostly by co-opting the conservative PAN (Partido Acción Nacional or National Action Party). This struggle between a decaying and degraded hegemonic regime, heavily dependent on the United States for economic and security support, and social classes struggling for real democracy is, once again, Mexico's central drama and Mexico's hope.

Substituting for a poorly developed capitalist class, the Mexican state provided capital investment and protected national industry through high tariffs and through import substitution. The state organized and coordinated the most important social and economic sectors under a populist, nationalist, corporatist party structure. The PRI maintained a revolutionary façade that allowed capital and its foreign allies to control Mexico through its 'popular' sector. When leftist resistance movements emerged opposed to misery and repression, they were destroyed to maintain an autocratic form of state capitalism based on wage exploitation and social destitution.[1] But lower international demand in the early 1970s, the saturation of the national market with manufactured goods not competitive in international markets, and a declining state capacity to continue to provide business subsidies sent Mexico into deep economic recession.

Economic recession in Europe and the United States, declining rates of profit, and a surplus of 'petrodollars' made Mexico and Latin America more attractive to European and American investors. Mexico's debt tripled in the 1970s as the government borrowed in order to develop newly-discovered petroleum resources. This gave greater leverage to the World Bank and the International Monetary Fund (IMF) to impose Structural Adjustment Programmes (SAPs) that required that Mexico promote open markets, foreign investment, and integrate its economy more closely into the world economy in ways that would facilitate debt payment. Mexico embarked on its latest cycle of economic globalization.

Globalization

Capital's strategy of globalization maximizes profits by penetrating and incorporating economies into the global economy to appropriate and exploit more fully their human and natural resources. International regimes such as the World Trade Organization, the International Monetary Fund and the proposed Multilateral Investment Agreement supervise and coordinate this process. Neo-liberalism is the tactical dimension of globalization, designed to achieve strategic objectives of economic globalization by privatizing state-owned enterprises, reducing tariffs, eliminating barriers to foreign investment, reducing the state's role in social provision, devaluating currencies, decentralizing decision-making and imposing market-oriented economic policies.

Neo-liberalism does not reduce state power (as is often assumed) because a stronger state is required to impose unpopular policies of austerity held necessary by foreign and domestic elites in order to pay debt. Neo-liberalism is neo-state capitalism without social provision. Jorge Nef labelled this state a 'receiver state' – a state whose 'power' is reduced primarily to the areas of social provision and the social regulation of capital.[2] Dropping the mask of class 'mediation', the state aligns forcefully with foreign capital and domestic interests with liquid assets.

Neo-liberal regimes override democratic accountability because tech-nocrats who now manage the state reject both accountability and social provision as 'demagogic'. They promote decentralization in the name of greater efficiency but also to deflect and fragment opposition to policies that lead to greater impoverishment. The state appears to be more democratic by making concessions, such as electoral reform, that do not compromise the market-oriented model but that foreclose altern-atives to neo-liberalism. Opposition alliances form, most often in the larger urban centers, to denounce corruption, lower living standards and the lack of social provision. But even when a political opposition gains control of national legislatures, it is unable to alter the economic model. The dynamics of globalization and its deleterious consequences reveal themselves most dramatically in Mexico where nearly two decades of economic restructuring has sunken most Mexicans into deeper pov-erty, more than doubled its national debt and given rise to movements of resistance against neo-liberalism and corruption.

Globalization in Mexico

The PRI moved from a state-centred to a market-centred economic man-agement model when an *eficientista* or hard market-oriented faction of the PRI gained control of the Mexican government during the fiscal crisis of the 1980s.[3] During the presidency of Miguel de la Madrid (1982–8), this faction of the PRI 'won out' over the state-oriented fac-tion headed by Alfredo del Mazo and a moderate, pragmatic faction headed by Jesus Silva Herzog. Understanding how the *eficientista* faction transformed Mexico's economy and the impact of that transformation on Mexico's state and society are fundamental to understanding the Mexican political system.

Under President José Lopez Portillo (1976–82), Mexico entered its most severe economic crisis. Encouraged by the availability of petro-dollars (aided by recessions in Europe and in the United States) and a doubling of proven oil reserves, the government pursued a debt-driven strategy of economic development. Oil had constituted only 10 per cent of Mexico's exports in 1972 but, by 1980, oil production surpassed 2 million barrels per day and accounted for 75 per cent of all Mexican exports.[4] Oil dependency, increasing debt and looting of public funds brought Mexico to bankruptcy. In 1981 alone, the Mexican government borrowed $24 billion. The $5 billion borrowed in the month of Septem-ber 1981 was equal to the loan obligations incurred by Mexico from its inception as an independent nation to 1970.[5] By 1982, Mexico's debt was $80 billion, mostly in dollar-denominated, short-term debt at a 15 per cent rate of interest.[6]

The head of the Secretariat of Budget and Planning, Carlos Salinas de Gortari, and technocrats in the government of Miguel de la Madrid imposed policies that included tightening money supply and wage controls that lowered wages by 40 per cent during his administration. Dissident unions opposed to his policies were repressed. Mexico joined the General Agreement on Tariffs and Trade (GATT) in 1986 to promote trade with the United States, especially in the *maquiladora* sector. As the economic and social crisis in Mexico worsened and PRI party stalwarts resisted party democratization, a faction emerged within the PRI known as the Democratic Current that later became an opposition party, the Partido Revoluciónario Democratico (Revolutionary Democratic Party or PRD). The PRD challenged the austerity programme of de la Madrid and supported the former PRI governor of Michoacan, Cuauhtémoc Cárdenas, for president of Mexico in the 1988 elections.

Carlos Salinas de Gortari was barely 'elected' president in one of the most corrupt elections in the post-revolutionary history of Mexico. Some 30,000 ballot boxes disappeared and the final ballots were declared a state secret in order to avoid the uncovering of the massive political fraud that led to Salinas's election. The new president tore up what little remained of the social contract that was the legacy of the Mexican Revolution. He modernized Article 27 of the Constitution, prohibiting the sale of communal lands, called *ejidos*. State-owned enterprises were sold to presidential cronies and laws requiring 51 per cent ownership by Mexicans in strategic industries were rescinded. Salinas then made his biggest decision: to make the Mexican economy an extension of the US economy through the North American Free Trade Agreement (NAFTA).

The major winners under de la Madrid and Salinas were financial conglomerates with liquid assets that enabled them to monopolize sectors of the Mexican economy. By 1990, the grossly uneven distribution of wealth in Mexico grew even worse as 2 per cent of the population controlled 78.5 per cent of national income. More than two dozen Mexicans became billionaires under the Salinas administration mostly through investments in newly privatized industries, while hardships were imposed on peasant farmers, workers and even on the middle class. The major losers were workers and small farmers, many of whom joined two million new rural poor as a result of the neo-liberal policies of Salinas.

The tumultuous year of 1994 included the assassinations of PRI presidential 'candidate' Luis Donaldo Colosio and José Ruiz Massieur,

General Secretary of the PRI. The 1994 election victory of Ernesto Zedillo presaged continuity as the 'devaluation crisis' of 1994–6 drove even more Mexicans into destitution:

- The cost of the basic food basket increased by 60 per cent while the minimum wage rose by only 31 per cent in 1995;
- One million Mexicans lost their jobs in 1995 as large companies 'streamlined';
- More than 45 per cent of the bank credits were not being serviced under the original terms of the agreements and 30 per cent of all bank loans were overdue.

Mexico's inability to meet short-term debt obligations and the subsequent currency devaluation led to a deep contraction in the Mexican economy in 1995 and 1996. An additional 40 billion dollars in debts was 'collaterized', in part, by Mexican oil sales receipts deposited directly at the First Federal Reserve Bank of New York. The net capital outflow for the years 1995 and 1996 was $36 billion per year and Mexico's debt surpassed $170 billion.[7] Yet in the midst of this crisis, tariff reductions continued as a signal of Mexico's commitment to NAFTA.[8]

While severe hardships were imposed on Mexico's majority, a study of 500 privatized Mexican corporations shows that they received increased government subsidies after they were privatized.[9] In the crisis year of 1995, 13.5 per cent of Mexico's GNP (a total of $47.2 billion) went to bail out faltering banks that had recently been 'privatized'.[10] A number of new bank owners had looted their banks of hundreds of millions of dollars and only 8 of 18 privatized banks remained under control of the original purchasers.

Under Zedillo, Mexico continues to function as a 'receiver state' servicing foreign debt and implementing structural adjustment policies to liquidate its own bankruptcy. Zedillo's 1997 poverty programme, that allocated $155 million for 177,416 poor families in ten of Mexico's states, pales in comparison to his payback of billions of dollars of debt by refinancing $6 billion at lower rates of interest.[11] By making a multi-billion-dollar debt payment to the United States three years in advance, Mexico maintained a façade of creditworthiness with lenders at the expense of Mexico's poor. Early debt payment only increased Mexico's debt load because the money for early payment was borrowed from European banks. This is the Receiver State at work. Quick debt service is a higher priority than meeting the needs of Mexico's desperate majority condemned to a seemingly endless cycle of belt-tightening.

The Mexican political opposition

Three forms of opposition to the PRI party-state have emerged: the ballot, social protest and armed struggle. Cuauhtémoc Cárdenas's election as mayor of Mexico City in July of 1997 makes him, arguably, the second most powerful political figure in Mexico and the most powerful voice in a state with one-quarter of Mexico's population.[12] But now Cárdenas and the PRD are 'the government' in the capital and can be saddled with blame for policy failures. Jesus Ignacio Carrola, who Cárdenas designated as chief of Mexico City's investigative police, resorted to a face-saving leave of absence within five days of Cardenas's inauguration when he was implicated in tortures and linked to Tijuana drug traffickers.[13] A second member of Cárdenas's team, Francisco Castellanos de la Garza, resigned the following day as head of the auto thefts department following revelations that he had been fired as the director of a prison under accusation of sexual abuse and drug trafficking.[14] Both the PRD's capacity to govern and to control corruption came under immediate challenge within the first week that Cárdenas assumed 'power' as mayor of the nation's capital.

If Cárdenas remains within the old school of Mexican politics, governing from the top, and does not resort to mass mobilization, he will not touch the major issues affecting Mexico City and he will lose prestige along with the mass base of the PRD. The PRD is limited at this juncture because it must operate within the narrow confines of a market-oriented model that it cannot reverse. Cárdenas's challenge is to disprove those who believe that, under neo-liberal regimes, people can be 'given more freedom to make political choices through formal democratic processes, leaving them free to choose governments with no power, politicians with no capacity to deliver on promises, or social movements with little possibility of mounting a coherent political challenge.'[15] In Mexico, the margin for action is a narrow one but the economic model does not preclude radical political mobilization – against crime, pollution, class exploitation, lack of democracy and political corruption. Cárdenas's willingness to trust the people of Mexico City is critical to his success, but he must encourage them to mobilize to solve their own problems – as they mobilized after the earthquake of 1985 when it became evident that the government was too incompetent and corrupt to help them.

Cárdenas has lowered the expectations of radical intellectuals and the mass base of the PRD who wanted him to challenge the neo-liberal model head-on. But this might have less relevance than his willingness to become a facilitator of the people's efforts in Mexico City to solve their own problems. For now, he is focused more on the incremental tasks of improving the delivery of services, increasing the efficiency of administration and decreasing corruption, in order to increase his chances for victory in the next presidential elections.[16] But by diffusing demands for more radical changes, the PRD runs the risk of becoming a shock-absorber for transnational capital.

Short of mass mobilization, there is no viable way for the PRD to govern Mexico City given the official culture of corruption and the sheer scale of the socio-economic problems of the world's largest city. Disruption of the current political game might be the only viable, albeit risky, course of action. Maintaining Cárdenas's connection to the mass base of the PRD is crucial if his election is to be something more than a hollow victory that allows the PRI to transit from being the party of hegemony to being the party of domination. Only by staying close to his mass base can Cárdenas deny the PRI's strategy of legitimation based on its cohabiting with the PRD while doing everything in its power to sabotage Cárdenas's chances for success as mayor.

The Partido Acción Nacional (National Action Party or PAN) differs little on substantive issues from the PRI but it has staked out the clean route to power, attacking the ruling group's long history of corruption in state management. It collaborates with the PRD in the Chamber of Deputies mostly in procedural matters to erode the power of the PRI.[17] In 1989, 'Salinas had adopted much of PAN's traditional platform, [and the PAN] party leadership opted for "co-governance" instead of what it saw as fruitless opposition.'[18] Zedillo's appointment of a PAN member, Antonio Garcia Lozano, to the important post of Attorney General was meant to signal both his commitment to legality and the lack of fundamental differences with the PAN. While in northern Mexico some PAN supporters are major capitalists, it is still the PRI that has the largest share of big business and upper-class support. The PAN has been mostly a middle-class party at its mass level, but by neglecting to address the problem of poverty, in a country where most people are poor, the PAN has limited its appeal among the mass of the national electorate.[19]

New PAN leaders such as Governor Vicente Fox are poised to transform the PAN into the perfect party for Mexico in an era of global capitalism. Fox is 'a nationalist with a global outlook, a corporate manager and exporter with a strong social and ecological conscience.'[20] Elected governor of Guanajuato in May of 1995 by a two-to-one majority, Fox campaigned for a decentralized Mexican federalism, democratic accountability and self-reliance. He has decentralized his administration; given more power to municipalities in his state; encouraged greater citizen participation in local government; and increased the return of 'federal' tax dollars to Guanajuato.[21]

A more modern and moderate PAN – the kind of PAN represented by Fox – could serve transnational business better than the PRI. The corporatist political model established by the PRI is no longer viable without a large and flexible state budget to buy social peace. Feuding cliques within the PRI turned the once unified party-state into a divided and leaky vessel with which to carry the balsam of neo-liberalism. Fox's prospects for winning the candidacy of the PAN in the next presidential election have improved since the defeat of the PAN governor of Chihuahua in early July 1998. But an internal feud between Fox and Diego Fernández de Ceballos, the PAN's presidential standard bearer in 1994, leaves that issue still in doubt.

Emerging from an emboldened civil society, social movements have produced odd political coalitions in Mexico. The middle-class debtor's movement, 'El Barzón' (The Yoke) has collaborated with the PRD and the FZLN not because they share class interests but out of the tactical political necessity of pressuring and opposing the PRI. 'El Barzón' represents small and medium businesses and mortgage holders who were faced with mounting interest rates in the early 1990s and large increases in their debts after the 1995 devaluation of the Mexican currency.[22] More than 200,000 lost their businesses in the first 18 months of the devaluation and many now fear they will fall into poverty. Their middle-class status, political acumen, and the threat posed to lending institutions should they default on their debt have enabled Barzonistas to force the government to absorb one-third of their debt.[23] Given the specificity of El Barzón's debt agenda, its alliance with the FZLN and the PRD has a built-in fragility. For now, however, they are united in their opposition to the policies and methods of the PRI that have impoverished them.

The Frente Zapatista de Liberación Nacional (Zapatista Front for National Liberation or FZLN) is the political offspring of the Ejercito Zapatista de Liberación Nacional (Zapatista National Liberation Army or EZLN). It holds that the current government is illegitimate because it has destroyed whatever bases of legitimacy it might have had as the heir of the Mexican Revolution.[24] Javier Elorriaga, an FZLN coordinator, has characterized what is now happening in Mexico as 'change which changes everything so that everything remains the same.'[25] The Mexican political elite, he argues, is not functional to the logic of capital because it is no longer a coherent and secure channel for capitalist development.

Thus it can be passed over or sacrificed and replaced by another elite from within Mexican 'political society' as long as such a passage respects the basic institutions of the old regime. But the PRD's Cárdenista base frightens the international and Mexican power elite, and the PAN's internal divisions and a lack of popular support for its 'reactionary project' place it in a similar light.[26] Thus a pacted transition in Mexico that involves the PAN or the PRD remains a dilemma for transnational capital.

The FZLN eschews partisan activity and elite-brokered democratic transitions that use state power through the current system to repress real popular participation (defined by the FZLN as popular self-determination). The FZLN holds that political parties want to control society through the state rather than promote the interests of the majority. In contrast, the FZLN favours a democratic transition that can come about only as a result of the 'break down of the current system of domination'.[27] The EZLN has a strained relationship to the PRD because it suspects that new political parties will replace the PRI-dominated corporate system with a new corporate system of domination.

The new labour coalitions that have broken from the PRI heighten the prospects for forging a rural/urban alliance against the PRI that the Zapatistas support. In August of 1997, unions representing 1.5 million members established an independent labour federation – the Union Nacional de Trabajadores (National Worker's Union or UNT). Within the UNT, the independent Frente Autentico de Trabajadores (Authentic Worker's Front or FAT) represents manufacturing workers in at least half of the states of Mexico and is particularly active in organizing *maquiladora* workers in collaboration with US trade unions and support groups. The more radical CIPM is a part of the Frente Zapatista. Despite these developments, 'the guts of the state-party system remain intact, and the next stage looks to be a drawn-out, uncertain, and ugly affair.'[28]

The EZLN which led the revolt in Chiapas on 1 January 1994 constitutes 'the most dramatic and coherent expression of a worldwide reaction against neoliberalism'.[29] For more than five years the government of Mexico has sought to contain the influence of the EZLN in Chiapas using endless dialogue to mask a military occupation of that state. Paramilitary groups are organized and paid by the local PRI bosses to commit mass killings of 'subversives'. The 22 December 1997 assassinations of 45 persons (mostly women and children) in Acteal, Chiapas by a paramilitary group linked to the state PRI organization has served only to erode further the legitimacy of the PRI locally and nationally.[30] The government's strategy has been to drag out dialogue with the Zapatistas and to renege on the agreements made, thus buying time to build roads (making EZLN strongholds more accessible) and occupy Chiapas militarily.[31] Similarly, in Guerrero, concern over the Ejercito Popular Revoluc005ónario (Popular Revolutionary Army) led the national government to send 10,000 additional troops to that state. Soon, there was a rapid increase in serious violations of human rights.[32]

Massive popular demonstrations, the formation of independent unions, guerrilla uprisings in Chiapas and Guerrero, and the loss of power in the Chamber of Deputies after the last legislative elections reveal the PRI's declining power. This allows local PRI bosses to exert greater political independence from the national party organization. Four PRI leaders changed party affiliation and were elected governors as leaders of the PRD. But the PRI party-state can hobble around as a degraded model of its former self for some time to come with the help of its neighbour to the north.

Conclusions

Real democracy in Mexico means ending broker-mediated politics and requires political parties with organic links to social forces in civil society, such as independent labour organizations who practise shop-floor democracy, independent peasant organizations and independent neighbourhood associations. Real democracy requires political parties that subscribe to what the Sandinistas called 'the logic of the majority'. Real democracy is incompatible with governing 'from above' and is incompatible with the very logic of neo-liberalism that imposes policies of austerity engineered by technocrats 'from above'.

Mexico's hope lies in the changes being wrought 'from below' to policies 'from above' that have crushed Mexico's poor and damaged all but those Mexicans with liquid assets involved in the dollar economy. The struggle for real democracy is now being waged in Mexico by an awakened civil society of independent labour movements, neighbourhood organizations, peasant-based organizations like the EZLN and the EPR, the FZLN and the PRD as they move from the margins to the centre stage of Mexico's political drama. The 60 year-old PRI hegemony is crumbling from within and challenged from without as disaffected PRI leaders have been elected governors of Zacatecas, Tlaxcala and Baja California Sur under the banner of the opposition PRD. The PRI 'has grown a cancer and as it spreads, the PRD grows healthier'.[33] Links to narco-traffickers also corrode the negligible legitimacy of the PRI. Manipulation and coercion reign in the countryside, where the PRI is strongest, and the party's strength has all but collapsed in large urban centres where it governs in only two of the twelve largest cities of Mexico. (Its biggest defeat was its loss of the mayoralty of the federal capital to the PRD in 1997.)

From without, social movements assert their independence from the PRI and seek to break away from the established corporatist political culture that has discredited Mexican political parties altogether. Only by building a viable alternative to the PRI can social movements gain room to negotiate; and, until recently, the only viable alternative to the PRI has been the PRD. But the relationship between parties and social movements is far from easy, even for the reformist PRD. Wary of political parties, Mexican social movements offer cyclical support to them at election time only to distance themselves in-between elections as part of a bargaining strategy of 'strategic, conjunctural alliances'.[34] Resource competition and differences in 'movement logic' and 'party logic' increase tensions between movements and parties because the former place greater priority on substantive goals and local struggles over the broader partisan goals of electoral success with the hope of controlling the nation's political mother lode – the presidency. The institutional context of Mexican politics, compensatory programmes to co-opt possible opposition, and competition in party–movement relationships that strain the PRD as a party built on top of pre-existing organizations – all constitute obstacles to stable party–movement relationships.[35]

Popular movement traditions of bargaining with the state once conflicted with the PRD's identity as a party of confrontation and non-negotiation. But relations between social movements and the PRD have been strained by the party's move toward the centre. Conjunctural alliances between social movements and the PRD lent a cyclical and unstable character to the relationship of many social movements and led the PRD in 1994 to reserve 50 per cent of its candidacies for leaders of popular organizations to bring some stability to the party–movement relationship.[36] Party activists resist turning over candidacies for political office to leaders of social movements who, while seeking office as PRD candidates, want to maintain autonomy and control over their movements.

The lustre of the PRD has dulled and it is under increasing attack as an inert organization that lacks a base of militants and that rests on the momentum of the 1988 elections and their aftermath. Even from the left the PRD is attacked for lacking institutionalization, ideological rigour or coherent programmes, and for undemocratic, caudillo-style leadership. Cárdenas's reputation has been damaged by the revelation that he met with Carlos Salinas in secret in the weeks following the 1988 elections. Because the election of all four of the PRD governors came shortly after they had switched over to the PRD from the PRI, the PRD is now perceived – even by some on the left like Enrique Semo – as a party that wins elections only where there are divisions within the PRI. The 14 March 1999 primary elections of the PRD were marred by sufficient irregularities to force their cancellation and further undermined the PRD's prestige and unity. Vicious attacks on Cárdenas by Porfirio Muñoz Ledo, accusing him of clientelism and bossism, have produced a loss of confidence in the PRD by its rank and file.[37]

Mexico is awash in rumours of a grand coalition of all major political parties against the PRI in the presidential elections in the year 2000. The Mexican party system was in shambles just 15 months before the next presidential election. This can be interpreted as a sign of growing 'democratic pluralism' or of the incapacity and irrelevance of the party system that is emerging in Mexico. In John Ross's view, 'the Zapatista *consulta* and indeed all the *consultas* (there are many) is a popular non-party way of doing politics and [is] gaining credibility [as] civil society doing politics. Meanwhile, the *suciedad* (dirtiness) that keeps leaking out of the parties sells lots of [news journals] but continues to alienate the average voter.'[38]

The political game 'from above' – involving dissident PRI leaders co-opted into the PRD – and possible 'conjunctural alliances' between the PRD and leading opposition parties have more to do with terminating the electoral hegemony of the PRI than with meeting the needs of Mexico's increasingly impoverished majority. Even should Mexico's fractured party system become stable, the battle for economic democracy still would have to be fought as all major political parties in Mexico support some variant of neo-liberalism (the PAN minus corruption and the PRD minus corruption and with support for mitigating social policies). Thus the politics 'from above' is necessary but only as a prelude that broadens the political space for a struggle for true democracy that can come only with political liberty, jobs, food, housing and education. Mexico remains one of the most inequitable societies in the world. The fundamental redistribution of wealth necessary to achieve real democracy cannot be achieved within the limits of Mexico's present neo-liberal regime, which relies, ultimately, on force.

A likely scenario for Mexico's future is the continued 'maquiladorization' of the Mexican economy with maquiladora growth and expansion to central and southern Mexico. The PRD and the PAN will expand as the PRI continues to fragment and as discontented PRI defectors run under the banner of 'the opposition'. As the political game 'from above' widens political spaces, a mass movement will grow 'from below' among those alienated from a political and economic system wedded to Mexico's historic pattern of low-wage exploitation. Only in these social movements is there any possibility for a continued broadening of political spaces in Mexico to wage the battle for economic democracy.

With the major political parties committed to the neo-liberal model, the real fissure that is exposed in Mexican politics is between those pressuring 'from below' and variants of the political game 'from above'. Forced by internal divisions, defections and declining resources to keep its local bosses under control, the PRI will move from an authoritarian and semi-authoritarian clientelism in the countryside – varying only in degrees of political subordination – to a greater associational autonomy in urban areas that reflects the degraded hegemony of the PRI. The movement from one-party authoritarian politics to multi-party electoral politics can stabilize far short of democracy, depending on the degree of mobilization by social movements at the shop floor, in the union halls, in the countryside and in the urban streets. Thus 'the prospects for democratization in Mexico depend on how conflict between more or less authoritarian policy currents within the state interact with growing civic pressures from below.'[39]

The globalization process itself – with its downsizing, lowering of wages, 'runaway industries' and corporatization of all social relations – is compelling Americans and Canadians to defend their self-interests by rendering assistance to social movements in Mexico.[40] The challenge is how to link the considerable social mobilization against neo-liberalism already in place within local and national arenas into a global movement and to overcome the social atomization that is the key resource of capital and its state and global apparatus.

Notes

1 J. Adler Hellman, *Mexico in Crisis*, 2nd edn (New York and London: Holmes and Meier, 1983), pp. 148–63.
2 J. Nef, 'Normalization, Popular Struggles, and the Receiver State', in J. Knippers Black, eds, *Latin America: Its Problems and Its Promise* (Boulder, Colo.: Westview, 1991), pp. 197–216.
3 H. Veltmeyer, J. Petras and S. Vieux, *Neoliberalism and Class Conflict in Latin America: a Comparative Perspective on the Political Economy of Structural Adjustment* (New York: St. Martin's, 1997), pp. 140–5.
4 J. Ross, *The Annexation of Mexico: from the Aztecs to the I.M.F.* (Monroe, Me.: Common Courage Press, 1988), p. 171. Half of these exports were destined for the United States market.

5   Ibid., p. 172.
6   Ibid.
7   C. Marichal, 'The Vicious Cycle of Mexican Debt', *NACLA Report on the Americas*, XXXI (Nov./Dec. 1997), pp. 25–31.
8   P. Muñoz Rios, 'El TLC seria chivo expiatorio del año electoral en EU: Kolbe', *La Jornada* (electronic), 20 Feb. 1995.
9   E.W. Butler, J. Pike and W.J. Hettrick, 'Economic Transformation in Mexico: the Mexican 500 Before and After NAFTA', paper presented at the Joint Conference of the Rocky Mountain Council for Latin American Studies and Pacific Coast Council on Latin American Studies, Santa Fe, New Mexico, 20 March 1996 (unpublished).
10 J. Smith, 'Banking on Change', *Los Angeles Times* (7 Dec. 1997), p. D1.
11 A. DePalma, 'Mexico's Recovery By Passes the Poor', *The New York Times* (12 Aug. 1997), p. A3.
12 A. Reding, 'Aztec Sun Rising: the Cárdenas Challenge', *World Policy Journal*, XIV, no. 3 (Fall 1997), pp. 63–70.
13 M.B. Sheridan and A. O'Connor, 'Mexico's New Police Chief Ousted', *Los Angeles Times* (11 Dec. 1997), p. A1.
14 See *Los Angeles Times* (13 Dec. 1997), p. A12.
15 M. Bienefeld, 'The New World Order: Echoes of a New Imperialism', *Third World Quarterly*, 15 (March 1994), pp. 31–48.
16 See Reding, 'Aztec Sun', p. 69.
17 Together the opposition constitutes a majority of 269 votes to 239 votes for the PRI in the Chamber.
18 A. Reding, 'The New Mexican Revolution', *World Policy Journal*, 13, no. 3 (Fall 1996), p. 63.
19 Ibid., p. 66.
20 Ibid., p. 61.
21 Had Fox been an American or British politician, he would qualify as a New Democrat or a leader of New Labour.
22 200,000 businesses closed in the first 18 months of the crisis. Forty per cent of the loans in Mexico's 18 private banks were not collectable, with the top three banks holding $6 billion in such loans. See Ross, *Annexation of Mexico*, pp. 258–60.
23 Ibid.
24 These bases are the *ejido* system: government control of oil resources; free public education; a social security system sufficient for the reproduction of the workforce; a state economic sector not guided by the logic of individual gain; and a foreign policy opposed to US economic intervention in Mexico. In place of these guarantees, the government has put in place an economic model that excludes the majority, de-industrializes Mexico and transfers resources abroad. I refer to J. Ellorriaga, 'La Transición: Continuidad o Ruptura', address given at California State Polytechnic University, Pomona (17 Nov. 1997), unpublished textual notes.
25 Ibid.
26 Ibid., p. 6.
27 Ibid., p. 7.
28 D.W. Payne, 'Mexican Labor: Cracks in the Monolith', *Dissent* (Winter 1998), p. 24.

29 Veltmeyer et al., *Neoliberalism*, p. 200.
30 Luis Hernandez Navarro, secretary of the commission charged with verifying compliance with the February 1996 peace agreements in Chiapas, charged that the local government in Chenalho municipality aided the paramilitary group Peace and Justice in fighting a dirty war against the EZLN. This has led to more than 200 deaths in northern Chiapas, documented by Human Rights Watch and other reputable human rights organizations. Declining support for the PRI in the state and 30 parallel Zapatista governments threaten to destroy the power base of PRI strongmen, who then resort to a dirty war to maintain their power. See L. Hernández Navarro, 'Red Harvest in Long-Bloodied Chiapas', *Los Angeles Times* (27 Dec. 1997), p. B6.
31 In Chiapas and other rural areas PRD members often take revolutionary positions, especially around land questions, that are more radical than those of the national PRD.
32 Ross, *Annexation of Mexico*, p. 271.
33 R. Riva Palacios, *Los Angeles Times* (5 March 1997), p. B7.
34 K. Bruhn, 'The Seven-Month Itch? Neoliberal Politics, Popular Movements, and the Left in Mexico', in D.A. Chalmers et al., eds, *The New Politics of Inequality in Latin America* (New York: Oxford, 1997), p. 162.
35 Ibid.
36 Ibid., p. 164.
37 See Riva Palacios in the *Los Angeles Times*; M. Scherer Ibarra, 'Enrique Semo: El PRD se mueve de acuerdo con los misteriosos impulsos de sus personajes y de sus grupos politicos', *Proceso* (11 April 1999).
38 *Consultas* are popular consultations in the form of mass rallies. Quote is from J. Ross, author of *The Annexation of Mexico*, correspondence, 19 April 1999.
39 J. Fox, 'The Difficult Transition from Clientelism to Citizenship: Lessons from Mexico', in Chalmers et al., *The New Politics*, p. 417.
40 See J.D. Cockcroft, *Mexico's Hope: an Encounter with Politics and History* (New York: Monthly Review Press, 1999), pp. 365–71. I concur with this excellent book's positive message that Mexico's hope lies in its growing social mobilization.

Part III

National and Transnational Policy-making

7
Anti-globalists and Agricultural Protection: the State Battles On

David N. Balaam

As is to be expected, supporters of globalization are usually quite critical of state agricultural protection measures that lead to production inefficiencies, drive up the budgetary costs of support programmes and distort and destabilize international trade. Opponents of globalization writing from a critical (Marxist) structuralist perspective, by contrast, often argue that it is increasingly difficult for the state to act autonomously in developing agricultural policy. This paper argues that these anti-globalists seriously underestimate the resilience of the state in dealing with agriculture. After briefly examining some of the anti-globalization literature to explain why the structuralists underestimate the state's role, this paper discusses the GATT (General Agreement on Tariffs and Trade) Uruguay round agricultural negotiations to demonstrate that the state continues to be a potent force in agriculture. Indeed, the GATT Uruguay round negotiations may have helped to strengthen the state's capacity to reconcile domestic and international interests and objectives in agriculture. While the state's role may be decreasing in some sectors of the economy, in agriculture it continues to exert a good deal of autonomous control over policy-making. Many anti-globalists have not been sufficiently attuned to the differences among sectoral areas when assessing the effects of globalization.

The anti-globalization literature and agriculture

Much of the structuralist literature portrays globalization as harming the most vulnerable groups in the agro-food system.[1] For example, most anti-globalists challenge the liberal economic assumption that the integrative forces of capitalism, whereby new technologies are applied to agricultural production and distribution, serve the interests of poorer people and peasants in less developed countries (LDCs). Capital, new technologies and other agricultural inputs enhance efficiency, but they also drive many farmers off the land.[2] Food security is weakened as family farms and rural communities everywhere are destroyed and peasants go hungry.

Friedman and McMichael view the world agro-food system as a regime of production and consumption that serves to intensify global capitalist integration.[3] Since the Second World War the rich nations of the North have demanded more exotic and high-protein meat, fruits and vegetables grown in Southern developing nations. New production technologies and biotechnologies along with pesticides and chemicals have been applied to the production process. Land concentration and a diffusion of US food consumption patterns have displaced traditional and seasonal foods with mass-produced items. Agribusiness mass-production techniques ('Global Fordism') have spread to a number of LDCs such as Brazil, Thailand, Argentina and emerging (former Soviet bloc) countries, such as Hungary. Footloose agribusinesses have attempted to make LDCs agro-export platforms or agro-export (free trade) zones.

The extension of commercial agriculture and corporate values into the global market intensifies North–South tensions in general as a result of inappropriate food production and growing dependent consumption patterns. Tropical growers who subsisted under colonial plantation structures today have become 'petty commodity producers' for agro-business exporters.[4] National and local food security goals are compromised by agro-industrial development strategies that emphasize production for export. Thus, at the same time as LDCs were increasing their exports of agricultural products of interest to the West, they were accounting for a growing percentage of global wheat imports.

Rural people are also disadvantaged by structural adjustment programmes sanctioned by the International Monetary Fund (IMF) and World Bank, whose development plans require LDC borrowers to eliminate welfare programmes and to devalue local currencies to encourage foreign-exchange earning exports. Financial credit often goes to the largest commercial farmers, while displaced peasants in countries such as Brazil and India are moved from local areas, and in some cases into rain forests, in search of land. Food prices in urban areas are kept low to maintain political support for the government, while taxes are invested in the production of semi-processed industrial goods for export. Demand for food in heavily populated urban areas is met with costly imports, which drives up debt and adds to LDC dependency on the industrialized states. Mexico, for instance, now imports corn from the

United States, while its own producers are driven off the land or forced to work for low wages in overpopulated urban areas. Thus, anti-globalists such as Lehman and Krebs chastise the IMF and World Bank for promoting investment in agro-export crops and fostering malnutrition and food dependency.[5]

Underlying the anti-globalists' criticisms of the negative impact of agribusiness on vulnerable groups is the assumption that the role of the state is rendered weak, or in many cases forced into 'retreat'.[6] From this perspective, the modern agro-food system virtually compels states to fulfil roles pursuant to extending the world capitalist system. At the global capitalist level, systemic economic structures and processes are transforming or 'restructuring' the agro-food system via the instruments of developed rich nations that include liberal economic trade and investment policies, the self-serving practices of agribusinesses and agro-corporations, and international finance institutions and agencies whose agenda is decidedly anti-food-security.[7] Thus, Alessandro Bonanno argues that 'the globalization of the agricultural and food system generates a dislocation between the transnationalization of the accumulation process and the national dimension of state action. More specifically, the national state is increasingly unable to perform its historical societal "functions", i.e., fostering economic development (accumulation) and guaranteeing mediation between social groups and social organization (legitimization).'[8]

McMichael argues that the state should be endeavouring to gain more autonomy from global business forces, and thus to act in the public interest and reclaim local forms of social organization.[9] He and other anti-globalists hope to see a growing anti-globalization movement to protect local producers as part of a new social movement that parallels the rise of citizenship politics, the Green movement, feminism, ethnonationalist movements, regional associations and Non-government Organizations (NGOs).[10] Nevertheless, anti-globalists are often pessimistic, arguing that local, regional and national governmental efforts to gain more autonomy offer little hope of providing a truly alternative paradigm to the globalized agro-industrial structure.

David Goodman contends that McMichael and others who focus on the restructuring impact of global capitalism are overly deterministic about the influence of megatrends on the international economy's structure and agent behaviour.[11] The agro-food picture is much more complex and idiosyncratic than the analysis offered by the structuralists. In Goodman's view, McMichael and others borrow too heavily from industrial sector studies and apply them to the agro-food sector.

Agricultural products and corporate strategies continue to be multi-domestic, not completely global in production or market orientation. Goodman recommends 'unpacking' globalization to look more closely at agents and the relationships – institutional or otherwise – they establish with one another, separate from the constraints of the total agro-food system. Indeed, in this chapter I contend that the most important agent in the international system when it comes to agricultural issues is still the nation-state.

Agriculture in the Uruguay round

The Uruguay round of GATT negotiations (1986–93) provides a good case study of the connection between constraining global and national conditions, state strategies and the behaviour of national and international actors. In past rounds, when officials could not reach an agreement to liberalize agricultural trade, they simply removed it from the trade negotiations. Thus, agriculture was largely exempt from GATT trade rules for almost forty years. In the Uruguay round agriculture became the centrepiece of the negotiations when trade officials agreed that success in other new trade items such as services and intellectual property rights was contingent upon an agreement to liberalize agricultural trade. At the eleventh hour in the negotiations, the world's major grain traders – the US, the European Community (EC) and the Cairns Group[12] (which included Australia and Canada), along with Japan (the world's second largest food importer – the US is first!) and a number of developing nations – reached an agreement that many praised for beginning the process of liberalizing agricultural trade.

The agricultural agreement itself dealt with a number of complicated and politically contentious issues. It had five major features.[13] Export subsidies are to be cut in value by 36 per cent and in volume by 21 per cent over the next 6 years; LDC cuts are to be 24 and 14 per cent respectively over a 10 year period. Second is a reduction of 20 per cent in aggregate domestic farm support. Third, 'tariffication' converts all quantitative restrictions on imports (or import quotas) to tariffs, then reduces them by 36 per cent over the next 6 years. Additionally, protection for the most sensitive products is to be reduced by at least 15 per cent, and countries have to allow for imports equal to 3 per cent of what is produced domestically. Two other measures include sanitary and phyto-sanitary (SPS) trade controls to protect human, animal and plant life or health. Finally, the Final Act of the Uruguay Round contained several provisions for the dispute settlement process.

Given its flexibility and rather modest cuts, why would GATT members accept this type of agreement, and, how much national decision-making authority in agriculture does the agreement in fact transfer to the new World Trade Organization (WTO)? My research indicates that the representatives of the major trading nations in the Uruguay round purposefully reached an accord that appears to liberalize agricultural trade, but in fact continues to permit the state to maintain agricultural policies that are quite protectionist.[14] There is much evidence to suggest that farm groups in the US, Japan and especially the EC, pressured their negotiators into watering down the final agreement.[15] However, an explanation that focuses on interest groups only partly accounts for the outcome of the talks.

If farm groups that opposed cuts in protection had been all that influential during the negotiations, chances are officials would have once again taken agriculture off the negotiating table. I contend that while the Agriculture Agreement did reflect a number of group interests as well as global constraints, more than anything else it mirrored the effort of state officials to reconcile a wide variety of national and international interests. Rather than adhering to systemic roles that compelled states to drop agricultural protection, national officials had considerable room to manoeuvre apart from the groups they represented. Thus, the major states were able to pursue a variety of strategies and options in their efforts to arrive at an accord, if only a modest one.

The Reagan administration used the negotiations primarily as part of an effort to cut farm-programme costs.[16] US officials sought to thwart protectionist pressures in Congress to continue farm assistance related to declining exports, increasing imports and mounting job losses. The administration also sought to correct a growing balance of trade problem, especially with Japan, by reaching an agreement that favoured the US comparative advantage in agriculture and that also extended trade discipline to services and intellectual property. Finally, US officials viewed the talks as an opportunity to reduce the protectionist measures of other exporters and importers whose commodities competed with those of the United States. These goals help to account for the hard driving and even combative style of US negotiators early in the talks. For example, President Reagan pressured the EC to accept his 'zero-option' proposal to do away with all import and export protectionist measures.[17] The EC as expected rejected his offer and countered that the President was not serious, and was only interested in killing the talks. Reagan appears to have wanted to put the Europeans on the defensive, forcing them to justify agriculture's protection.

Due to EC intransigence, the US gradually came to accept more politically realistic proposals to reduce protection only marginally and over a long period of time. Throughout the talks, however, the US continued to employ a variety of heavy-handed measures to gain compliance with its objective of significant reductions in agricultural protection. It threatened Japan, Brazil and India, among others, with Super 301 trade legislation that required the President to economically punish those nations whose trade practices hurt US producers. Furthermore, countries in the GATT felt pressured by concurrent negotiations between the US and its NAFTA and later its Asia Pacific Economic Cooperation forum (APEC) neighbours, which threatened to regionalize trade if a multilateral agreement could not be reached in the Uruguay Round.

The EC began the talks in favour of opening up trade that covered new items, yet it was also reluctant to significantly reform its Common Agricultural Policy (CAP) or limit the use of import levies and export subsidies.[18] The British favoured reform of the CAP because of its drain on the EC's budget, while the French opposed the talks because of their impact on its farmers. For all intents and purposes, EC officials stalled early on in the talks while the Council of Ministers and commissioners wrangled over how much and where the CAP would be reformed. After two years of effort within EC institutions, agricultural commissioner Ray MacSharry was able to get through a proposal to reform the CAP, thereby bringing it into line with GATT efforts to reduce agricultural protection. Just as US officials did, some EC officials used the Uruguay Round to counter protectionist pressure within the Community. Even though the new agreement reduces domestic protection by 30 per cent over a 10-year period of time for cereals, rice, olive oil, oilseeds and protein crops, along with sugar beets and livestock products, EC officials had to buy off French farmers with an increase in set-asides and Community payments directed to smaller farmers.

In the 1980s Japan made a conscious effort to reduce its expensive commodity programmes and import protection measures for rice, citrus products and beef. Post-Second World War Japanese farm programmes and trade policies reflected state efforts to sustain commodity production in conjunction with Japan's economic recovery and its export-led growth and industrial development strategies.[19] As the farm base of Japan's Liberal Democratic Party (LDP) deteriorated, and consumers demanded cheaper and more imported food items, officials found it difficult to negotiate reductions in agricultural protection. Japanese officials were interested in cutting farm programme costs and also in improving bilateral relations with the US and playing a positive role in the Uruguay round talks. Through it all they generally kept a low profile, while US and EC officials routinely battled one another.

Australian officials pursued trade liberalization quite aggressively early in the negotiations, heading up the Cairns Group of countries committed to freer trade in agriculture. Because Australia found itself in agreement with the US on a variety of issues, it took on the role of an 'honest broker' between the parties. A number of LDCs, especially Argentina, Brazil, Mexico, Thailand, India and China, took an interest in the agricultural part of the talks based on their advantages in agricultural production. Yet, during the talks on agricultural issues LDCs did not act as a cohesive unit because of major divisions between agricultural exporters and importers. However, LDCs did play an important role in other areas of the trade talks, especially those concerning services and intellectual property rights.

Despite threats to end the talks, and occasions when some states walked out of the trade talks over agriculture, the promise of economic gains or 'sweet deals' emerging from trade liberalization in other areas, kept state officials in the game. The modest agricultural agreement allowed officials to claim they had made enough progress on agricultural trade without selling out domestic interests. In the end, the industrialized nations gained more access to each other and to LDC markets in new areas such as services. Some LDCs gained more access to industrialized markets for their primary commodities and for an increasing number of their semi-processed and finished products along with more time to implement the agreement and adjust to its domestic effects.

Contrary to the deterministic arguments of some anti-globalists, one outcome of the Uruguay round was that states *chose* to put only a minor dent in agricultural protection. They could have liberalized agricultural trade more than they did given that, since the 1970s, national officials have gradually been able to separate themselves from the interests of farm groups (more so in the US and Japan than in the EC). During the negotiations state officials made a number of bargains and deals that only marginally hurt, and may in fact have helped to further protect farmers.

Rather than state power being weakened by globalization, this case study of agriculture in the GATT demonstrates that the state held its own in the battle to manage globalization. In contrast to other sectors, agriculture was not liberalized as much as many had hoped. In fact, some supporters of free trade were quite disappointed in the accord, mainly because, they argue, it did not go far enough in eliminating domestic and international trade protection measures.[20] Export subsidy cuts are not commodity specific. Countries can group them in any combination to arrive at the required average needed to show a decrease in support. Countries can also shift support for farm programmes as long as they stay beneath the required ceiling of reduction, while other support programmes such as milk remain exempted from the new rules. Ambiguous rules also allow national officials to employ 'dirty tariffs' whereby they inflate tariff rate equivalents used as base levels, essentially negating the effort to cut tariffs. Finally, the agreement does not bite hard enough into export subsidies. Thus, it has the effect of *continuing* to sanction remaining subsidies and tariffs in the new WTO.

Contrary to globalization weakening the state in this sector, it may actually have helped to strengthen state power to the extent that the negotiations helped crystallize a number of conflicting issues and interests state officials had to reconcile. Capable of trading away the interests of some farm groups, state officials used the talks to help reform their domestic support policies and programmes. Officials may have also reached a limit when it came to their willingness to make agriculture any more competitive. This finding complements the work of Palan and Abbott, for instance, who argue that globalization's impact on the state is both overestimated and overstated.[21] States react differently to globalization in accordance with unique combinations of socio-economic structures within each nation-state. Even more interestingly, Palan and Abbott argue that globalization does not engender a unified reaction. States continue to be relatively powerful actors who draw on a variety of instruments to achieve their political and economic objectives.

What of the anti-globalist's claim that the expansion of global trading rules under the new World Trade Organization (WTO) that replaced the GATT signifies a loss of sovereignty by member states? Noted trade expert Jeffrey Schott argues that the member countries, not the new WTO, are basically responsible for ensuring compliance to new rules. This is because the WTO has no means to force countries to honour their obligations.[22] WTO decisions are not self-executing in national legal systems. Furthermore, its decisions are normally made by consensus, or decided by majority vote if no consensus is reached. Even if Schott's arguments do not deal with the charge that the WTO's ardent support of free trade is misplaced based on its many negative effects on both industrialized and developing nations, the most important point here is that WTO rules cannot be separated from state interests and policies.

Conclusion: the state's role in the anti-globalization campaign

The anti-globalization literature tends to relegate state agricultural policies to economically deterministic forces that compel the state into retreat. Little hope is left for states or local groups to counter the effects of globalization. Yet, examination of developments in agriculture in the Uruguay Round show that in this sector the state is not as limited as it is often portrayed. There is a range of choices available to states to counter the effects of globalization. States play a reconciling role when it comes to deciding which domestic interests to support in the face of global constraints.

In the future researchers should pay more attention to the connection between developments in agriculture at the international, regional, state and local levels.[23] Solutions to food security problems in particular are well served by efforts to make local communities self-sufficient. However, these strategies might not be appropriate for parts of the world where large numbers of people face a variety of agro-food problems. At the state and international levels, anti-globalists are correct to point out that free trade is no panacea to solving food security issues. Yet the anti-globalization campaign should look more to the state for help to sort out when, under what circumstances and by which policy instruments, agriculture protection would best serve regional, national and local community interests. For instance, as part of the recent efforts to reform the European Union (EU), community officials have directed more support to smaller farmers, and at times the US government has also made efforts to ensure that greater numbers of small farmers receive support benefits.

Another important issue is whether states can collectively manage the international economy on a more equal basis. New WTO trade rules move states in that direction, even if the values of the WTO remain uncritically liberal economic in outlook. Efforts to reform the WTO so as to make its decision-making processes more democratic should continue. In the US Congress critics of globalization have pushed President Clinton to move the WTO toward adopting policies that emphasize concerns for inequality as much as economic growth.[24] When it comes to issues of food security and hunger, state power could be used to create conditions under which global competition leads to a global levelling up.

Notes

1 See for example K. Lehman and A. Krebs, 'Control Over the World's Food Supply', in J. Mander and E. Goldsmith, eds, *The Case Against the Global Economy and For A Turn Toward the Local* (San Francisco, Calif.: Sierra Club Books, 1996), pp. 122–30.

2 This is one of the themes of R. Schaeffer's 'Technology, Food, and Hunger' in his *Understanding Globalization: the Social Consequences of Political, Economic, and Environmental Change* (Lanham, Md.: Rowman & Littlefield, 1997), pp. 143–82.

3 For example, see the entire issue of the *Review of International Political Economy*, 4, no. 4 (Winter 1997).

4 P. McMichael 'Rethinking Globalization: the Agrarian Question Revisited', in *Review of International Political Economy*, 4, no. 4 (Winter 1997), p. 637.

5 Lehman and Krebs, 'Control Over the World's Food Supply'.

6 For a different view see Linda Weiss, *The Myth of the Powerless State* (Ithaca: Cornell University Press, 1998).

7 McMichael 'Rethinking Globalization'.

8 A. Bonanno, 'The Locus of Polity Action in a Global Setting', in A. Bonanno, L. Busch, W. Friedland, L. Gouveia and E. Mingione, eds, *From Columbus to Conagra: the Globalization of Agriculture and Food* (Lawrence, Kan.: University of Kansas Press, 1994), p. 257.

9 McMichael, 'Rethinking Globalization'.

10 See D. Imhoff, 'Community Supported Agriculture: Farming with a Face on It', in Mander and Goldsmith, *The Case Against the Global Economy*, pp. 434–5.

11 D. Goodman, 'World-Scale Processes and Agro-Food Systems: Critique and Research Needs', in *Review of International Political Economy*, 4, no. 4 (Winter 1997), pp. 663–87.

12 The Cairns Group was named for the Australian city in which it originated and was composed of Argentina, Australia, Brazil, Canada, Chile, Columbia, Hungary, Fiji, Uruguay, Indonesia, the Philippines, Malaysia, New Zealand and Thailand.

13 For a more detailed discussion of all the results of the Uruguay round see J. Schott, *The Uruguay Round* (Washington, DC: Institute for International Economics, 1994).

14 For a more detailed discussion see D.N. Balaam, 'Agricultural Trade Policy', in B. Hocking and S. Smith, eds, *The New Trade Policy* (London: Routledge, 1999).

15 See for example R. Paarlberg, 'Agricultural Policy Reform and the Uruguay Round: Synergistic Linkage in a Two-Level Game?', *International Organization*, 51, no. 3 (Summer 1997), pp. 413–44.

16 See Paarlberg, 'Agricultural Policy Reform and the Uruguay Round', and A. Oxley, *The Challenge of Free Trade* (New York: Harvester Wheatsheaf, 1990).

17 The term 'zero option' originated in President Reagan's arms control proposal in 1985 to reduce to zero US missiles in Europe provided the Soviet Union did the same.

18 For a detailed account of the EC and the issue of agriculture during the Uruguay round see A. Swinbank and C. Tanner, *Farm Policy and Trade Conflict* (Ann Arbor, Mich.: University of Michigan Press, 1996).

19 For a more detailed discussion see D.N. Balaam 'Self-Sufficiency in Japanese Agriculture: Telescoping and Reconciling the Food Security–Efficiency Dilemma', *Policy Studies Review*, 4, no. 2 (Nov. 1984), pp. 281–90.

20 See for example Paarlberg, 'Agricultural Policy Reform and the Uruguay Round'.

21 R. Palan and J. Abbott with P. Deans, *State Strategies in the Global Political Economy* (London: Pinter, 1996).

22 See J. Schott, ed., *The World Trading System: Challenges Ahead* (Washington, DC: Institute for International Economics, 1996), p. 6.

23 An excellent example is J.M. Paige, *Coffee and Power: Revolution and the Rise of Democracy in Central America* (Cambridge, Mass.: Harvard University Press, 1997).

24 See E.J. Dione, Jr., 'Globalism with a Human Face', *The Washington Post*, 29 May 1998, p. A27.

8
The Influence of Globalization and Internationalization on Domestic Policy Change

Steven Bernstein and Ben Cashore

Introduction

For many, the term 'globalization' evokes the spectre of an impersonal global marketplace that threatens to overwhelm domestic policy and policy-making independence.[1]

Resistance to the market's inexorable logic may be possible at the margins, but adaptation appears the most rational response. The welfare state becomes the 'competition state',[2] corporate power grows at the expense of non-business civil society, and pressure mounts for a race to the neo-liberal bottom. Although these pressures are real, talk of globalization conflates a variety of processes that do not necessarily all push public policy in the same direction. The *political* transcendence of borders has created a range of potential non-domestic pressures on domestic public policies ignored in much of the globalization literature, which has stressed the logic of global markets.

We thus make an important distinction between globalization, which primarily concerns increasing economic transactions that cross or transcend borders, and internationalization, which concerns increased activities and influence of transnational or international actors and institutions. Both sets of factors are important, but analytic leverage increases by differentiating them in order to show their independent effects and interaction. An examination of the processes of internationalization then shows how these actor-based and institutional forces from beyond state borders can directly influence policies and policy-making.

The argument focuses especially on transnational actors as agents of change through which internationalization of public policy occurs. Transnational actors – non-state actors who regularly engage in interactions across national boundaries and who do not operate on behalf of a national government or intergovernmental organization[3] – are key sources of influence because they often deliberately attempt to affect domestic policies. We examine two paths of transnational influence: the use of the global market/international political economy to pressure for change, and the infiltration of domestic policy processes.[4] These two paths highlight potential sources of influence largely ignored in the globalization literature and explore the most direct strategies employed by transnational actors to achieve policy change.

The chapter then explains how transnational actors influenced domestic policy change in eco-forest policy in British Columbia in the early to mid-1990s, a case chosen for two reasons. First, it usefully illustrates the independent effects of globalization and internationalization. The forest sector in British Columbia has a long history of dependence on foreign markets for its products and significant foreign ownership (globalization),[5] yet major change in policies to incorporate environmental goals occurred only recently, in the face of intense international scrutiny (internationalization).

Second, it illustrates how a growing global consciousness – about ecological concerns in this instance – can direct world-wide attention to local problems with global significance. Global conferences like the 1972 UN Conference on the Human Environment in Stockholm and the 1992 UN Conference on Environment and Development in Rio, increases in the scope of international environmental agreements, and increases in the activities of transnational environmental groups all attest to this growing global ecological consciousness. Much of it has been directed toward local and regional environmental problems, where policy authority ultimately remains in the hands of domestic governments.

Such concerns contextualize the BC case, which drew international attention because the province contains much of the world's remaining temperate old growth forests. Similarly the dominant mode of forest harvesting in BC is clearcutting, a controversial practice criticized by many transnational environmental groups. Since eco-forestry was formerly considered a domestic issue, its elevation to a global concern subject to non-domestic pressures provides a useful illustration of how transnational influences might work across a wide range of similarly internationalized policies.

Disentangling internationalization and globalization

The important distinction made between 'globalization' and 'internationalization' clarifies the role of various non-domestic pressures and shows the value added of focusing on transnational actors as drivers of domestic policy change. *Globalization* refers specifically to structural economic factors, mainly 'rising levels of trade, finance and foreign direct investment'.[6] In contrast, the term *internationalization* refers to situations when policies within domestic jurisdictions face increased scrutiny, participation or influence from transnational actors and international institutions, and the rules and norms they embody.

This distinction partially remedies contradictory findings over whether increasing global transactions lead to domestic policy convergence, and whether that convergence is likely to be 'upward' or 'downward'.[7] For example, many theoretical and empirical findings support Berger's proposition that in the absence of international rules and norms to the contrary, increased market integration and capital mobility (globalization) places *downward* pressure on 'wages, working conditions ... or environmental protection',[8] or encourage companies to relocate where standards are low. If left unchecked, companies will have an incentive to invest in those regions/countries with lower wages, taxes and regulations. Yet, others find that standards may harmonize up as easily as down in response to free trade.[9]

These differences stem partly from the conflation of structural economic factors with actors and institutions so that the independent effects of each are poorly understood. Global economic factors alone do not generally determine the direction of domestic policy responses. Vogel shows that trade liberalization can lead to domestic consumer and environmental protection when 'wealthy, powerful states' prefer such standards.[10] He demonstrates that actors within and across borders, the ideas and identities they promote, and the institutions through which they work can all influence state preferences. Protection of standards may then occur if trade liberalization is accompanied by agreements among states to coordinate their regulatory policies, which can occur in strong institutional settings such as the EU; and where non-governmental actors successfully influence powerful governments to require or permit regulatory protection in international agreements.[11] Seen in this light, Vogel's argument is partly about the potential of organized interests or advocacy groups to counter the trends of globalization.[12]

A second set of factors that can mediate the effects of globalization on domestic policy is differences in the nature of the state, society, policy-making institutions and values. But more needs to be known as well about the conditions under which these various domestic factors matter in mediating *internationalization*, that is, why and how transnational actors and international institutions have influence.

To understand better these processes we delineate below two distinct pathways of transnational influence, each with its own logic: *market dependence* and *direct infiltration of the domestic policy-making process*. Actors following the first path aim to force governments to make policy choices in response to direct pressures from outside the domestic political jurisdiction. Action along the second path does not employ coercion or directly use international mechanisms. Instead, it requires direct 'infiltration' of the domestic policy-making process by attempting to alter the balance of power among existing domestic organized interests and their participation in policy networks. Transnational actors accomplish their mission through the sharing of resources, ideas and expertise with existing groups, or by facilitating the creation of new groups or coalitions. Globalization, to the degree that it creates dependence on foreign markets, is a necessary condition of the first path, but is not required with the second path.[13]

Path one: market dependence

Here, transnational actors directly use global markets to force policy responses by practising 'leverage politics'.[14] Boycott campaigns are the most common strategy. A company or government faces market loss and economic hardship if they do not bow to demands of foreign consumers. Sometimes domestic groups initially bring the issue to the attention of transnational actors.

This path largely bypasses domestic politics. The key factor is the ability of transnational actors to convince consumers of the need to change the target's 'detrimental' policies. Strategies to achieve this goal may vary depending on what works best in consuming countries, but can include education, influencing media coverage, normative/moral arguments, and even targeting suppliers of the foreign product in the domestic market (who themselves are coerced into supporting a boycott or risk being boycotted themselves). The causal mechanism here is primarily the threat or reality of economic reprisals. This strategy is coercive, rather than based on moral suasion. It requires globalization to the degree that the target government or firms must be relatively dependent on the external markets in which the boycotts are launched.

On the market path, domestic politics does not influence the strength of this pressure, since it emanates from external markets. While domestic politics influence the specifics of the policy response, the relationship between the state, business and non-business interests (the policy network) is relatively unimportant for success because the coercive force of the market dependence path affects business interests as much as the state. The struggle for power shifts to consumer countries, with the targeted government and industry associations often participating as a counter lobby to the environmental or consumer boycott campaign.

Importantly, this path does not reverse the downward effects of globalization. Rather, these international pressures act as countervailing forces; the strength of each will influence the type of policy responses considered by the domestic government. For example, targeted companies and / or governments may weigh the costs in lost income and reputation versus the risks of being standard-leaders or the loss of competitive advantage that may result by forgoing practices or policies allowed in other countries that push prices lower.

Upward policy responses to market pressures could be relatively unstable if transnational groups vacated this path. Alone it is unlikely to result in the kind of value changes sought by transnational actors that we argue can make policy change more durable.

Path two: infiltration of the domestic policy-making process

Here, transnational actors attempt to participate (directly or indirectly) in the domestic policy-making process, in effect internalizing the external influence. Two related factors are important: the structure of and membership of domestic policy networks, and the ability of transnational actors to penetrate networks in such a way that does not open them up to charges of violating national sovereignty.

The term policy network refers to the nature of exchange between the state and societal interests in policy-making over a particular issue.[15] International relations scholars have turned to the domestic policy network literature because it helps explain why some transnational actors are more successful than others in their efforts to directly penetrate domestic policy-making processes.[16] Three network characteristics are most important: the degree of openness, state autonomy, and state capacity.

Openness refers to the ability of the existing networks to accommodate new organizations and interests into network deliberations. Where networks are closed and rigid, transnational influence will be difficult. In these cases blockage will usually occur and groups will be forced to find other more open networks, or other paths.[17]

Related to but distinct from openness is the degree of state autonomy within a given network. State autonomy refers to the *degree* of independence of state officials when realizing goals and making policy choices, which is most often manifest when state officials' choices depart from the goals of traditional business interests. (In this treatment, state officials often deliberate upon an array of societal pressures, rather than ignoring them.)

The greater the relative autonomy of state officials from traditional business interests, the more potential for transnational actors' arguments for change to be considered. Even in the case of relatively closed networks, the argument holds since transnational actors can use persuasion on autonomous state decision makers, although direct access, or access of domestic coalition partners, would be limited. When networks are characterized by openness and autonomy, strategies of coalition-building and direct action through networks becomes possible. However, where state officials rely on a business association for advice and expertise on a particular policy, and are not autonomous from such an association, other organizations' proposals will face difficulty in getting consideration from state officials, whatever the strategy employed.

State capacity refers to the ability of state actors to implement policy choices. Where state structures are fragmented and/or decentralized, policy success will be more limited than in those networks where authority is concentrated, because relatively quick and wide-ranging decisions are possible.

On this path, transnational actors provide resources, knowledge, training and financing to existing domestic groups, or help organize or finance new domestic-based groups or coalitions. Resources and expertise are important, for even if the network is open and state autonomy is high, new organizations must also be able to participate in the often highly technical policy networks.

The preceding arguments could just as easily apply to non-internationalized policy-making, except for the fundamental issue that non-domestic actors cannot directly participate in policy-making without risking accusations of violating national sovereignty. A charge that foreign organizations have violated sovereignty is a powerful slogan that domestic opposition groups employ in order to counter transnational influence. Here, Risse-Kappen asserts that transnational groups' successes depend largely on their coalition building strategies – particularly with domestic groups able to penetrate existing networks. These and other indirect strategies somewhat shield transnational organizations from charges of violating sovereignty because they can work with or through domestic organizations. Coalition building, in turn, depends on transnational actors' knowledge of extant policy networks' structures and the persuasiveness of their beliefs on potential domestic allies. In addition to sharing resources and other coalition strategies listed above, transnational groups might also engage in behind-the-scenes quiet lobbying.

International institutions can also play an important facilitative role. For example, they may provide forums for governmental, sub-governmental and transnational actors to interact, which may facilitate coalition building, government learning, or an extra avenue of access to government officials. Unlike path one, globalization is not a prerequisite for influence since strategies here rely on 'tipping the scales' within domestic struggles rather than on taking advantage of or manipulating economic vulnerabilities.

The above discussion highlights that transnational actors can travel various paths in their efforts to influence domestic policy-making. Domestic politics matter, but its importance varies, being much greater in the second path. Similarly, globalization can matter, but not in all cases of internationalization and not to the same degree. The BC case will illustrate these arguments.

Internationalization and change in British Columbia eco-forestry policy[18]

Non-domestic actors became interested in BC forest policy in the early 1990s for three reasons. First, many US-based environmental groups and foundations focused on BC after successful efforts in the US Pacific North-west to increase forest preservation and regulations and improve practices.[19] Second, international media coverage of the 1993 decision to allow widespread logging in Clayoquot Sound's old-growth forests led to criticism by environmental groups and negative public opinion in Europe and the US of BC forest practices. Third, intensified global concern over the state of the world's forests led many actors to scrutinize British Columbia, as it contained much of the world's remaining old-growth temperate rain forests.

The BC case illustrates the different opportunities and constraints that each path provided to transnational actors, who had varying degrees of influence on key policy responses. In evaluating responses to external pressures, we focus mainly on policy decisions (statutes, regulations and policy statements that carry the force of the state). Although formal policies are just one stage of the policy-making process,[20] anything less fails to indicate the actual choices of governments. The effects of policy change on behaviour 'on the ground' and on performance (e.g., reducing environmental degradation) are important areas of research, and represent the ultimate goals of most transnational actors, but they fall outside the scope of this study. Thus policy change is measured by the degree to which new policy initiatives conform to the new goals or values promoted by transnational actors.

Policy responses

In the early 1990s the BC government undertook a host of forest preservation/land use (where to log) and forest practices (how to log) policy initiatives. Policies addressed land use issues through three mechanisms: the Protected Area Strategy (PAS); the Commission on Resources and the Environment (CORE); and Land and Resource Management Plan (LRMP) processes. PAS focused on attaining the stated target of preserving 12 per cent of the province's land. The latter two initiatives were designed to facilitate regional consensus-oriented land use planning processes, which would offer specific advice on which areas to preserve. In areas not covered by CORE or LRMPs processes, local Protected Area Strategy processes were developed to advise on which areas to protect from logging.

The government largely addressed forest practices through the Forest Practices Code. It promised a new way of managing the forests through the inclusion of Ministry of Environment officials and the incorporation of biodiversity norms over previous conceptions such as sustained yield or 'multiple use' management. The Code also created new rules, including maximum clearcut sizes and no logging 'riparian zones' in fish-bearing streams. The government also dramatically increased the price for logging publicly owned timber, and used some of the increased revenues to offset the negative employment effects of the Code. Sharp increases in logging costs also affected forest practices, as did audits that reduced the traditional annual allowable cut (AAC). From 1996, the government backtracked in some areas, streamlining the Code and reducing stumpage rates. These policy fluctuations allow us to examine the durability of policy responses to transnational pressures.

We also focus on the local area of Clayoquot Sound, which received international scrutiny after government decisions on the Sound's development in 1993 and 1995. First, BC permitted widespread logging in the area. But, following intense international and domestic protests, the government embraced ecosystem management principles for Clayoquot, representing the most comprehensive and wide-ranging normative changes among all policy responses.

Path one: markets

Transnational actors began to vigorously travel the market-dependence path in the early 1990s after the BC government opened two-thirds of Clayoquot Sound to logging. They launched boycott campaigns in two of the province's largest markets: Europe and the United States.[21] Greenpeace UK, Greenpeace Germany, Greenpeace International, the World Wildlife Fund (UK) and the UK Women's Environmental Network led European boycotts. The California-based Rainforest Action Network orchestrated the US boycotts, which included the active participation of the Natural Resources Defence Council (NRDC). The BC-based Western Canada Wilderness Committee (WCWC) supported both boycotts.[22] The campaigns criticized BC forestry, using the Clayoquot example to argue that the province did not protect enough of its old-growth forests, and that forest companies conducted most of their harvesting by 'clearcutting.'

The BC government responded by announcing that it was reforming its forest practices rules and by lobbying European nations to counter transnational criticisms. As our arguments about this path predicted, loss of markets motivated state actors. Premier Harcourt explained in the summer of 1994: 'in California, legislation has been proposed to ban BC forest products. The *New York Times* is under pressure to stop printing on BC paper. In England, Scott Paper suspended a $5.5-billion wood-pulp contract. In Europe alone, $3-billion a year in BC forest exports are on the line.'[23]

Reflecting later, Harcourt noted that transnational groups' efforts had led to European Parliament scrutiny and that prominent US activists had mobilized political support there. Harcourt felt he had no choice but to go to Europe and the US, '[to] acknowledge we made mistakes' and to fight the boycott efforts, not by defending previous practices, but to show how things had changed.[24] Otherwise, Harcourt later argued, 'We would be [known] as "Brazil of the North"', and the province would have been devastated economically. The Forest Practices Code allowed him to make swift changes. While industry officials quibbled over the exact nature of the Code, most forest industry associations supported the need to demonstrate forest practices reform. The BC forest industry's newly created Forest Alliance association also sent senior officials to Europe and the US to fight boycotts. They argued that the Code was 'proof' that forest practices reform was being undertaken.[25]

The government's response supports the hypothesis that domestic policy networks matter very little under the market path, as formulation of the Code actually bypassed previous closed industry/government collaborative relationships. The BC government undertook such changes partly to facilitate a quick response to international boycott efforts.

Transnational boycott pressures also contributed to the provincial government's ultimate 1995 Clayoquot Sound policy, which reversed its 1993 decision, permitting only limited logging under an 'ecosystem management regime'. While transnational pressure was by no means the only cause of this decision, its influence was apparent. The BC Premier personally contacted the NRDC, one of the lead supporters of the US boycott campaign, to explore its views on the BC government's Clayoquot policy response deliberations.

The BC case also supports the argument that the durability of changes in response to the market path is often weak. For example, when the BC forest industry headed into a painful downturn in 1996, accelerated by the Asian economic collapse, the provincial government announced a series of changes to the Forest Practices Code and stumpage rate decreases that environmental groups felt significantly weakened eco-forestry reforms.[26] These measures occurred at a time environmental groups, buoyed by apparent successes, had allowed boycott efforts to wane. Such policy reversals support the argument that coercive pressure must be maintained to be durable, and that the 'downward' effects of globalization do not disappear under this route. In response, transnational actors launched a new round of boycotts, the influence of which is being offset by the continued decline in the province's forest industry.[27] Thus, the market path did not appear to produce responses aimed at long-term policy change, but primarily to preserve markets. When an economic downturn threatened markets, corporate profitability and jobs, the government moved swiftly to alter the very policies it initially used to pacify first-path pressures.

Path two: direct influence through policy networks

Many transnational groups and organizations sought to influence BC policy by infiltrating the domestic policy-making process. As predicted, the structure of domestic policy networks appeared to affect the type of influence that transnational actors could achieve. Indeed, transnational groups only began to travel this path after some traditionally closed, business-dominated forest policy networks changed in the early 1990s.

Three groups of policy network structures emerged in the province in the 1990s. Forest land use policy networks, characterized by a high degree of state autonomy and capacity to implement its policy choices, were the most open to new interests. These networks became open largely because new institutions required the accommodation of a diversity of actors in policy choices. Consequently, these networks received the most attention by transnational actors. The forest practices rules network permitted only minimal openness, but a high degree of state autonomy and capacity resulted in well-calculated attempts to influence state deliberations by transnational actors. The local forest management networks, where the government relied most heavily on industry for advice and policy implementation, were the least open, and exhibited only limited state autonomy. As a result, they received scant attention from transnational actors.

Aware of the changes in network structure in the early 1990s, transnational actors undertook a variety of resource-sharing and coalition-building strategies. The US Wilderness Society lent expertise and resources to assist the Sierra Club of Western Canada in a joint production of an expensive mapping project of Vancouver Island forests. In turn, the Sierra Club used this expertise to become a policy participant in land use policy networks.[28]

Other groups used their expertise to become directly involved in policy networks. The World Wide Fund for Nature (WWF) became heavily focused on protected areas in BC in the late 1980s.[29] Such efforts began with the WWF's promotion of protected areas in BC by using the UN-sponsored Bruntland Commission's notion of sustainable development and its explicit call for 12 per cent of the world's land to be protected. The 12 per cent target quickly became the new government's official policy. Moreover, conscious of sovereignty sensitivities, the WWF established a BC office in 1992, and hired a well-known BC protected area advocate, with instructions to become an active, but low key, member of the forest land use policy network. The openness of most land use policy networks post-1991 facilitated this entry. Knowledge of network structures, sovereignty sensitivities, and detailed technical expertise led to a dominant place in the land use policy network. As a result, this organization became highly successful in removing from the industrial forest land base many of the specific areas sought by the WWF.

The US Natural Resources Defense Council also sought to influence the Clayoquot Sound policy network by developing coalitions not only with local environmental groups, but also local aboriginal people, whose aspirations carried great symbolic weight with both the BC and

US governments. Indeed, the NRDC sought to solidify its coalition with Clayoquot aboriginal groups by bringing them to the United Nations, the White House and the US Congress.

Transnational groups also used international institutions to facilitate coalition building with domestic groups, particularly over their efforts to focus provincial policy on new ideas like 'biodiversity' and ecosystem management. The 1992 Earth Summit in Rio de Janeiro became a platform to actively communicate to the BC and Canadian governments the value of preserving forest biological diversity. This concept had gained increased global legitimacy during negotiations leading to the signing of the Convention on Biological Diversity at Rio. Transnational actors' emphasis on 'biodiversity' held importance because it recast the conception of forests as a land subject to 'multiple uses' and competing demands that policy-makers must balance, to a view that all forests contained an underlying support mechanism for the world's ecosystems. Transnational groups such as the NRDC then urged domestic environmental groups to push these new concepts within forest policy networks. Subsequently the forest practices network deliberated over biodiversity issues, which resulted in the development of guidelines that later accompanied the BC Forest Practice Code. Similarly transnational groups strongly pushed 'ecosystem management' principles with their domestic partners who participated in the Clayoquot Sound policy network. The BC government subsequently embraced these concepts in its decision to initiate holistic ecosystem management planning in Clayoquot Sound.

One striking development was how transnational actors worked to assist in the creation of new domestic groups as a way to increase domestic actors' involvement in the policy-making process. Thus, in 1991, the Sierra Legal Defence Fund (SLDF) was created with financial support from US interests.[30] The SLDF provides the environmental community with legal expertise to assist groups who participate in open forest policy networks. For example, its research on riparian zones facilitated advocacy efforts in the forest practices rule network to increase logging restrictions near streams. Though access to this network was only slightly open, SLDF's technical expertise convinced state officials to revise upward riparian rule standards, which they did quickly owing to the high degree of state autonomy and concentrated authority that characterized this network.

US environmental groups also convinced key US foundations to expand their funding efforts beyond Pacific Northwest forestry to British Columbia, in part to increase access to the domestic policy process. Well aware of sovereignty concerns and network structures, US foundation officials in turn asked prominent BC environmental activists to join a province-wide organization through which funds could be channelled and the activities of BC's environmental groups strategically coordinated.[31] They thus created BC Wild in the early 1990s, whose Board of Directors included leaders of some of BC's most high profile environmental groups.[32] Among its activities, BC Wild transferred expertise and resources to local and provincial environmental groups so they could effectively participate in the new regional land use policy networks across the province. After deliberating upon different societal pressures, the state used its high level of autonomy and capacity in many of these networks to establish an array of new protected areas and 'low impact' harvesting zones.

Conclusion

Our distinction between globalization and internationalization has allowed us to explore important non-domestic causes of policy change ignored by much of the globalization literature. Structural economic factors do affect domestic politics and policies, but actors, ideas and institutions from beyond state borders often interact with forces of globalization, channelling them in ways not predictable by economic logic alone.

Whereas the above analysis indicated various obstacles and opportunities for transnational influence, they were not meant as sole predictors of specific policy outcomes. Domestic policy develops in response to a variety of factors, of which transnational pressure is but one.

Internationalization is by no means the only source of domestic policy change. But it can be an important one. Furthermore, the unique nature of such pressures cannot simply be added onto existing theories of public policy, nor be reduced to the blunt pressure of the global marketplace. As the lines between domestic, international and transnational politics become blurred, more attention needs to be paid to better specifying the relationships between factors thought previously to operate in each of these realms, rather than grouping all non-domestic influences under the nebulous rubric of 'globalization'.

Notes

1 An earlier version of this chapter was published as 'Globalization and Four Paths of Internationalization', *Canadian Journal of Political Science*, Spring 2000.

2 P.G. Cerny, *The Changing Architecture of Politics: Structure, Agency, and the Future of the State* (London: Sage, 1990).

3 T. Risse-Kappen, 'Introduction', in Risse-Kappen, ed., *Bringing Transnational Relations Back In: Non-state Actors, Domestic Structures and International Institutions* (Cambridge: Cambridge University Press, 1995), p. 3.

4 Risse-Kappen, *Bringing Transnational Relations Back In*. These paths are not exhaustive of how transnational influence occurs. For example, in S. Bernstein and B. Cashore, 'Globalization and Four Paths of Internationalization: Exploring Eco-Forest Policy Change in British Columbia', *Canadian Journal of Political Science* (forthcoming), we also identify an 'international rules' and 'normative path'.

5 See P. Marchak, *Green Gold: the Forest Industry in British Columbia* (Vancouver: University of British Columbia Press, 1983); and R. Schwindt and T. Heaps, *Chopping Up the Money Tree: Distributing the Wealth from British Columbia's Forests* (Vancouver: the David Suzuki Foundation, 1996), pp. 80–1.

6 S. Berger, 'Introduction', in Berger and R. Dore, eds, *National Diversity and Global Capitalism* (Ithaca: Cornell University Press, 1996), p. 9.

7 See Berger and Dore, *National Diversity* for a range of views.

8 Berger, 'Introduction', p. 12.

9 David Vogel, *Trading Up: Consumer and Environmental Regulation in a Global Economy* (Cambridge, Mass.: Harvard University Press, 1995).

10 Ibid., p. 5.

11 Ibid., pp. 2–5.

12 Vogel argues this only occurs when organized interests in rich and powerful countries pressure their leaders to negotiate such international agreements. Vogel, *Trading Up*, p. 268.

13 We focus less on why non-domestic groups decide to target particular policies than on their ability to affect domestic policy.

14 M.E. Keck and K. Sikkink, *Activists Beyond Borders: Advocacy Networks in International Politics* (Ithaca: Cornell University Press, 1998).

15 See W. Coleman and G. Skogstad, 'Policy Communities and Policy Networks: a Structural Approach', in *Policy Communities and Public Policy in Canada: a Structural Approach* (Mississauga, Ont.: Copp Clark Pitman Ltd, 1990), pp. 14–33.

16 Risse-Kappen, *Bringing Transnational Relations Back In*; and A.P. Cortell and J.W. Davis, Jr., 'How Do International Institutions Matter? the Domestic Impact of International Rules and Norms', *International Studies Quarterly*, 40 (1996), pp. 451–78.

17 Whereas some research asserts that a single national-level policy network exists, our research supports studies that find different policy networks within the same country, and often within the same policy sector.

18 This section is based in part on interviews with senior government officials, politicians, members of transnational and domestic environmental groups and business associations. Interviewees are only cited when quoted directly.

19 S.L. Yaffee, *The Wisdom of the Spotted Owl: Policy Lessons for a New Century* (Covelo, Calif.: Island Press, 1994).
20 Other stages include agenda setting, policy formation, implementation and evaluation. See M. Howlett and M. Ramesh, *Studying Public Policy: Policy Cycles and Policy Subsystems* (Toronto: Oxford University Press, 1995).
21 The United States accounts for 59 per cent of BC's forest products export market, the European Union 11 per cent and Japan 21 per cent. Natural Resources Canada, *The State of Canada's Forests: 1997–1998* (Ottawa: Government of Canada, Natural Resources Canada, 1998).
22 W.T. Stanbury and I.B. Vertinsky, 'The Challenge to Canadian Forest Products in Europe: Managing a Complex Environmental Issue' (Vancouver: Forest Economics and Policy Analysis Research Unit, University of British Columbia, 1995).
23 M. Cernetig, 'BC Park Plan Will End Loggers' Jobs: Harcourt Says Province Must Yield to Global Pressures on Harvesting', *Globe and Mail* (23 June 1994), pp. A1, A4. By not renewing its contract with MacMillan Bloedel, the *New York Times* joined Scott Paper and UK-based Kimberly Clark in suspending contracts over BC clearcutting. 'Costs of Clearcutting', *Environment*, 38, no. 1 (Jan./Feb. 1996), p. 21.
24 Personal interview.
25 Forest Alliance of British Columbia, *U.K. Tour Report* (Vancouver: Forest Alliance of British Columbia, 1994).
26 G. Hamilton, 'Don't Lower Stumpage, US tells BC', *The Vancouver Sun* (11 April 1997), p. D1.
27 See H. Bernton, 'Coalition for Forests Gets Help of Firms', *The Oregonian* (9 Dec. 1998).
28 Government ministers said that the maps provided new information their own bureaucratic officials could not produce.
29 World Wildlife Fund Canada, *Making Choices: a Submission to the Government of British Columbia Regarding Protected Areas and Forest Land Use* (Toronto: World Wildlife Fund Canada, 1993).
30 *Sierra Legal Defence Fund Newsletter*, 1 (1992).
31 Even then, a coalition of BC labour and business groups attacked the environmental movement in 1998 revealing the amount of money US-based foundations had invested in the province.
32 BC Wild, Report as of 31 Oct. 1994 (Vancouver: BC Wild and Earthlife Canada, 1994).

9

Domestic Institutions and Non-state Actors in International Governance: Lessons from the US–Canada Migratory Birds Convention

Luc Juillet

Introduction

Current debates about the nature of globalization raise interesting questions about its consequences for non-state actors in contemporary politics. While some critics have warned of dire consequences for communities and social groups as the expansion of global capitalism seems to increasingly disempower them, other authors have observed the development of a correspondingly global reach for an increasingly sophisticated community of non-governmental organizations dedicated to influencing the global world that is shaping itself before them. How should we think about the influence of non-state actors in an era of globalized politics? Are non-state actors significant players in the evolution of supranational governance regimes?

In this chapter, I argue that, in an era of eroding state sovereignty, state actors remain central players in the production of supranational governance but that they must increasingly contend with the influence of non-state actors who have both acquired the means and the mindset to act transnationally in order to influence these regimes. Moreover, the processes of globalization put into question the usefulness of the distinction between international and domestic politics. Given the increasingly integrated nature of international and domestic politics, domestic institutions also have an important effect on contemporary governance by structuring transnational politics and affecting the strategic decisions of political actors. In this perspective, an interpretative framework accounting for the role of transnational actors and domestic institutions in shaping supranational governance appears to offer greater analytical purview than a traditional focus on national states as actors in a separated international realm.

In order to explore the relevance of these hypotheses empirically, the chapter examines, in its second half, the attempt by the American and Canadian governments to amend the Migratory Birds Convention in the early 1980s. The failure of both national governments to amend this continental environmental treaty in order to recognize the subsistence needs of their northern and aboriginal populations reveals the significant impact of transnational action by non-state and subnational actors on the evolution of continental governance regimes. The case shows that, through the effective use of American Congressional institutions, Canadian and American non-state and subnational state actors have forced the abandonment of a continental agreement signed and defended with considerable insistence by both national states. As such, the case confirms that an interpretative framework recognizing the importance of non-state actors and domestic institutions seems better tailored to the contemporary conditions of globalized politics than the traditional, more exclusive focus on states for explaining the evolution of supranational governance.

Globalization and the domestic–international divide

Globalization refers to a series of processes, most notably the internationalization of production and finance as well as the expansion of international communication, that are having a significant impact on the structure of politics by undermining one of the main pillars of political organization since the seventeenth century: the principle of state sovereignty.[1] State sovereignty is essentially an historical claim about the organization of political life – one resting on the ability of state bureaucracies to control the activities of social actors within their territories, by resorting to the use of legitimate coercion if necessary, thereby establishing a secular order conducive to the development of an orderly and more prosperous social life.[2]

However, by their very nature, historical claims are liable to become less compelling over time as the changing historical context undermines their relevance and credibility or undercuts the instrumental effectiveness that made their real-world implementation possible. As such, the interactive duo of capitalist expansionism and technological innovation appears to be progressively superseding state sovereignty as the determinant principle of political organization.

In this perspective, the processes of integration and fragmentation that we associate with globalization derive essentially from a profound structural change in social systems: the nature and pace of technological innovation. Technological innovation made the globalization of production and finance possible and, through the explosion of cheap and better transnational communication and transportation, contributed to the increase in awareness of many citizens in previously isolated regions and to the growth in citizens' activism on the world stage.[3]

In effect, these technological innovations are leading to some fundamental changes in the nature of politics. They are not only altering the power relationship between national states and transnational firms; but they are also leading many citizens to redefine their previous conceptions of political community and the boundaries of their political engagement.[4] In this sense, globalization is not solely about the erosion of state sovereignty and rising influence of global businesses. It is also partly constitutive of a new transnational politics corresponding to a growing integration of domestic and international politics.[5] In this respect, three fundamental developments are worth noting.

First, globalization is creating a deeper interdependence among communities, irrespective of borders, forcing the redefinition of many policy problems. Global environmental problems are prominent examples. On these issues, local communities cannot act effectively by themselves. Planetary problems call for planetary solutions; but these solutions will require locally tailored interventions to effectively modify the local behaviours that are constitutive of these global problems. At the same time, the increased mobility of capital, made possible by globalization, has weakened the capacity and will of national states to deal with thorny local problems either for fear of capital flight (e.g., pollution, social justice) or for lack of legal and technical capacity (e.g., local culture and morality). In sum, global processes increasingly have direct consequences for domestic political choices, while adequately addressing domestic problems increasingly necessitates global involvement. The domestic and the global are increasingly integrated.

These developments have had a significant impact on the role of states in a globalized world. But they have equally affected non-state actors. Because the local is increasingly global (local decisions have extra-territorial or global consequences) and the global increasingly local (global economic and communication systems affect domestic political and social choices), non-state actors are finding it necessary to redefine the boundaries of their political activism, reaching across borders in the hope of having some influence on the supranational conditions that affect their local environment.

Secondly, the globalization of communications contributed significantly to the explosion in the number and activism of non-state actors. The growing ability to communicate cheaply and rapidly across national boundaries has helped citizens to mobilize in response to local and global events. Global communication networks are diffusing more effectively information about world events, improving citizens' understanding of the social trends that shape their world, and providing examples of alternative forms of social organization that can be emulated locally. These developments in global communication contribute to what Rosenau has termed the 'skills revolution' that is increasingly empowering citizens across the world.[6] Consequently, authors have noted a growing influence of non-state actors in world politics,[7] increasingly forcing states to cope with these new actors in defining supranational governance arrangements.[8]

Finally, globalization is a process of cultural change. It includes 'a process of cultural homogenisation – emanating from the centres of world power, spread by the world media, and sustained by a convergence in modes of thought and practices among business and political elites'.[9] But the influence of this dominant world-view should not mask the concomitant presence of alternative discourses developed and diffused with some success by many citizens and non-governmental organizations. Faced with growing social complexity, declining effectiveness of state controls, and the erosion of dominant cultural and moral referents, individuals are reconsidering the hierarchy of their loyalties and re-examining their sense of belonging to alternative communities. They are also developing 'counter-hegemonic' world-views.

In this perspective, some authors have argued that we are slowly witnessing the development of a global civil society, populated by non-state actors that are driven by the realization of projects representing their alternative view of the world.[10] For example, through their struggles to alter the allocation of environmental resources and to further environmental protection, transnational non-state actors are *de facto* engaging in the mutual construction of an alternative intersubjective conception of the world, which seeks to redefine the essential meaning of human–nature relationships.[11] The world-wide public movement to save the Brazilian rainforest offers an interesting example of an emerging alternative world-view, which embodies a different conception of political space and which is contesting national sovereignty.[12] Similar

examples can be found in the realm of human rights.[13] These alternative discourses may not be about to supplant the hegemonic discourse of
global capitalism. But they are constitutive of new understandings of
political space and new conceptions of citizens' engagement.

The preceding analysis does not suggest the disappearance or irrelevance of the state-as-actor in the realm of world politics. The claim of
national sovereignty has been and remains the most effective claim to
ground the legitimate exercise of authority at both the domestic and
international levels. Consequently, states remain central actors in
supranational governance, even in this era of globalization. But the
technological and social processes undermining the traditional effectiveness of this claim, by weakening the states' ability to control social
behaviour within their borders and by weakening their pretension of
effectively representing their citizens, have empowered other actors to
act within and across national boundaries. Non-state actors are no
longer insignificant players on the world stage and, by themselves and
through transnational coalitions, they increasingly pursue their objectives by acting beyond national boundaries.

The rise of transnational activism bears consequences for our analysis
of politics. In some ways, there are no longer two conceptually distinct
yet related politics, the international and the domestic, but a series of
integrated political spaces, enmeshing the global and the domestic in
multiple ways, whose boundaries are drawn by actors themselves as
they cognitively frame the issues facing them and define for themselves
the realm of their political action. States, even if they remain crucial
actors in shaping supranational governance regimes, are no longer the
sole significant agents.

To account for the integrated nature of this globalized politics, scholars
need to think across disciplinary divisions between international relations and domestic politics. Moving away from the notion of international politics as a distinct sphere of social relations, politics in the age
of globalization is more usefully interpreted as a series of strategic interactions among state and non-state actors which occurs within unified
political spaces, i.e. ones where policy actors cross national boundaries
and where claims of sovereignty no longer serve as foundational, onto-
logical categories as much as represent privileged power resources in the
hands of state actors.

Crossing the international–domestic divide also requires recognizing
the richness of domestic political life. Freed from the state-as-unitary-
actor conceptual shorthand of realism, the national state reveals its
fragmented nature. A diversity of state actors composing fragmented

bureaucracies, federal systems and legislatures pursue multiple and often conflicting interests. Coalitions of state and non-state actors vie for influence in pursuit of their interest and their conception of desirable public policy. And, in the context of a globalized politics, these coalitions cross borders both by incorporating actors from relevant foreign countries and by pursuing their objectives through transnational lobbying.[14]

Recognizing the richness of domestic politics also ascribes a new importance to domestic institutions in shaping supranational governance. The particularities of national institutions matter by structuring transnational politics and contribute to shaping the outcomes of political contests. Within the constraints of these institutions, policy actors seek to influence political outcomes by deploying strategically the resources that they can mobilize, such as legitimacy, money, command of infrastructures, or information. But different institutional contexts make policy processes more or less permeable for different actors. Consequently, while merely representing intervening variables, domestic institutions nevertheless have an independent effect on policy decisions. As a significant determinant of the dynamics and outcomes of politics, they affect the strategic choices and the ultimate success of competing coalitions.[15]

With regard to the evolution of supranational regimes, domestic procedures for the ratification of international treaties bear particular importance. More restrictive ratification procedures would tend to restrain the manoeuvring room of state actors and enhance the influence of non-state actors.[16] More generally, the institutional configuration of domestic institutions partly determines the access and influence of non-state actors to the policy process of respective countries.[17] As comparative neo-institutionalists have established, more fragmented and open institutions, such as the US Congress, provide more access points to interest groups to influence decisions and voice ideas as well as more opportunities for vetoing policy proposals than more centralized institutions, such as those of cabinet government.[18] As such, it would appear that countries with more fragmented and open domestic institutions would be more vulnerable to the influence of transnational coalitions.

The analytical value of integrating transnational coalitions and domestic institutions in our analysis of politics in a globalized era will ultimately reveal itself through empirical testing. Below, I begin this empirical work by examining a case in environmental governance in North America. The failure of the Canadian and American governments to secure ratification of an international agreement for amending the Migratory Birds Convention in the face of significant opposition by non-state and subnational state actors suggests that transnational coalitions and domestic institutions constitute important variables in explaining the evolution of supranational governance regimes.

Amending the Migratory Birds Convention

The Protocol Amending the Migratory Birds Convention between Canada and the US (hereafter the Protocol) sought to grant the right to northern residents of both countries (especially aboriginal peoples) to hunt migratory game birds during the spring in order to meet their subsistence needs.[19] Signed in 1916 in order to protect bird populations that were endangered by excessive harvesting, the Migratory Birds Convention (hereafter the Convention) had established a ban on spring hunting in order to protect the birds during their reproductive season. Unfortunately, due to migratory patterns, these birds with great spiritual and nutritional value for many Aboriginal Peoples arrived and departed northern Canada and Alaska during the closed season, essentially placing them out of reach of those who depended most on them.

From the early 1920s, the ban on spring hunting became a major point of contention between national governments and their respective northern residents, eventually emerging as an important point of discord in relations with aboriginal communities for whom the Convention had unilaterally abrogated aboriginal and treaty rights. In the late 1970s, in part to alleviate aboriginal opposition to their development of northern natural resources, Canadian and American governments finally undertook serious negotiations to amend the Convention to account for the needs of northern residents. The resulting protocol of amendment, signed in 1979, generated strong opposition by many stakeholders, triggering a wide-ranging political campaign for its defeat.

While broadly worded, the Protocol would have provided a limited exemption for aboriginal hunting in the spring for 'subsistence and other essential needs' in the North. Despite the rather limited nature of the proposed amendment, environmental groups, particularly the Canadian Wildlife Federation (CWF) and the US National Wildlife Federation (NWF), opposed any opening of the spring harvest for fear of detrimental consequences for bird population levels. A large number of other non-state actors, including hunters, were also strongly opposed to the Protocol, finding its wording ambiguous and dangerously generous. Subnational state actors were also opposed to the Protocol, with the exception of Canadian northern territories and Alaska. Canadian provinces and American states similarly feared the environmental impact of a spring harvest, but the Americans were additionally concerned by a corresponding decline in their annual share of the sport harvest.

The negotiation and signature of the Protocol constitutes a testimony to the predominance of unitary states in the realm of international politics. After about 60 years of protests and grievances by Aboriginal Peoples and northern residents, a mere six months were sufficient for national governments to reach an agreement for amending the Convention. The process was almost exclusively the purview of high-level bureaucrats in national wildlife agencies. Subnational state agencies, environmentalists, hunters and even aboriginal organizations were not consulted on the negotiations. Despite early protests by Canadian provinces, the Protocol was swiftly approved by the Canadian cabinet. While the formal process was essentially complete in Canada, the exchange of instruments sealing the international ratification of the agreement needed to await the Protocol's approval by the US Senate.

However, while the first six months of the Protocol's history revealed the dominance of national states in shaping international governance regimes, its subsequent defeat as a result of mounting opposition by non-state and subnational state actors show the necessity of taking these actors seriously in explaining globalized politics. Less than six months after the Protocol's signing, both the CWF and the NWF were publicly expressing strong concerns over the Protocol and had launched a joint campaign to oppose it in the US, mainly by lobbying against Senate approval. The environmentalists' efforts added strength to the Canadian provinces' opposition who, under the leadership of western provinces, continued to denounce the Protocol both in bilateral meetings with Ottawa and in intergovernmental fora (e.g., Eastern and Western Wildlife Advisory Committees, the Canadian Council of Resources and Environment Ministers).

Despite the barrier of internal opposition by non-state and subnational state actors, in April 1980 the Canadian government, relying on its privileged position at the apex of centralized political institutions, decided to move ahead with the implementation of the Protocol. However, in a revealing turn of events, successful lobbying abroad stopped the Canadian government's resolve. At that time, the US Department of the Interior notified the Canadian Wildlife Service that 'there was no possibility of the protocol going to the US Congress that spring due to the lobbying and opposition of the principal interest groups'.[20] The lobbying of the US Senate by the transnational coalition had made it very unlikely that the Protocol would be approved by the required two-thirds of American senators, essentially stalling the international ratification of the agreement. The inability to push the Protocol in its original form through the US Senate essentially forced the Canadian government to seek to accommodate some of its opponents.

In seeking a compromise that would not jeopardize the Protocol, the Canadian government explored some limited grounds for renegotiation and offered to involve provinces in drafting the regulations implementing the amendment. But these efforts failed as western provinces eventually threatened to sue the federal government to challenge the Protocol's constitutional validity. In the US, state concerns led the International Association of Fish and Wildlife Agencies (IAFWA), which despite its name is mainly an umbrella lobby for state wildlife agencies in Washington, to officially express 'its opposition to ratification of the protocol by either the United States or Canada until it is clarified which peoples will qualify for subsistence taking of waterfowl and their eggs, what this utilization is estimated to be by species, and how regulations are to be enforced'.[21] By withdrawing its support, IAFWA, which embodied the states' opposition for US senators, added a powerful voice to the lobby against the Protocol.

Contemplating mounting political opposition abroad and at home as well as a potential defeat in the Senate, in January 1981 the US Department of the Interior finally asked the Senate Foreign Relations Committee to delay action on the Protocol until it had had an opportunity to deal with the growing objections to its ratification. Two years after the signature of the original document, Canadian and American governments were still unable to force the agreement through the US Senate veto without overcoming opposition by non-state actors and subnational state actors.

The final attempt at salvaging the Protocol came from the initiative of the American government. In exploring alternatives for resolving the deadlock, the Department of the Interior and the Senate Foreign Relations Committee favoured the drafting of an 'implementation report' to accompany the Protocol through ratification. The implementation report would be negotiated with non-state and subnational actors from both countries and it would spell out how the Protocol would be implemented (e.g., where and to whom it would apply, how resources would be monitored, etc.). It would then be ratified along with the Protocol, allowing for the alleviation of some opponents' concerns without reopening completely the negotiations of an amendment to the Convention.

In order to envisage this possibility and explore grounds for compromise, the IAFWA organized a meeting of all parties in early 1982 in
Washington. In addition to Canadian and US federal wildlife agencies,
conservation and hunting organizations, including the CWF and the
NWF, representatives of Senate Foreign Relations Committee, and officials from the US State Department were invited to the meeting. While
some support for an implementation report was found among state
agencies, non-state actors proved difficult to convince. Despite previous
assurances to the contrary, the CWF raised the spectre of a million
Métis getting access to the spring subsistence harvest and threatening
the sustainability of bird populations. Most non-state actors, including
Ducks Unlimited, the NWF, the Waterfowl Habitat Owners Alliance and
the Wildlife Management Institute, also expressed their disapproval and
argued instead for the renegotiation of the Protocol.

In early 1982, Canadian and American governments decided to seek
the development of an implementation report through broad consultations in both countries. While realistic about the prospect of winning
over environmentalists and hunters, national governments hoped that
the implementation report would make sufficient inroads into the
coalition of non-state and subnational state actors to get the Protocol
through the Senate. Unfortunately, domestic events, this time in Canada,
would again come to derail the amendment of the continental regime.
In 1982, Canadians were in the midst of constitutional reforms, which
included the entrenchment of ill-defined aboriginal rights. The process
of constitutional reform foreclosed any extra-constitutional attempt at
defining the nature of aboriginal resource rights, including hunting
rights, and consequently prevented the immediate negotiation of an
implementation report.

By the time the constitutional discussion on aboriginal rights had
closed, the legal and political contexts surrounding native rights issues
had changed significantly. The terminology and approach of the Protocol, essentially concerned with granting privileged access to the spring
hunt to northern aboriginal hunters on the basis of discretionary state
regulations, were no longer consistent with the dominant legal and
political discourse of aboriginal and treaty rights. In particular, limiting
the access to the spring harvest to aboriginal communities living in the
north (as opposed to all aboriginal hunters across the country as a matter
of rights) was increasingly an untenable position for the Canadian
Wildlife Service. By 1984, the Protocol was, for all practical purposes,
left to die on the agenda of the Foreign Relations Committee of the US
Senate.

Conclusion: international governance and transnational politics

What lessons can we draw from the failure to amend the Migratory Birds Convention in this period? Firstly, our analysis provides a strong indication that transnational lobbying by non-state and subnational actors is indeed an important variable for understanding the evolution of supranational governance in the context of a globalized politics. The outcome of the case would be impossible to account for by focusing our analysis exclusively on national state actors. In the end, the Protocol was defeated by the opposition of a transnational coalition of non-state actors and subnational state agencies despite the clear preference and substantial efforts deployed by national states in both countries.

Secondly, the analysis also offers strong support for taking into account the intervening role of domestic institutions in explanations of international governance. The key role of the US Senate veto, established by American constitutional requirements for the approval of international treaties, in structuring the transnational politics around the Protocol is particularly revealing. It played a key role for both US and Canadian non-state and subnational state actors for delaying the approval of the Protocol and eventually stopping its adoption entirely. The more open and fragmented American institutions made the Senate the focal point of opposition for transnational opposition. It seems clear that the more centralized Canadian institutions bore less opportunities for transnational influence.

The role of the Senate veto for Canadian non-state actors, in coalition with American non-state actors, is particularly revealing of the potential consequences of the new transnational politics for non-state actors. In this particular case, it suggests that globalization, as far as it suggests a growth in transnational activism on their part, could in fact empower non-state actors in the realm of supranational governance by providing them with a broader access to foreign institutional veto points. In our case, the CWF used effectively the US Senate veto point, in coalition with the NWF and other groups, to improve its leverage at home and eventually defeat the Protocol. It is by relying on transnational lobbying that it actually forced the Canadian government to reconsider its position at home. It could do abroad, due to the fragmented institutions of the US political system, what it could not do at home due to the centralized nature of Canadian institutions.

Finally, the behaviour of Canadian state actors also raises interesting questions about the strategic competencies of state actors in international bargaining. The repeated decisions of the Canadian government to push ahead despite opposition by domestic non-state and subnational state actors suggest a mindset of state actors that is out of touch with the existing transnational realities. Canadian state actors did not appear to fully understand the potential effectiveness of transnational action, repeatedly underestimating the impact of the transnational coalition in the US and seemingly relying on traditional claims of sovereignty to downplay the importance of non-state and subnational state opposition abroad. Such miscalculations raise interesting questions about the ability of national state actors to adapt to a world of declining sovereignty and about the role of policy learning in the adaptation of political actors to the new world brought into existence by globalization processes. Would subsequent bilateral negotiations for supranational wildlife governance reveal the same strategic errors by Canadian state actors? Would similar strategic miscalculations be common in other fields of international governance?

The impact of globalization on politics and governance is complex and multifaceted. More than simply shifting the determinants of governance to higher levels of social organization, it is affecting how actors relate to political space and conceive of their political engagement. To account for the increasingly transnational nature of politics, analytical models of politics must break traditional barriers between the analysis of domestic and international politics. The examination of the Migratory Birds Convention case illustrates the need to recognize transnational coalitions of non-state and subnational state actors as well as domestic institutions as important factors in shaping the evolution of international governance regimes.

Notes

1 R.B.J. Walker and S. Mendlovitz, 'Interrogating State Sovereignty', in Walker and Mendlovitz, eds, *Contending Sovereignties* (Boulder: Lynne Reinner, 1990), p. 1.
2 J. Camilleri, 'Rethinking Sovereignty in a Shrinking, Fragmented World', in Walker and Mendlovitz, *Contending Sovereignties*, pp. 13–44.
3 S. Strange, 'Rethinking Structural Change in the International Political Economy: States, Firms, and Diplomacy', in R. Stubbs and G. Underhill, eds, *Political Economy and the Changing Global Order* (Toronto: McClelland and Stewart, 1993), pp. 104–5.
4 J.N. Rosenau, 'Citizenship in a Changing Global Order', in Rosenau and E.-O. Czempiel, eds, *Governance without Government* (Cambridge: Cambridge University Press, 1992), pp. 272–94.
5 J.N. Rosenau, *Along the Domestic–Foreign Frontier* (Cambridge: Cambridge University Press, 1997).

6 J.N. Rosenau, *Turbulence in World Politics* (Princeton: Princeton University Press, 1990).
7 K. Liftin, 'Ecoregimes: Playing Tug of War with the Nation-State', in R.D. Lipschutz and K. Conca, eds, *The State and Social Power in Global Environmental Politics* (New York: Columbia University Press, 1993), pp. 94–117; A. Hawkins, 'Contested Ground: International Environmentalism and Global Climate Change', in Lipschutz and Conca, pp. 221–45; and O.R. Young, 'Rights, Rules, and Resources in World Affairs', in Young, ed., *Global Governance* (Cambridge: MIT Press, 1997), pp. 1–23.
8 M.W. Zacher, 'The Decaying Pillars of the Westphalian Temple: Implications for International Order and Governance', in Rosenau and Czempiel, *Governance without Government*, pp. 58–101.
9 R. Cox, 'Globalization, Multilateralism, and Social Choice', in *Work in Progress* (New York: United Nations University, 1990), p. 2; an alternative, more popular account is found in B. Barber, *Jihad vs McWorld* (New York: Times Book, 1995).
10 P. Wapner, 'Governance in Global Civil Society', in Young, *Global Governance*, pp. 65–84; P. Wapner, *Environmental Activism and World Civic Politics* (New York: SUNY Press, 1996); and R.D. Lipschutz, *Global Civil Society and Global Environmental Governance* (New York: SUNY Press, 1996).
11 Lipschutz, *Global Civil Society*, pp. 60–2; and R.D. Lipschutz and J. Mayer, 'Not Seeing the Forest for the Trees: Rights, Rules, and the Renegotiation of Resource Management Regimes', in Lipschutz and Conca, *The State and Social Power*, p. 252.
12 L.C. Hempel, *Environmental Governance* (Washington: Island Press, 1996), pp. 209–13.
13 N.H. Sambat, 'International Regime as Political Community', *Millennium*, 26 (1997), pp. 349–78.
14 The literature has produced a vast array of concepts for defining these coalitions of actors. This chapter relies on a broad conception of transnational coalitions potentially including both state and non-state actors regrouped through common circumstantial interests. Alternative conceptions (some excluding state actors, some emphasizing common world-views or epistemes) can be found in T. Risse-Kappen, ed., *Bringing Transnational Relations Back In* (Cambridge: Cambridge University Press, 1995); K. Sikkink, 'Human Rights, Principled Issue-Networks, and Sovereignty in Latin America', *International Organization*, 47 (1993), p. 411; and P. Haas, 'Epistemic Communities and International Policy Co-ordination', *International Organization*, 46 (1992), pp. 1–35.
15 K. Thelen and S. Steinmo, 'Historical institutionalism in Comparative Politics', in Steinmo et al., *Structural Politics: Historical Institutionalism and Comparative Analysis* (New York: Cambridge University Press, 1992), pp. 1–31.
16 A. Moravcsik, 'Integrating International and Domestic Theories of International Bargaining', in P.B. Evans, H.K. Jacobson and R.D. Putnam, eds, *Double-Edged Diplomacy* (Berkeley: University of California Press, 1993), pp. 24–6.
17 T. Risse-Kappen 'Ideas Do Not Float Freely: Transnational Coalitions, Domestic Structures, and the End of the Cold War', *International Organization*, 48 (1994), pp. 185–214.

18   K. Weaver and B. Rockman, eds, *Do Institutions Matter?* (Washington: Brookings Institution, 1993).
19   The following case analysis is based on archival material provided by the Canadian Wildlife Service as well as on a series of unstructured and semi-structured interviews with public servants involved in these events. The files are held at the Canadian Wildlife Service headquarters (Place Vincent Massey, 351 St-Joseph Blvd, Hull, Québec, Canada, K1A 0H3) and at the National Wildlife Research Centre (100 Gamelin Blvd, Hull, Québec, Canada, K1A 0H3). Audio tapes and notes from the interviews, as well as copies of some of the key documents, are available from the author. For sake of brevity and with the exception of direct quotations, I have kept references to archival documents to a minimum but sources are available on demand.
20   Canadian Wildlife Service, internal briefing note entitled 'Protocol: Chronological Summary of Significant Developments', personal files of J.A. Keith, undated, p. 3.
21   International Association of Fish and Wildlife Agencies, *Resolution No. 17 – Protocol on Migratory Bird Treaty*, Washington, 1981.

Part IV
Subnational Initiatives

10

'Globalist' versus 'Globalized' Cities: Redefining Urban Responses to Globalization

Patrick J. Smith

What is a Global City? One answer is that a Global or World Class city is an international business city or *globalized* world economic centre. In that case cities in Canada, Australia and many other countries will hardly qualify. An alternative would include commitment to and evidence of a broader and deeper global citizenship. Here, cities in countries like Canada have a better claim. Indeed such cities are already undertaking what might be termed a broader 'globalist' stance. The central question regarding these essentially contesting globalized vs globalist options is which is most likely to prevail as an urban response to globalization into the twenty-first century.

Some analysts suggest that there is a link between a capacity to play a major economic role globally and qualifying for 'International' or 'World Class' city status.[1] This seems too narrow a view; it misses much of what is at play in subnational, urban settings in a global age. Cities in countries like Canada and Australia can play inclusive globalist World City roles in several ways – both as models and by taking broader globalist policy stances. The experience of many city-regions supports the possibility of this emerging globalist stance of urban solutions to global problems.[2] Examples from cities such as Vancouver and its suburban neighbours in Canada offer evidence for such an urban globalist citizenship,[3] just as the experience of many so-called 'world class cities' presents a much more negative, less inclusive interpretation.[4] The tally to date suggests that the experience of 'world cities' exhibits both globalized and globalist responses to globalization.

This chapter addresses the two conflicting definitions of city responses to globalization through an assessment of municipal international

activities in the metropolitan Vancouver region. Both globalized and globalist city policy stances are evident, but city responses to globalization
increasingly demonstrate characteristics of a globalist citizenship broader
than that contained in narrower, economic or globalized definitions.

Definitions

Part of the discourse on globalization focuses on the emergence of a
New International Cities Era.[5] New notions are emerging which suggest
more fundamental shifts in understanding the impacts of, and urban
responses to, globalization. These include:

1. The argument that major urban city-regions, having become dominant explanators of national economies (Jacobs),[6] are now coming to
dominate as 'the core locations of the global system';[7] here, as Friedmann
has suggested, the network of world cities is continuously 'under
tension', and the order of world cities can undergo significant changes
in less than a decade. There are 5 elements in Friedmann's world city
definition:

- they serve as *economic centres*;
- they provide *space for global capital accumulation*;
- they are more than cities – they are *urban regions*;
- they constitute a *hierarchy of spatial articulations, tied to their economic
  power*;
- their *dominant culture is cosmopolitan*.

There are at least four variants of 'world cities':

Global Financial Articulations – the 'command and control' forms
(London, New York, Tokyo);
Multinational Articulations (e.g., Miami, LA, Frankfurt, Amsterdam,
Singapore);
Important National Articulations – such as Paris, Zurich, Madrid, Mexico
City, Sao Paolo, Seoul, Sydney;
Subnational/Regional Articulations – such as Osaka, San Francisco, Hous-
ton, Chicago, Boston, Seattle/Vancouver, Toronto, Montreal, Hong Kong,
Milan, Lyon, Barcelona, Munich, the Rhein-Ruhr.

2. The counterpoint that an understanding which limits definitional
aspects of world class cities to the economic omits at least half, perhaps
two-thirds, of the globe, referred to variously as 'techno-apartheid for a
global underclass',[8] and the '20:80 Society'.[9]

3. The notion that a focus solely on the state system – international, national as well as subnational/local – misses much that is necessary in explaining contemporary politics, and real alternative responses to globalization and new modes of governance.[10] As Warren Magnusson argued, 'world politics has to be understood as a type of urban politics – the global city – in which inter-state relations occur as a particular form of activity.'

The development of 'global cities', 'world class cities' and, simply, 'world cities' has most usually been seen as local/urban responses to the economic forces of globalization. This defines cities as 'global', essentially 'globalized', economic and business components of a new world order where cities are understood as 'global spheres of production, consumption and exchange'. However, Friedmann concludes that it is not helpful to focus *only* on global cities and the space of global accumulation which they articulate. 'We must understand global cities in relation to their respective peripheries. It opens up questions of international labour flows and investment, etc. It also raises obvious questions about the possible limits to growth, not only in the ecological sense so popular today, but also in a political sense. If the global periphery becomes destabilized, or if migrant workers arrive at the core in numbers that cannot be assimilated, the whole project of capitalism is put in jeopardy.'[11]

Any critical rethinking must confront these notions of global/world class/'world cities': 'the beauty of the world city paradigm is its ability to synthesize what would otherwise be disparate and diverging researches into labour markets, information technology, international migration, cultural studies, city building processes, industrial location, social class formation, massive disempowerment, and urban politics – into a single meta-narrative . . . And if meta-narratives, like dualism, are no longer fashionable, surely that is only because the meta-narrative of capital remains largely invisible. Without a counter-narrative to place in high relief, it is as if it didn't exist. The world city paradigm not only allows us to make portions of the meta-narrative of capital visible but also provides us with a basis for a critical perspective.'[12] A system unable to hold out the promise of a better life to a majority of the world's population – the 'dualism of the excluded' – is what Friedmann calls the Achilles' heel of capitalism.

The world city cases: globalized vs globalist options – policy lessons from the metropolitan Vancouver region

The 'West–Pacific Northwest' region has been one of the most internationally activist areas in North America – both historically and today. In this region, city-based constituent diplomacy has *expanded* significantly.

Vancouver first twinned with Odessa in 1944 – the first such muni-cipal international link in North America. By 1967, nine Canadian cities had twinned with other non-Canadian cities; currently there are several hundred such Canadian examples. Similarly in the US, after a slow beginning in the 1950s, with Seattle in the forefront, over 1,000 cities with more than 2,000 sister-city affiliations exist.

More importantly, as the number of subnational governments involved in international activities has grown, so too have the types of activities. Often initially cultural and educational, these activities eventually transformed to more strategic, business-oriented ventures; now, increas-ingly, many shift to an even broader, more mature 'globalist' citizenship/ involvement. The analysis of such constituent diplomacy in metropol-itan Vancouver, and elsewhere, and its globalized vs globalist potential, can be organized around four policy phases.

Vancouver's global policy phases

The *ad hoc* policy phase: 1940s–1970s

The first city twinning established in North America was between Odessa and Vancouver in 1944. This appears to be the first 'modern' twinning anywhere. The local rationale for Vancouver's action was rooted in humanitarian assistance to a war-devastated sister port. There was also, and continues to be, a cultural link between the Jewish com-munities in both cities. Cold War relations after 1945 limited further contact, but the sister-city link was never broken.[13]

Vancouver added the sister cities of Yokohama in 1965 and Edin-burgh in 1978. In each instance, the incremental pattern was the same: intense initial involvement by parts of the community creating pressure for formal municipal linkages to be established, followed by consider-able periods of relative neglect. The basis of these early international exchanges for Vancouver was cultural and educational. The incremental phase was, as then Vancouver Alderman Libby Davies stated, 'never a set program; it was just a matter of evolution'.[14] This was consistent with Federation of Canadian Municipalities (FCM) objectives for such twinnings: to provide direct contact between diverse peoples to foster international understanding, to expand contact between homelands of new Canadians and Canadian communities, to develop an appreciation of foreign culture, history and traditions and to develop better perspec-tives on problems/opportunities at home.[15]

The sporadic nature of Vancouver's global exchange was noteworthy. Depending on the interest of a particular mayor, or city councillor, or on the interest of a particular, usually ethno-cultural segment of the community, there would be brief bursts of interaction followed by more extensive periods of inactivity. For some, this was an entirely natural situation; for others, particularly city officials feeling the early effects of increased global interdependence, by the end of the 1970s this was increasingly 'not enough'.[16]

The rational policy phase: 1980–6

In 1980, Mike Harcourt was elected as Vancouver's mayor, with substantial leftist support. During his three terms (1980–6), Harcourt sought to put the city's internationalist links on a less *ad hoc* basis. Apart from active participation in the FCM, and in the discussions of 'Big City' mayors, Harcourt promoted the case of Vancouver as Canada's Pacific Gateway. The City's international focus began to shift to a more economic rationale.

This involved work with the Conservative Federal Government to establish Vancouver as one of two Canadian International Banking Centres,[17] and to strengthen Vancouver's Pacific Rim links. The Yokohama/Japan link was revitalized under Harcourt and in 1985 Guangzhou, China was added as a sister city, drawing on the significant Cantonese base in Vancouver. Gaungzhou's increasing ties to the Hong Kong/Pearl River region were an additional consideration. This was consistent with the more rational policy phase; as expressed by the City's Economic Development Manager, 'your sister city program has to focus on something'. That something in this first rational phase was 'on economics' with a 'Pacific focus'.[18] This was also evident in the 1986 choice of Los Angeles as Vancouver's US twin. Harcourt, supported by the Board of Trade, pushed for Los Angeles because of business opportunities, particularly in the film industry.

The more 'rational' policy stance was also reflected in the organization and funding of City international initiatives between 1980 and 1986. Prior to 1980, there had been no obvious organizational centre for this activity. Prior to 1982, budgetary allocations had been *ad hoc*. In 1982, Harcourt instructed the City Council to establish an annual budget for Vancouver's International Programme which grew to $100,000 (out of a total city budget of $300 million) by 1985. Despite the limited nature of City funding, when private sector multipliers (dinners, air travel, etc.) and senior governmental grants (such as travel funding for cultural/artistic groups to participate abroad) were added, the impact of this City seed funding was considerable. Organizationally, day to day staff responsibility for Vancouver's global activities was shifted to the City's Economic Development Office, with protocol placed in the City Clerk's Office.

More importantly, the Harcourt initiatives of this policy phase contained the seeds of the third, and emerging fourth, phases of the City's international policy-making. The third, strategic phase reflected a more obvious business focus; the fourth, globalist, contained a broader, more prescriptive orientation, emphasizing city contributions on issues such as foreign aid, world peace and the environment. Under Harcourt, Vancouver was designated a Nuclear Weapons Free Zone, reflecting a City view that issues such as peace and disarmament were clearly within the city's policy purview. Harcourt was also instrumental in foreign aid initiatives such as the Canadian International Development Agency (CIDA) funded and FCM administered China Open Cities Programme, Africa 2000, and the Municipal Professional Exchange Project.

The very success of this more rational City diplomacy under Harcourt highlighted the limitations of the incremental phase with its emphasis on formal sister-city links. The confluence of increased interdependence, a proactive, internationalist mayor and senior governments with coincident Pacific policy goals, all created important global opportunities – and a policy window[19] – for Vancouver. Harcourt's departure to lead the Official (leftist New Democratic) Opposition in the province, the October 1986 election of a new (rightist Social Credit) Provincial Government[20] and the November 1986 election of a rightist, business-backed Vancouver Mayor, Gordon Campbell, all paved the way for a redefinition of the rational policy phase.

The strategic policy phase: 1987 to the early 1990s

Campbell placed a 'quiet moratorium' on additional sister-city links and a new emphasis on economic considerations: 'a sister city rationale for the 1980s must recognize that in addition to friendship, economic and cultural opportunities must be reinforced. It is vital that governmental and non-governmental institutions coordinate their efforts to optimize their economic benefits.'[21] To ensure this policy goal, Campbell had council create a Sister City Commission and five sister-city Citizen Committees. This was followed by a major policy review which produced the Strategic City programme in August 1987. Its key policy goals included flexibility, rather than the formal requirements of twinnings; stronger business links, rather than a mixed range of relationships, with business often a limited priority; access to foreign cities that acted as gateways to significant national and regional economies and which could provide a discernible niche for Vancouver business, with the potential for generating frequent contact between a considerable number of Vancouver and overseas business people and centres where such activity accorded with federal priorities. Except for the early established Edinburgh and Odessa twinnings, all other cities considered by Vancouver were in the Pacific Rim, each with cultural components to complement economic exchange.[22]

Perhaps the most innovative dimension of the 'strategic city' policy thrust was the idea that there was no necessity to even let the targeted city know of its place in Vancouver's international policy. This allowed Vancouver to add other collateral cities to its strategic plan; for example, Yokohama is Vancouver's Japan link, but the City seldom went to Yokohama without economic development/cultural stops in neighbouring Osaka and Tokyo.

The 1988 Strategic City programme budget was $92,000 plus a one-time $200,000 city grant for Yokohama's International Exposition. This city seeding again illustrated the impact of multipliers: the city grant was matched by the federal government and the province. With this start-up, the Vancouver–Yokohama Society was able to raise an additional $1 million – a total of $1.6 million for one international event. When budgetary restraint returned at the end of the 1980s, cutting the City's strategic city spending by two-thirds, many of the global links had reached the self-standing take-off point.

By the end of the 1980s other policy dilemmas were emerging which placed the city's strategic policy considerations in a much broader setting. Economic considerations remained important, but city/regional activities related to concerns identified by the Brundtland Report,[23] the Summer 1992 United Nations Conference on Environment and Development, the 1996 Habitat II 'City Summit'[24] and local studies on preserving livability now were becoming integral parts of city constituent diplomacy.

The globalist policy phase: late 1990s/2000s

Soldatos's definition of an 'International City' substantially corresponds to Vancouver's *strategic* definition: a primarily economic focus, with key cultural components.[25] The policy reality of the late 1990s and 2000s suggested pressure for an altered and expanded city international role *and* less fiscal capacity to support such activity. The latter was evident in the international city policy stance of current Vancouver Mayor, Philip Owen. Under Owen, the international city budget has been slashed and much of the activity contracted out. Neighbouring Seattle has managed to marry expanded capacity and tighter fiscal circumstances better with a partnership approach costing the City relatively little money.[26]

Greater Vancouver municipal variants

Greater Vancouver is Canada's third largest metropolis. It is one of the four fastest growing urban areas in North America.[27] It is projected that the population will grow to 2.5 million by 2025. Established in 1967, the GVRD is now an amalgam of 20 municipalities and 2 unincorporated electoral areas, covering 3250 sq. kms containing a little under half (1.867 million people – 48.2 per cent) of the provincial population and a majority of the largest (over 50,000 population) local authorities in the province.

One byproduct of this rapid growth is that the ethnic makeup of the Vancouver-centred region's population has become increasingly multicultural; almost half of the public school population of Vancouver has English as a second language. This translates, increasingly, into the region's politics representation and interest in international exchanges for the cities of the region.

Yet, if examination of Vancouver's international policy activity – on economic development and other areas – suggests a clear role for public involvement in sustaining international policy advances over time, then the picture presented by an assessment of the internationalist strategies of Vancouver's municipal neighbours is more varied.[28]

Surrey, the second largest city in British Columbia, has a limited range of international activity: two 'Sister Cities' – Koto-Ku, Japan (1986) and Zhuhai, China (1987), plus an informal 'twinning' with Cloverdale, California. The linkages have some cultural base: for example, the Chinese link was developed through a lawyer from the Surrey Chinese community. Activities around this link have been cultural and educational, and have begun to add an economic development component; Zhuhai is 'favoured' as one of four special economic zones in China. However, despite a degree of community involvement in developing and maintaining such global linkages, there are counter-pressures to limit this type of activity.[29]

The international initiatives of Burnaby are more broadly-based and older than Surrey's. Formal relations exist with Kushiro, Japan (1965), Loughborough, England (1986) and the Village of El Zapotal, El Salvador. Less formal links – with a more economic focus – have been established with Beaverton, Oregon (1993). The Japanese exchange is active – and since 1990 has had a stronger economic focus. The England link was mostly a result of the historical connection for Burnaby's 'founder', a Royal Visit to Burnaby – and a return in 1998. It is largely inactive.

The 'globalist' response to El Salvador came from a request for local assistance, and a strong Central American interest in the community. Local social democrat Member of Parliament Svend Robinson and a leftist city council were both supportive and responsive to this public push to provide aid to help rebuild the Salvadoran village. As a result, Burnaby raised thousands of dollars and general public awareness of the war in El Salvador. The overall city budget for international activity is limited, but there is a view that the City has 'benefited' economically and politically from its international activities. The city now actively pursues foreign investment and economic development through its formal and informal international links. The latter have been expanded to California and Washington states, though no further 'formal links' are sought due to financial constraints.

Richmond, Vancouver's southern neighbour, is the fourth largest GVRD city; its two formal municipal twins currently represent opposite ends of the community-based spectrum. Wayakama, Japan (1972) is the home of many of Richmond's early (1900) Japanese settlers in the Steveston-area fishery. Pierfonds, Quebec, was 'twinned' because a former Richmond resident moved there and worked to develop this pan-Canadian link. As with many municipalities, due to limited resources no other formal links were sought until recently. Despite that, increasing business links with Japan – Richmond has offices for virtually all the major Japanese corporations – and with Hong Kong, Taiwan and China have grown. Export promotions have been added, and cultural links strengthened. Richmond's advice to other municipalities wishing to develop international links is 'to be cautious – budgets can be high'; and 'to establish a strong base of community volunteers'. Even where there has been an important cultural base in the community, as with Richmond's Japanese population, City encouragement remains a useful component of ensuring ongoing international activity.

Coquitlam, Greater Vancouver's 'sixth' city, has no formal international activities. There has been no local push for these and Council has decided that it is 'not seen as an appropriate local government activity'. Coquitlam is involved in 'no' foreign investment or export promotion programmes, 'no' cultural or educational exchanges, and 'no' tourism promotion abroad. Despite that, over fifty foreign 'visits' a year to Coquitlam occur. The council recently began to reconsider its view.

Langley Township, the largest of the mid-sized cities (70,000), has only one formal link, essentially a government-to-government one, with Lynden, Washington, its geographic neighbour. Its only action around this link has been to apply pressure on the federal and provincial governments on cross-border shopping and the Goods and Services Tax. New Westminster has a long-standing link with Moriguchi, Japan (1963) and a recent one with Quezon, Philippines (1991). The Japanese link developed out of meetings between the cities' mayors. Other formal links are prohibited by limited budgets; much of New Westminster's activity is funded 'by individual citizens'. Most international activity is coordinated out of the Mayor's Office and the Mayor, retiring in 1996, noted that most exchanges had been educational and cultural rather than economic. Despite that orientation, the current Mayor added that 'communities are better than senior governments on facilitating peace, understanding and economic development. The federal government is ineffective and wastes money.'

The City of North Vancouver has just one international link – with Chiba, China (1970), the result of a Mayors' meeting. It has been mainly cultural, involving student exchanges; and with little community base. Maple Ridge, one of the newest GVRD members, has had a formal 'sister-city' link to Ying-Ko, Taiwan since 1988. That actually prompted a call from Canada's External Affairs Department to discuss Canada's rejection of a 'two-China' policy. The then Mayor of Maple Ridge indicated that he did not care about External's concerns, and felt he had been encouraged by the Vander Zalm provincial government to develop this Taiwan link. While the initial activities were cultural and educational, the intent was economic development, with the City actively seeking foreign investment through its sister-city agreements. A linkage with a Japanese city was a priority in 1994 but the only formal links have been educational and cultural. 'Global economics' was the primary motivator for such activity in Maple Ridge, with initiation at the City versus community level.

Amongst the seven 'small' municipalities in Greater Vancouver – from 1,000 to 20,000 population – Port Moody has one formal 'pairing' – chosen by the Africa 2000 (CIDA-funded Aid) Programme: Kariba, Zimbabwe. Africa 2000 is a city-to-city aid with costs being provided by the FCM from CIDA, with local fund-raising ($10,000, matched by $20,000 from CIDA). This international link was begun in 1992. There are no plans to expand global activity in Port Moody.

Langley City has no international activities, because it is 'small' and primarily concentrating on 'purely local issues'. Pitt Meadows, which joined the GVRD in July 1995, has no formal international links but is active in seeking foreign investment; such as a $200million Japanese investment in a local golf course/resort. White Rock, population

17,000, has two 'twins', both initiated by its sister cities: Imperial Beach, California (1980) and St Andrew's, New Brunswick (1984). Contact is minimal as the 'size of the city prohibits cost of travel, etc.' That theme, of fiscal constraints on smaller and even larger municipal actors, has been common in the Canadian experience.

Policy lessons: globalist vs globalized urban responses

A brief outline of what a 'globalist' city might look like in policy terms is presented below. In no one city in Canada – indeed throughout North America or elsewhere – could it be argued that a fully coherent *globalist* policy stance exists. The experience of Canadian municipalities in the Vancouver region suggests the probable characteristics of this emerging globalist policy phase, however.

It is only a small step for a significant number of major cities in the world to move to a globalist city policy position, and the potential for significant globalist policy diffusion is high. Globalization has also meant that the emergence of the globalist city will occur with or without senior governmental support. In Vancouver and in other settings, city cases suggest a high degree of municipal internationalism, some of it globalist in nature. That suggests the possibility of expanding globalist responses – with city-regions at the core. In this, the city experiences of North America are not alone. In South America, 19 cities of the four-nation Mercusor trade zone have become integral partners in redefining an initial economic focus.[30] In the EU, city-regional international responses are also more commonplace.

To sustain themselves, such city-based initiatives will need globalist orientations – an appropriate outcome for the twenty-first century. This globalist response will include the following components:

1. A World Peace/Disarmament component
2. A Foreign Aid component
3. A Global Ecological component
4. A Social Equity component
5. A Community/Cultural Diversity component
6. An Economic component

The globalist alternative would include what has been described as a *moral economy*: an economy where ecological issues are not played off against social values, or either of these against growth.[31] The *moral economy* from a globalist perspective is, as Paul Ekins argues, more community sensitive.[32] This globalist potential has begun to be demonstrated by cities in the Vancouver region. All that remains is its achievement.

Notes

1 See J. Friedmann, 'The World City Hypothesis', in *Development And Change*, 17, no. 1 (Jan. 1986), pp. 69–84, and P. Soldatos, 'Atlanta and Boston in the New International Cities Era: Does Age Matter?', in Earl Fry et al., eds, *The New International Cities Era: the Global Activities of North American Municipal Governments* (Provo, Utah: Brigham Young, 1989).
2 See P.J. Smith, H. Oberlander and T. Hutton, eds, *Urban Solutions to Global Problems: Vancouver–Canada–Habitat II* (Vancouver: Centre for Human Settlements, University of British Columbia, 1996).
3 Much of the discussion of the Pacific NorthWest Canada/US cases is based on earlier research, some of it done with my colleague, Ted Cohn.
4 On non-inclusive city developments see, for example, M. Levine, 'Tourism, Urban Redevelopment and the World Class City: the Cases of Baltimore and Montreal', in C. Andrew, P. Armstrong and A. Lapierre, eds, *World Class Cities: Can Canada Play?* (Ottawa: University of Ottawa Press, 1999).
5 E. Fry et al., eds, *The New International Cities Era. See also* P. Hall, *The World Cities* (New York: McGraw Hill, 1971); D. Clark, *Urban World/Global City* (New York: Routledge, 1996); S. Brunn and J. Williams, eds, *Cities of the World: World Regional Urban Development*, 2nd edn (New York: Harper Collins, 1993); M. Crahan and A. Vourvoulias-Bush, eds, *The City and the World: New York's Global Future* (New York: Council of Foreign Relations, 1997); Fu-chen Lo and Yue-man Yeung, eds, *Emerging World Cities in Pacific Asia* (Tokyo/New York: United Nations University Press, 1996); G. Moffitt, *Global Population Growth: 21st Century Challenges* (Ithaca, NY: Foreign Policy Association, 1994); L. Sharpe, *The Government of World Cities: the Future of the Metro Model* (New York: J. Wiley, 1995); W. Robson and D. Reagan, eds, *Great Cities of the World: Their Government, Politics and Planning* (Maplewood, NJ: Hammond, 1958/1972).
6 J. Jacobs, *Cities and the Wealth of Nations: Principles of Economic Life* (New York: Random House, 1984), p. 45.
7 J. Friedmann, 'Where We Stand: a Decade of World City Research', paper for the *World Cities in a World System* Conference, Center for Innovative Technology, Sterling, Va.: April 1993; J. Friedmann and G. Wolff, 'World City Formation', *International Journal of Urban and Regional Research*, 6, no. 3 (Sept. 1982), pp. 309–44.
8 R. Petrella cited in Friedmann, 'Where We Stand'.
9 H. Martin and H. Schumann, *The Global Trap: Globalization and the Assault on Democracy and Prosperity*, trans. P. Camilleri (Montreal: Black Rose Books, 1997).
10 See H. Bastrup-Birk et al., of the Forward Studies Unit, European Commission: *Governance: Progress Report* (European Commission, Brussels, December 1996).
11 Friedmann, 'Where We Stand', p. 31.

12 Ibid., pp. 32–3.
13 P. Smith, 'The Making of a Global City: Fifty Years of Constituent Diplomacy – The Case of Vancouver', *Canadian Journal of Urban Research*, 1, no. 1 (June 1992), pp. 90–112.
14 Interview, then Vancouver Alderman Libby Davies (6 Oct. 1988).
15 Federation of Canadian Municipalities, *A Practical Guide to Twinning* (Ottawa: FCM, 1988).
16 Interview, Sid Fancy, then Manager, then Economic Development, City of Vancouver (27 Oct. 1989).
17 See M. Goldrick, 'The Impact of Global Finance in Urban Structural Change: the International Banking Controversy', in J. Caulfield and L. Peake, eds, *City Lives and City Forms: Critical Research and Canadian Urbanism* (Toronto: University of Toronto Press, 1996), pp. 195–214.
18 Ibid.
19 See J. Kingdon, *Agendas, Alternatives and Public Policies* (Boston: Little, Brown, 1984).
20 P.J. Smith, 'Labour Markets and Neo-Conservative Policy in British Columbia, 1986–1991', in A. Johnson, S. McBride and P. Smith, eds, *Continuities and Discontinuities: the Political Economy of Social Welfare and Labour Market Policy in Canada* (Toronto: University of Toronto Press, 1994), pp. 291–305.
21 Interview Janet Fraser, then Executive Assistant to Vancouver Mayor Gordon Campbell (30 Sept. 1988) and interview then Vancouver Mayor Gordon Campbell (17 Oct. 1988).
22 Smith, 'The Making of a Global City'.
23 Gro Harlem Brundtland, *Our Common Future* (New York: World Commission on Environment and Development, United Nations, 1987).
24 On City–Habitat II links see Smith, et al., *Urban Solutions To Global Problems*.
25 Soldatos, 'Atlanta and Boston', p. 39.
26 On Seattle comparisons see, for example, P.J. Smith, 'Policy Phases, Subnational Foreign Relations, and Constituent Diplomacy in the United States and Canada: City, Provincial and State Global Activity in British Columbia and Washington', in B. Hocking, ed., *Foreign Relations And Federal States* (London: Leicester University Press, 1993), pp. 211–35.
27 The Canadian Dicennial Census of 1996 confirmed the Vancouver CMA as the 3rd largest metropolitan region in Canada, and the 27th largest in the United States and Canada. See A. Sancton, 'Introduction', in D. Rothblatt and A. Sancton, eds, *Metropolitan Governance Revisited: American/Canadian Intergovernmental Comparisons* (Berkeley: IGS Press, 1998), pp. 2–3, table 1, for a list of North American city-regional comparisons.
28 This survey of elected and staff municipal officials was conducted in late 1993–early 1994 and updated in 1996 and 1999.
29 J. Kincaid, 'Rainclouds Over Municipal Diplomacy: Dimensions and Possible Sources of Negative Public Opinion', in E. Fry, L. Radebaugh and P. Soldatos, eds, *The New International Cities Era: the Global Activities of North American Municipal Governments* (Provo, Utah: Brigham Young University, 1989), pp. 223–49.
30 O. Saavedra, 'Micromunicipios: Entre El Mercosur Y La Decentralizacion', in Ofelia Stahringer de Caramuti, Coordinadora, *El Mercosur En El Siglo XXI* (Buenos Aires: Ediciones Ciudad Argentina, 1998), pp. 163–79.

31 J. Biehl, *The Politics of Social Ecology: Libertarian Municipalism* (Montreal: Black Rose, 1998).

32 P. Ekins, *A New World Order: Grassroots Movements for Global Change* (London: Routledge, 1992).

11

The Global Economy and the Local State

Christopher Leo

Introduction

Local politics has long been subject to influences originating in the global economy, but it is only lately that students of urban political economy have begun to appropriate a language and a set of concepts intended to comprehend that reality.[1] Much work remains to be done. In this article, I look at urban politics in North America and Europe, with special attention to the politics of planning and development, ask how globalization is changing the political landscape, and enquire into the local political response to the challenge of globalization.

This question has not been given the attention it deserves. Much of the literature tends either to assume that globalization is bringing about a massive homogenization in the development of cities; or it observes significant political differences in different jurisdictions without reference to the literature that points to homogenization. In these pages, we will observe substantial homogenization, and take a look at the dynamics that drive it, but we will also note local and national political differences that are capable of exerting significant influence on the way globalization affects city development. Comparing continental Europe with the United States, I argue that the greater involvement of the European national state in local politics produces a more nearly level playing-field in bargaining between the state and capital. At the same time, I find a greater American penchant for involvement of the public in decision-making about urban development, a penchant that is likely to prove an important asset in the local politics that is emerging under the aegis of globalization.

The argument is that, as a result of technological and economic developments that are global in scope, cities are being subjected to a wide range of pressures for homogenization, of urban built form, of urban physical structure and of administrative and political arrangements. At the same time, urban governance asserts local particularity – local ideas of how cities should be governed, how they should look and what the social milieu should be – in the face of these homogenizing pressures. I find that these two pressures – the push for homogenization and the assertion of particularity – are both important, both help to shape cities and the ways they are governed, but neither enjoys absolute dominance. Therefore, although cities in Europe and North America are facing many of the same problems and often reacting to them in similar ways, important and deeply rooted differences remain, and exert major influence.

Global homogenization

Norms and practices based in the global economy have a 'homogenizing' effect on local and national political cultures. Among the homogenizing forces are the spread of technologies that have an impact on urban form, for example the private automobile which confers greater mobility upon a large number of people, and encourages lower-density development; computer and communications technology, which allows for further decentralization of residence and workplace; and the subway, which provides a transportation infrastructure that encourages the development of high-density commercial and residential concentrations around subway stations.[2] The result is similar suburban subdivisions, 'edge cities', and high-density developments in widely scattered cities.[3]

A more personalized homogenizing influence is the demands of developers who seek to make their developments conform to international architectural norms and technical standards. Often, meeting those demands necessitates compromises with, or abandonment of, locally set standards of design or local administrative and political practices. Another homogenizing stimulus is the example of other jurisdictions. Administrators and politicians are constantly on the alert for ideas originating elsewhere that can be applied locally.

Two examples of ideas that have spread and had an important impact on cities in different parts of the world are urban development corporations as an administrative mechanism for downtown redevelopment projects, and design controls as a way of creating a supposedly unique character for each neighbourhood – a 'uniqueness' that is often replicated in Chinatowns, coffee house districts and downtown malls in city after city. Yet another homogenizing influence can be seen in international agreements and organizational structures, such as the North American Free Trade Agreement and the European Union, which compel many changes in local as well as national administrative norms.

Much of the literature on globalization, especially the earlier literature, has tended to stress homogenization. For example, in a discussion of the impact of the global economy on cities, Logan and Molotch classify all American cities into only 5 types, according to their economic function: headquarters cities, innovation centres, retirement centres, and so forth. Noyelle and Stanbach, approaching the same problematic from a different ideological perspective, identify 4 categories, albeit 11 subtypes. Storper and Walker consider how cities are shaped by industrial growth, while Scott enquires into how cities are shaped by the division of labour. All of them, of course, allow for differences among cities, but all concentrate on differences created by variations in the economic forces acting on them. The cities become, in effect, urban units whose differences are seen primarily in terms of conditions and changes that are global in scope.[4]

Likewise, Fainstein looks at the influence of property development upon London and New York City, and strongly stresses similarities in the property developments she investigates. Sorkin offers perhaps the ultimate expression of this emphasis. Complaining about the impact upon cities of technology and current development styles, he says, 'The new city eradicates genuine particularity in favour of a continuous urban field, a conceptual grid of boundless reach.'[5]

Studies that emphasize the way global economic and cultural influences exert pressure for homogenization have contributed a great deal to our understanding of cities today, and the politics of planning offers much evidence in support of their perspective. Canadians, for example, have watched since the 1950s as their cities changed to resemble the way American cities had already begun to look before the Second World War. The first American-style suburb was Don Mills in Toronto, which was being built in the 1950s and early 1960s. In the 1960s, the Place Ville Marie office tower complex in Montreal, an enterprise of the New York developer William Zeckendorf, and the Toronto Dominion Centre, an office tower complex designed by the eminent Chicago-based modernist architect Mies van der Rohe, initiated the Americanization of Canadian downtowns.[6]

Today both suburbs and downtown cores across the country resemble those of American cities, the overall urban structure more compact,[7] but the style indistinguishable at ground level, as witness the fact that many American movies are shot on location in Toronto, Vancouver, Montreal and other Canadian cities. More recently, the influences have spread to Europe. La Défence in Paris is a forest of high-rises and London's Covent Garden, a long-established wholesale food market and working-class neighbourhood, has become a sort of fashionable mall surrounded by upscale shopping, restaurants and entertainment. The area has more historical depth than any city in North America can manage, but otherwise it is patterned on many similar developments across the Atlantic. La Défence and Covent Garden are only two of many similar examples.

The politics of particularity

If much of the globalization literature stresses, or even assumes, homogenization of cities in the face of global pressures, there is also an emerging literature that cultivates an eye for local particularity, while placing local politics in a global context. If we cull that literature, and add to it some material from a growing stock of cross-nationally comparative studies of urban politics, we can gain some insights into the degree to which politics 'still matters',[8] despite the overwhelming importance of global economic forces. We will focus on the politics of urban planning and development. Given the practical necessity of tailoring our investigation to the available literature in a field that is still young, we will pay special attention to the politics of inner city redevelopment.

It is useful to think of the bargaining over urban development as involving three parties: the state, capital and citizens. We will begin by comparing the relationship between the state and citizens on the two continents and then look at the more crucial relationship between the state and capital. The database is slender, and our findings are preliminary. The intention is to contribute to the attempt to gain an overview of the differences between European and North American city politics, a subject that is addressed elsewhere,[9] but has not received the attention it deserves.

The role of citizens

Case studies comparing Paris with New York show a marked difference in the degree of legitimacy accorded to direct participation of citizens in the process of urban development. For example, Savitch, in comparing New York with Paris, classifies New York City's decision-making process as 'a blend of corporatism and pluralism'. He finds corporatism in both cities, but it is New York's distinctive feature that 'non-established groups, with few resources and no privileged access' can wield pivotal influence, especially if the corporatist decision-making process, involving 'top politicians . . . business, labour, interest groups and community boards' gets bogged down.[10]

His strongest example of the potential of citizen opposition is the case of Westway, a massive Manhattan road-building scheme, which was first proposed in 1969, encountered fierce resistance, and had still not been built at the writing of his study. In Paris, by contrast, where 'mobilizing corporatism' holds sway, '[m]ass opposition to the political elite is surprisingly limited . . . Relatively few decisions evoke the ire of the citizenry.' In three case studies, Savitch found citizen opposition once, and then only 'at the eleventh hour'.[11] In that case, the opposition, as he demonstrates in some detail, did not significantly influence the outcome.

Savitch's findings are supported in Body-Gendrot, a study of a rare Parisian case of relatively successful neighbourhood resistance to a major development that came only after a large part of the neighbourhood had already been redeveloped with '35-floor towers'. The author prefaces her account with a characterization of France as a 'strong-state society' where 'particular wills' are 'not as well-protected as in the United States'.[12] It is clear, from both her account and Savitch's three case studies, that the position of ordinary citizens in Parisian development politics is very different from that in New York. Two of Fainstein's case studies confirm New York's side of that dichotomy, while making it clear that, although the legitimacy of citizen involvement is well-established, its ultimate effect is often marginal. Broadly, her findings coincide with the others.[13]

In these studies New York and Paris are poles in the North American–European dichotomy, and it is clear that they respectively reflect *modi operandi* that are observable elsewhere on the two continents. At the same time, there is intracontinental variation – perhaps, given the slender database, more than anyone suspects. Some of that variation is visible in case studies of British and Canadian urban development politics, and it suggests that those nations occupy a middle position between the poles represented by New York and Paris. Both Savitch and Fainstein include London in their comparative case studies, and their findings are interesting.

Savitch, having found a corporatist-pluralist hybrid in New York, and mobilizing corporatism in Paris, characterizes London politics with the term 'liberal corporatism'. In brief, his argument is that in London, as in New York, but not Paris, citizen input is a regular feature of development politics, but the response of the state is different. In New York, he observes, citizen groups remain independent of the state throughout the decision-making process, battering the state from outside when they disagree with proposals. In London, representatives of protesting groups that prove their mettle in the political arena are incorporated into the decision-making process, thereby on one hand giving them a direct role in decision-making and, on the other, neutralizing them as opponents.

For example, in the chic commercial redevelopment of the rooted working-class neighbourhood of Covent Garden, the Covent Garden Community Association (CCGA), 'a fiery and effective pressure group' with a radical political style, 'embarrassed public officials with its skill and thoroughness'. The response of the state was the formation of a representative body, elected from the community. As a result, '[w]hat had once been an opposition was suddenly converted into a collaborative organization with special access to decision-makers'.[14]

The upshot was a redevelopment that was humanized in scale and appearance, and more protective of the neighbourhood's environment and history, than the original proposals, and that incorporated some benefits to local residents. At the same time, a working-class neighbourhood was gentrified and transformed into 'one of the most chic locales in Central London'. The example suggests a much greater seriousness about citizen input in London than in Paris, but a very different style than in New York.

In four comparative case studies of development projects in New York and London – two in each city – Fainstein produces broadly similar findings.[15] In all four cases, citizen participation occurred, and was accepted by the authorities, as a matter of course. And although Fainstein does not report any actual co-optation of community representatives onto government bodies, as Savitch does, it is notable that in both the London cases the citizen groups were given financial assistance by the government, while no government finance for citizens was reported in either New York case. On this evidence, as on Savitch's, if Paris and New York are the poles, London is somewhere in the middle of the spectrum.

Comparable observations could be made about the Canadian situation. Citizen participation in urban development decisions is a legitimized, though sporadic, part of the political process. In the 1970s, there were a number of high-profile citizen rebellions against development initiatives. Among the best-known of these cases was the Marlborough Avenue campaign against Marathon Realty's Summerhill Square development in Toronto, in which local residents fought a tenacious battle before city council and in the court of local public opinion to win a modest list of concessions from the developer. Also in the 1970s, a series of citizen uprisings against urban expressway schemes proved partly responsible for the fact that most Canadian inner city neighbourhoods remain largely unscathed by multi-lane highways. A major factor in the greater success of such initiatives in Canada than the United States, however, was the paucity of federal government funding for expressways. In the 1980s, the Downtown Eastside Residents' Association, representing the residents of Vancouver's Skid Road area, won a number of remarkable concessions from local government in the area of cooperative housing and tenants' rights. These and similar efforts, however, have been sporadic, and have been preceded and followed by periods of dormancy.[16]

Perhaps the most striking example of institutionalized citizen participation in Canada is the development permit approval process in Vancouver, in which notice of any new development is posted in the neighbourhood affected, details of the plans are made available to the public, and then a process of consultations and hearings takes place in which the developer is required to respond to the concerns of citizens and to conform to a rigorous set of design guidelines.[17] This, however, has the earmarks of the co-optation evident in the Savitch data on Covent Garden. On the available evidence, Canada, like Britain, appears to be a mid-Atlantic case: Canadian urban politics is clearly more amenable than French to citizen initiatives, but operates differently than it does in the United States, or at least New York City.

The state and capital

However important citizen participation may be in the political scheme of things, it is also clear, from what we have seen, and from a variety of other evidence, that the actual impact of citizen initiatives on the shape of urban development is limited. At its most potent, citizen participation can score some successes, usually partial ones. At its least influential, it is window-dressing or is altogether absent.

The same cannot be said of the influence of capital. Therefore, we turn now to the more interesting and more crucial question of how the relationship between the state and capital differ in European and North American politics of downtown redevelopment. The available literature points to a striking contrast that directly affects the interactions, and the respective roles, of capital and the state in the process of urban development: the European national state has a markedly more prominent role in local decision-making than the American one.

For example, in an Italian case study, Vicari and Molotch argued that growth machines do not exist there as they do in the United States because of national regulation of land use, a highly centralized party machinery, 'systematically integrated with lower echelons', and the fact that 'local government is not financially or legislatively independent of the central state'. All of these factors, according to them, combine to insulate local government from the kind of development pressures that are a familiar feature of North American politics. The influence of capital is wielded at the national level, especially through party machinery, where land development interests must vie with much more powerful industrial, financial and other political interests for attention.[18]

Body-Gendrot's and Savitch's Parisian case studies paint a comparable picture of French politics. There, a strong, activist, centralized government and a powerful national bureaucracy play a more directive role in development than any found in North America. Savitch comments: 'It is not uncommon for French developers to behave as suppliants to a powerful class of technocrats.'[19] Here, as in Italy, pressures from land developers are only one of a wider array of influences upon a state marked by a high degree of integration between national and local levels.

Savitch's studies of New York find decision-making on development matters lodged primarily at the local level, and far more exposed to direct pressures from developers. He notes that decision-making is marked by 'the city's perceived need to attract investment, increase the value of land, augment tax revenues, provide jobs...' Fainstein, drawing conclusions from a series of case studies comparing New York and London, adds that both Mayors Koch and Dinkins 'felt compelled to respond to every notice by a major firm that it was considering a move to New Jersey with a counter-offer', and observes: 'In both London and New York...projects had government sponsors, but the willingness of government to offer direct subsidy to the developer was far greater in the latter city.'[20]

Savitch's British cases offer an interesting comparison and contrast. The central government's creation and subsequent abolition of the Greater London Council, both by fiat, have earned it a formidable reputation for high-handedness. However, Savitch's studies of development politics find a less centralized situation there than in France. The national government is actively involved in development decisions, but

Savitch finds a relationship more marked by central–local competition in Britain than in France, and his case studies picture a robustly competitive political arena, with local governments that do not appear as agents of the centre. He comments: 'If it wishes, the central government can override the local opposition with impunity, but it rarely does... relative to interest groups, French government is far more centralized and monolithic than British government.'[21] From that evidence, it would appear that here, as in the matter of citizen participation, Britain occupies a mid-Atlantic position.

Canada occupies a different, but similarly ambivalent, mid-Atlantic position. Canadian cities, like American ones, are directly exposed to developer pressures, because they are primarily responsible for decisions relating to land use. City governments negotiate with developers, as Toronto's local authorities did in the Marlborough Avenue case referred to above, and if their bargaining position is weak, they may find themselves making massive financial and material concessions, as Edmonton did in its Bank of Montreal and Eaton Centre developments and Winnipeg did in dealings with Trizec.[22]

However, although the federal government does not exercise supervision over local land use, it has involved itself very significantly in local development, through a wide range of measures, including federally owned corporations that sponsored such redevelopments as Toronto's Harbourfront and Vancouver's Granville Island; participation in a tri-level bureaucracy that managed the Core Area Initiative, a multifaceted programme for the revitalization of Winnipeg's inner city; and federal programmes to finance the relocation of downtown railway properties and the construction of convention centres.[23] Canada's non-directive but interventionist federal government places Canada, like Britain, in a mid-Atlantic position in our comparison.

Conclusions

In these pages, we have considered what happens to the study of the politics of urban development and planning when it is placed in a global context. We looked first at how pressures that are global in scope are having a homogenizing effect and then how politics asserts itself to forge important local differences in the responses to globalization. It was not, however, local politics *per se* that made the crucial difference, it was the role of the national state in city politics.

Drawing upon case studies, we found that the strong national state presence in urban politics that was evident in France and Italy was associated, on one hand, with a political environment that tended to be unreceptive to grassroots participation in urban development decisions and, on the other, with more state control and less clout for developers in urban development decisions. In the United States, by contrast, we found the opposite situation: a more receptive environment for grassroots participation and developers who were better placed to exert direct influence upon urban development. In Britain and Canada, a more complex, mixed picture, a mid-Atlantic state of affairs, was discernable in the data.

Another way of summarizing our findings about national power and the character of local politics is to say that, in the United States, power is more fragmented than it is in Europe, and that this fragmentation is not just a matter of a different way of doing things, but also has consequences for political outcomes. The fact that the national state has less say over local affairs enhances the power of one group, the development industry, in relation to other social groups and this, in turn, affects the way cities are governed and ultimately the way they look and the kind of society that develops there.

Our findings are based on careful, detailed case studies, but it needs to be stressed that it is an emerging, and therefore slender, database. Any conclusions we can draw from it are necessarily tentative and hypothetical. However, such tentative findings can play a useful role in mapping out directions for research, even if some of them are subsequently invalidated. It is appropriate, therefore, to end this investigation on a somewhat speculative note, offering clues to future research by drawing out some of the possible implications of current findings.

Implications

In our New York cases, we found a considerable degree of local autonomy in land development matters, with local authorities that had a great deal of control over their own land use policies, while the national government tended to keep hands off. This is a common state of affairs in the United States. Decisions about land use, typically, are a result of bargaining between local authorities, the developers or other corporate interests that are proposing new developments, and any citizens that become involved in the decision-making process.

Two sets of power relationships emerge from this constellation of political forces. One is that between corporations, some of them with deep pockets and far-flung international interests, and local governments that may be very vulnerable. Their vulnerability may be heightened by the ever-increasing mobility of finance and of corporate offices and industrial branches.[24] In many cases, corporations deliberately ignite bidding wars between municipalities to see where they can get the most generous assistance and the most liberal land use regimes.

The other power relationship typical of decisions about urban development is that between the local state and citizens, sometimes representing the neighbourhoods most affected by a development proposal, and sometimes constituting broader coalitions. Our case studies suggest that direct citizen participation in the making of particular development decisions is a more important factor in the United States than in continental Europe. All of these political conventions are reinforced by characteristic features of American political culture, including a widely-held belief in the importance of allowing private enterprise to operate with a minimum of hindrance; a belief in local autonomy, which takes the concrete form of the widely-observed principle of local 'home rule'; a suspicion of 'big government', especially if that government is a national government; and a suspicion of powerful, interventionist government, whether local, regional or national.

In the continental European examples that are available for this study, by contrast, there is much more involvement by national-level politicians and officials in the process of making decisions about land use. Greater national government involvement in urban affairs tends to shift the determination of urban policy from competition between corporations and relatively weak municipal governments to a bargaining process involving national governments with corporations that are able to wield influence at that level. Many or most of these are not in the land development business.

The fact that interurban competition for development is not as prominent a feature of European as of American urban politics stems in part from the frequently active role of national governments in urban development, a role that necessarily includes centralized allocation of development opportunities, together with at least some presumption that each city will get a share.[25] Likewise, the fact that decay of inner cities is a less pressing problem in Europe than in the United States is undoubtedly traceable to the stronger national political role in cities. This implies in some degree, a national commitment to the health of those cities.

Not only does the more powerful role of the national state enhance the state's position in its bargaining with corporate interests. It creates a situation that, from an American perspective, might appear as undue subordination to the state. From a European perspective, a more apt formulation might be that the involvement of national-level politicians in land use decisions produces something closer to a level playing-field in the bargaining between the state and capital than is found in the United States. At the same time, direct citizen participation is much less of a factor in continental European urban politics than in the United States.

Application

The comparative study of urban political economy, and of the various responses to the pressures of globalization, is not only a theoretical matter. It has immediate practical significance as well. The ubiquity of the pressures of globalization upon cities means that they have more and more to learn from each other's experiences. A globally oriented analysis of city politics can play a useful role in that process of learning and adaptation. It may be that the fates of some American inner cities are an object lesson to America and the world, but there are also more edifying lessons to be learned from the way United States cities are governed.

If urban politics in a wired world is to have any prospects of constructively channelling the forces of globalization, it is unlikely to be accomplished without involving the public far more actively in decision-making than they were in some of the European examples we have considered in this chapter. Usable models are much more likely to be found in the United States where a tradition of individualism and populist politics has forced urban politicians and administrators to develop habits and techniques of public involvement that may well be applicable and useful elsewhere.

Another lesson we can learn from a study of the impact of global economic forces on local politics is the need to rethink the disciplinary isolationism that characterizes much of the study of local politics, which often proceeds as if municipal government were an entity separated from the more rarefied politics of regions, nations and international relations. In a global perspective that is not possible, because, once we start looking at cities comparatively in terms of the global influences that help to shape them, we cannot carry out meaningful comparisons without considering the full range of things governments do, or refrain from doing, in cities.

Our unit of analysis must become, not just the local state, but all of the forces that help to shape political decision-making in and for the city, whether they originate at the local, regional or national level. What is more, the influence of such supranational governmental and quasi-governmental institutions as the European Union and the North American Free Trade Agreement are unquestionably felt in the administration of cities, and they too will have to be included in our understanding of urban politics. It is a fascinating challenge, that poses interesting and complex analytical problems.

Notes

1   This paper is a revised version of one that was previously published under the title 'City Politics in an Era of Globalization', in *Reconstructing Urban Regime Theory: Regulating Urban Politics in a Global Economy*, ed. Mickey Lauria (Thousand Oaks: Sage, 1997). Thanks to Joe Painter, Mark Goodwin, Bob Jessop and Mickey Lauria for helpful critiques. I also very much appreciate the research assistance that I received from Mike Gray, Michelle Mathae and Krista Boryskavich. And I am grateful to the Social Science and Humanities Research Council of Canada, the University of Winnipeg and the University's Institute of Urban Studies for financial and other support, but do not hold them responsible for any shortcomings.

2   H. Blumenfeld, *The Modern Metropolis: Its Origins, Growth, Characteristics, and Planning* (Cambridge, Mass.: MIT Press, 1967).

3   To be sure, the global economy not only homogenizes, it also differentiates, through uneven development of different cities and different neighbourhoods, for example, and through cycles of urban decline and regeneration. Likewise, politics not only resists homogenization, it also homogenizes. The policies associated with the names of Ronald Reagan and Margaret Thatcher played an important role in changing the character of economic policy-making around the world. The example of Reaganism and Thatcherism also illustrates that the economy, in addition to acting upon politics, is also acted upon by it. However, a recognition of all these complexities, and many more, does not prevent us from identifying relationships, and drawing out their implications, one at a time, as I am doing in these pages.

4   J.R. Logan and H.L. Molotch, *Urban Fortunes: the Political Economy of Place* (Berkeley: University of California Press, 1987), ch. 7; T.J. Noyelle and T.M. Stanback, *Economic Transformation of American Cities* (Totowa, NJ: Allanheld and Rowman, 1983); A.J. Scott, *Metropolis: from the Division of Labor to Urban Form* (Berkeley: University of California, 1990); M. Storper and R. Walker, *The Capitalist Imperative: Territory, Technology and Industrial Growth* (Oxford: Blackwell, 1989).

5   S.S. Fainstein, *The City Builders: Property, Politics, and Planning in London and New York* (Cambridge, Mass.: Blackwell, 1994); M. Sorkin, ed., *Variations on a Theme Park: the New American City and the End of Public Space* (New York: The Noonday Press, 1992), p. xii.

6   J. Sewell, *The Shape of the City: Toronto Struggles with Modern Planning* (Toronto: University of Toronto Press, 1993), ch. 3; R.W. Collier, *Contemporary Cathedrals: Large-Scale Developments in Canadian Cities* (Montreal: Harvest House, 1974), pp. 9–21, 122–3.

7   M.A. Goldberg and J. Mercer, *The Myth of the North American City: Continentalism Challenged* (Vancouver: University of British Columbia Press, 1986), ch. 7.

8   C.N. Stone, 'The Study of the Politics of Urban Development', in Stone and H.T. Sanders, eds, *The Politics of Urban Development* (Lawrence, Kan.: University Press of Kansas, 1987), p. 4.

9   Fainstein, *The City Builders*; H.V. Savitch, *Post-Industrial Cities: Politics and Planning in New York, Paris and London* (Princeton: Princeton University Press, 1988); H.V. Savitch and Paul Kantor, 'City Business: an International Perspective on Market Place Politics', conference paper, School for Advanced Urban Studies, University of Bristol, 1994; L.H. Klaassen and P.C. Cheshire, 'Urban Analysis Across the Atlantic Divide', in A.A. Summers, P.C. Cheshire and L. Senn, eds, *Urban Change in the United States and Western Europe: Comparative Analysis and Policy* (Washington, DC: The Urban Institute, 1993), ch. 20; C. Leo and W. Brown, 'Slow Growth and Urban Development Policy', conference paper, Urban Affairs Association, Louisville, Kentucky, 1999.

10 Savitch, *Post-Industrial Cities*, pp. 59, 60.

11 Ibid., p. 137.

12 S.N. Body-Gendrot, 'Grass-roots Mobilization in the Thirteenth Arrondissement', in Stone and Sanders, *The Politics of Urban Development*, pp. 129–30.

13 Fainstein (*The City Builders*, chs 6, 7) could be interpreted as arguing the ultimate marginality of citizen participation somewhat more strongly than Savitch.

14 Savitch, *Post-Industrial Cities*, pp. 219–22.

15 Fainstein's book actually contains six case studies in all, but since neither of the two others – Docklands and Battery Park – involved new development in the middle of established neighbourhoods, they are less helpful in comparing the role of citizens in the making of development decisions.

16 A. Sancton, 'The Municipal Role in the Governance of Canadian Cities', in T. Bunting and P. Filion, *Canadian Cities in Transition* (Toronto: Oxford University Press, 1991), p. 473; J.L. Granatstein, *Marlborough Marathon* (Toronto: A.M. Hakkert, 1971); C. Leo, *The Politics of Urban Development: Canadian Urban Expressway Disputes* (Toronto: Institute of Public Administration of Canada, 1977); D. Ley, 'Social Polarization and Community Response: Contesting Marginality in Vancouver's Downtown Eastside', in F. Frisken, ed., *The Changing Canadian Metropolis: a Public Policy Perspective* (Berkeley: Institute of Governmental Studies, University of California at Berkeley, 1994), vol. 2, ch. 21.

17 C. Leo, 'The Urban Economy and the Power of the Local State: the Politics of Planning in Edmonton and Vancouver', in Frisken, ed., *The Changing Canadian Metropolis*.

18 S. Vicari and H. Molotch, 'Building Milan: Alternative Machines of Growth', *International Journal of Urban and Regional Research*, 14, no. 4 (1990), p. 619; H. Molotch and S. Vicari, 'Three Ways to Build: the Development Process in the United States, Japan and Italy', *Urban Affairs Quarterly*, 24, no. 2 (1988), pp. 188–210.

19 Savitch, *Post-Industrial Cities*, p. 134.

20 Ibid., p. 59; Fainstein, *The City Builders*, pp. 164, 166.

21 Savitch, *Post-Industrial Cities*, p. 203 n. 4.

22 C. Leo, 'Global Change and Local Politics: Economic Decline and the Local Regime in Edmonton', *Journal of Urban Affairs*, 17, no. 3 (1995), pp. 277–99; D. Walker, *The Great Winnipeg Dream: the Redevelopment of Portage and Main* (Oakville, Ont.: Mosaic Press, 1979).

23 C. Leo and R. Fenton ' "Mediated Enforcement" and the Evolution of the State: Urban Development Corporations in Canadian City Centres', *International*

Journal of Urban and Regional Research, 14, no. 2 (1990), pp. 185–206; C. Leo, 'The State in the City: a Political Economy Perspective on Growth and Decay', in J. Lightbody, ed., *Canadian Metropolitics: Governing Our Cities* (Toronto: Copp Clark, 1995), pp. 27–50.

24 By the same token, it can be minimized by a city's superior attractiveness as a location for business. See Leo in Frisken, *Changing Canadian Metropolis*; P. Kantor 'The Dependent City: the Changing Political Economy of Urban Economic Development in the United States', *Urban Affairs Quarterly*, 22, no. 4 (June, 1987), p. 496.

25 The national government's doling-out of its share of development to each city and region is also a conspicuous feature of Canadian politics. H. Bakvis, *Regional Ministers: Power and Influence in the Canadian Cabinet* (Toronto: University of Toronto Press, 1991).

Part V

Labour and the Challenge of Globalization

12
Globalization, Unemployment and the Redistribution of Working Time

Andrew Molloy and John Shields

The polarization of work between those who have too little, or none, and those with too much is a pressing societal problem. Redistribution of work time has been largely driven by the market, although, especially in Western Europe, it has been more consciously encouraged through collective bargaining and public policy in an effort to spread 'scarce' work around. Along with the shifts in work time, parallel income redistribution effects occurred, which are contributing to significant economic and social inequalities.

The pressures from global economic restructuring, with its demands for just-in-time production and a corresponding flexible workforce, have been a major force influencing work time reorganization. This has resulted in a decline of standard work and the rapid rise of more flexible work forms such as part-time, temporary help and contract employment. At another level, the forces of globalization and the slowing of the rate of economic growth have undermined nationally centred Keynesian production and employment structures in the industrially developed world. OECD countries have witnessed the return of persistent mass levels of unemployment unparalleled since the Great Depression of the 1930s.

The demands of the new economy have fostered an employer strategy based on the utilization of an ever smaller core of workers whose work time has been intensified through the extensive use of overtime. To supplement the core workforce, employers have drawn upon cheap pools of non-standard and disposable workers employed according to the logic of a volatile just-in-time and lean production system. High levels of unemployment and underemployment exerted discipline on workers, restraining labour militancy, maintaining a ready army of skilled and educated workers for flexible utilization by capital and magnifying levels of polarization and social exclusion.

This chapter explores the various dimensions of the restructuring of work time and its relationship to the social and economic health of Canadian society. A comparative perspective is used since other countries, especially in Western Europe, have a longer history of active experimentation with work time reforms to address the problem of unemployment.

Governments in a more globalized and deregulated environment are increasingly constrained in their capacity to positively influence employment creation. Moreover, the broad trend towards more insecure and contingent forms of work means that new job creation (whether it is encouraged through work time reform or other means) consists of non-standard employment. None the less, while work time reform does not offer a panacea, it can play a supporting role in a policy package designed to manage high unemployment. Even in a more 'globalized' world national governments retain significant policy capacity.

Work week reduction with no loss of pay is a key part of a progressive agenda because it is a demand concerned with gaining greater state control of the labour process. It moves beyond the issue of job creation to the question of control over work time and working conditions. The political movement around work week reduction has the potential to challenge many of the tenets of neo-liberal globalization.

The global economy and the restructuring of work time

The most pressing economic problem facing policy-makers today is the employment crisis. Empirically the validity of this concern is not difficult to substantiate. Globally the International Labour Organization has estimated that 30 per cent of the world's workforce is either unemployed or seriously underemployed. Some 820 million workers fail to earn a subsistence wage.[1] Within the OECD by the mid-1990s there were some 35 million unemployed (over 3 million more than in 1983) and likely another 15 million who have given up looking for work or who refuse to take part-time employment. Underemployment could add another 30 to 40 per cent to the unemployment total.[2]

Prior to 1975, unemployment in Canada never exceeded 7.5 per cent; since then it has never fallen below this level.[3] Since the 1980s, average Canadian unemployment rates have rested at well over 9 per cent.[4] In late 1997, unemployment finally declined to under 9 per cent but this was achieved only after five years of sustained growth following the deep recession of the early 1990s. In 1993 unemployment averaged 1.6 million; but over 3 million experienced a bout of unemployment, representing 24 per cent of the labour force.[5] Unemployment is particularly acute for young people and the less skilled and educated. However, all groupings have experienced considerably greater job insecurity. Moreover, the duration of unemployment spells have also increased over time.[6]

Globalization is the central concept which has been used 'to make sense of the present situation'.[7] Globalization, however, embodies a dual character. It is a real material force involved with the extension of cross-border trade and communication, and the internationalization of finance and production. At another level it is a concept which captures the politics of deregulating labour markets, slashing state social spending and promoting neo-liberal approaches to public policy. Neo-liberal political forces have successfully pushed national governments to sign regional and international trade and investment deals which have placed significant constraints on policy-makers' autonomy. A good deal of the limitation on national policy capacity has been self-induced,[8] but remains a real constraint which will be difficult to reverse.

With the advent of globalization, flexibility has become a key word, especially regarding work organization. While in aggregate terms 'the average work week has remained remarkably static over the past 20 years, this stability masks considerable polarization in actual hours of work'.[9] In North America fewer than one-half of all workers enjoyed a standard 40 to 48-hour work week by 1995,[10] with workers increasingly being polarized between working long hours and short. Between 1983 and 1995 in Canada part-time employment expanded by 35 per cent while full-time work rose by only 19 per cent. Fully some 28 per cent of employed workers in 1995 would have liked more work.[11]

The pattern of work time distribution has also played an important role in enhanced income polarization, as many core workers work excess hours while other workers are underemployed.[12] Income polarization and social exclusion has increased within the OECD.[13] The greatest increases have occurred in North America.

In Canada, the 'increase in earnings inequality is associated with a decrease in the real earnings of workers at the bottom quintile and with a marked decline in the number of individuals earning "middle class" wages and salaries.'[14] Overall, in Canada between 1984 and 1995 there has been virtually no increase in real earnings even though labour productivity advanced by 9.7 per cent.[15] The increased incidence of part-time work has accelerated income polarization.[16]

Because of growing polarization and the weakening of job security many workers want to accumulate as much work time as possible in case tomorrow brings pay and/or job loss. The hoarding of work time is a conservative response generated by greater economic insecurity. Unsurprisingly, more workers within all occupational and demographic groups 'would work more hours for more pay than fewer hours for less pay (a ratio of 4:1)'.[17]

Paradoxically, contemporary labour markets exhibit overemployment and underemployment. Indeed the existence of high levels of over-employment can be explained by underemployment. 'Men are working overtime to compensate for expected job loss in the future. Women have expanded their work effort to cover for what otherwise would be a sharp reduction in family living standards'.[18] To a significant extent these labour market changes have been driven by the systematic intensification of competition brought about through globalization. Business has reacted to this 'by both intensifying work for some workers and then on the other hand, by casualizing work – moving to part-time, casual work'.[19]

Work time reductions, employment creation and politics of flexible labour

Slow economic growth and high levels of structural unemployment, which threaten social cohesion, have led to the idea that reduced work-ing could increase employment opportunities, or, minimally, help to stabilize existing workforce patterns. The underlying philosophy is that when the growth of jobs is smaller than the growth of job seekers, then a more equitable distribution of the available volume of work should be made available.

In continental Europe, major trade unions have embraced work time reduction, 'as a means of safeguarding existing jobs, or creating employ-ment in a context of high unemployment'.[20] For example, the shorter working week became the focus of much of the debate, resulting in the 1993 European Community Directive on the organization of working time. The Directive instructed member countries to amend a number of antiquated labour acts by promoting minimal standards on such mat-ters as a maximum daily and weekly working time, a minimum period of annual leave, 'mandated' rest breaks and specific health and safety safeguards for night working.[21]

Historically, the European labour movement has been in the vanguard of the battle for a shorter working week, arguing that such a move, without a cut in pay, would serve to open up job opportunities and reduce unemployment.[22] From the mid-1980s German trade unions advanced the demand that the work week be reduced without a loss in pay. They contended that a move to a 35-hour week would create over a million jobs. In October 1995 IG Metall, the largest union, secured contracts with its employers after conducting a major campaign.[23] Building on that success, IG Metall signed a 1997 agreement which provided workers over the age of 61 with the right to work half the normal working week for 82 per cent of full-time wages.[24] Working time issues have been adopted by Volkswagen as a method for saving some 30,000 jobs, 'by cutting working time by 20 per cent to 28.8 hours over four days, together with a 15 per cent wage reduction'.[25]

France and Italy are committed to reducing the work week to 35 hours by 1 January 2000 and 1 January 2001 respectively. As well as tackling unemployment and avoiding layoffs, workers in both countries 'are pressing for reductions in their working hours – or at any rate their adjustment – so that they can devote themselves to caring tasks' – hence providing a better balance between work and family responsibilities. Government reports which review collective agreements on working time confirm a number of measures agreed upon by 'the social partners'. Examples include flexible part-time contracts, different clocking in and out times, virtual offices, caring leave, and time off for overtime and holidays. Reducing the work week in this sense means trying to balance work with 'socio-familial commitments'.[26]

Both countries have phase-in periods designed to allow employers and trade unions to negotiate at the company and sectoral level before the new regulations are applied. Any new laws or amendments can simply take into account 'what will have been decided in bargaining, and will establish the ways in which the reduction of hours will be implemented.'[27] Both governments hope that when the new laws come into effect, the working time environment will already have been established to substantially lessen any transition costs and minimize political opposition.

Minimizing political opposition to working time reform may prove difficult given the negative response from employers and some academics to the 35-hour work week in France and Italy. Employer groups have protested at government interference in their businesses particularly when (from an employer perspective) the employment gains resulting from a 35-hour work week have yet to be proven.

In Canada, the Canadian Auto Workers has been in the forefront of negotiations around reduced work time as a job creation measure. In the fall of 1996, the CAW made work time a key issue in the central bargaining process with the big 3 auto manufacturers (Chrysler, Ford and General Motors). The result was a contract that gave workers between '8.7 and 10.2 weeks each year paid time off the job, or the equivalent of a 32 hour work week', creating thousands of new work openings.[28] In the Minivan plant in Windsor, the CAW negotiated a third shift and a reduced work day which combined to create about 1,000 new jobs.[29] These measures resulted in no loss of base pay for workers.

In 1993 Bell Canada, aiming to reduce costs and avoid layoffs, offered its employees a variety of shorter working week options including a 4-day work week, a 4-day week every second week, and a 10-week holiday period with corresponding percentage drops in pay. To address sched-uling issues and meet fluctuating consumer demand, workers were to negotiate their time off with their managers.[30] From management's per-spective, the work time experiment was unsuccessful; it failed to deliver the anticipated cost efficiencies. The reasons lie less in the move to shorter work time itself than lack of pre-planning and organizational change needed to accommodate the changed work environment. Other shorter work time experiments in Canada, such as work week reduc-tions at SaskTel, have resulted in productivity improvements.

Both management and labour at Bell came to the conclusion that the new system needed more flexibility and Bell has recently offered union members the 'option' of returning to a 5-day work week. Interestingly, only about 20 per cent of the workers have opted to return to the old 5-day work schedule even though a majority of workers were resistant to the shortened work week initially. 'The point here is that it is not just the move to shorter hours that is relevant, but how the transition is handled.'[31]

At the 1994 G7 Jobs Summit, labour in the industrialized countries prepared a paper, 'Trade Union Statement to the Detroit "G7" Conference on Unemployment and Job Creation', distributed via Robert Reich, the US Secretary of State. The paper called for familiar job creation policies such as investment in infrastructure, regional development, environ-mental improvement and military conversion. It concluded, however, that these moves would be insufficient. A broader solution would involve reducing and reorganizing working time by

1. facilitating voluntary and negotiated time off for the employed; and
2. extending equal employment rights to part-time workers and job sharers, hence, placing them on the same footing as full time workers.[32]

Canadian labour has grown more sympathetic to work time reform as a job creation strategy.[33] The United Steel Workers have argued that demand management policies aimed at achieving full employment were no longer sufficient and that they must be supplemented by complementary supply-side labour market policy including limiting excessive overtime and reducing standard working hours while maintaining high standards of living. Canadian labour has, however, been firmly resistant to proposals which call for work time reductions with basic pay cuts.[34]

Reduced working time became a 'side' issue in North America as a result of the post-war consensus between capital and labour, whereby each side concentrated on the increasing economic pie which was being produced by economic growth and consumer demand. The American AFL-CIO dropped its longstanding policy of a 30-hour work week in 1957, arguing that such a strategy could be an admission of failure if 'the nation's total level of production is not keeping up the pace.' This strategic positioning has made the US quite a distinctive labour society today, '[as] there is no single important US union that is committed to reducing work time as its primary bargaining or public policy agenda'.[35] However, a recent industrial dispute has broken with this American pattern. A successful 15-day strike in August 1997 by the Teamsters against the United Parcel Service demanded 'the transformation of thousands of part-time jobs into full-time jobs, [and] the reduction of the gap between part-time and full-time wages'. What was unusual but revealing was that popular opinion sided heavily with the strikers. The workers' demand for secure employment which offered a living wage struck a popular chord, an important factor in helping the union win the strike: 'The fight for full-time jobs had become a social issue for much of the working class.'[36]

Recent working time trends in Europe, North America and Australia indicate awareness and public concern over working time reduction and employment flexibility. Recent empirical studies have attempted to measure the employment effects of work time reductions. Proponents of working time reductions argued that such 'work sharing' would be an effective policy for reducing unemployment. Critics argued, however, 'that policies designed to shorten the work week or to increase work hour flexibility have created labour market rigidities which may actually raise the level of unemployment, regardless of policy intent'.[37] An analysis of these and other findings offers an opportunity to reconsider the work time debate.

First, studies indicate that there is no simple one-to-one relationship between work time reductions and job creation. The work time and employment relationship is complex and related to other forces in the economy, e.g. fixed costs per employee, increased use of overtime and higher wage rates. Therefore, it remains methodologically suspect to separate the effects of work time reduction from other economic variables in trying to determine its impact on employment creation.[38]

The empirical literature suggests that the employment generating potential of reduced work time, and the reduced work week in particular, is somewhat exaggerated. Western European studies have estimated employment effects ranging from 0.6 per cent increase to 0.15 per cent decrease resulting from a 1 per cent reduction in the standard work week.[39] The much-publicized French legislation would reduce the standard work week from 39 to 35 hours by 2000. Various studies project an employment effect ranging from 0.1 to +2 per cent.[40] If accurate, the effect of reduced working time on French unemployment would be marginal since unemployment currently stands at over 12 per cent.

Moreover, such factors as technological and organizational change, globalization and macroeconomic policy may have more of an impact on employment than the job creation effects of reduced work time.[41] Australian studies found that reduced working hours corresponded to increased employment in a rather limited number of industries and that the unemployment generated in those industries was mostly composed of part-time work. Overall, these studies found very modest job creation effects associated with reduced work time.[42]

The work time studies strongly suggest that the impact of work time reductions vary by industry. Consistent positive employment creation appears to be produced in a limited range of industries. Traditional manufacturing sectors are still more likely to produce full-time jobs than the service sector which continues to 'pump out' part-time jobs (a conventional pattern of employment which follows general trends within these sectors).[43] Another strong relationship continues to exist between the potential for reduced working time and employer cost structures and lost employee wages.[44] The obvious key issue for employers is the fixed costs per worker, while employees are likely to be torn between leisure and real buying power, with the latter winning out.

In 1986–7, the Donner Task Force addressed the issue of shorter work time. Its conclusion, based on US and European studies, was that the job-creation effects of reductions in the standard work week are usually insignificant because the cost increase associated with hours of work and overtime restrictions also reduce the demand for labour in general.

The task force argued that legislative changes do not automatically lead to hours reductions, nor do hours reductions automatically lead to new jobs. There are several limiting factors, such as the mismatch between the skills of the unemployed and those whose hours are being reduced, increased moonlighting, and alternative compensation arrangements to offset the overtime costs. However, the task force did see benefits in modifying the employment standards rules regarding hours of work and overtime to lessen the standard work week to 40 from 48 hours and limit mandatory overtime.[45] In a similar vein, a 1994 report raised concerns over work time polarization and its effects, but 'it strongly suggests that any movement to significantly shorten hours has to be the end result of largely voluntary and pragmatic agreement between the parties themselves in individual workplaces.' Consequently, the report did not recommend 'a legislated move to a four-and-one-half-day work week'.[46]

The benefits of reducing the work week remain unclear. However, if pre-existing studies caution us about exaggerated or unproven claims associated with work time reductions, we must be equally cautious in regard to the limitations of those empirical studies which have, for example, tended to focus upon the purported impact of minor reductions in hours. Under those conditions, employers are more able to make slight productivity adjustments to accommodate shorter working time. Significantly greater levels of job creation could result from a single large reduction of hours. One cannot discount the possibility, however, that employers may simply choose to replace labour with more investments in capital with corresponding job losses.[47]

As a political project, working time reform has potential. The idea of creating jobs through the reduction of work time embodies a popular logic and is easy to grasp – there is a 'common sense' to it. It is 'also something that people can see themselves actually doing and accomplishing something with'.[48] Past demands for the reduction of the work day became a significant political movement among workers and had an international appeal. The demand for working time reduction has the potential to forge a politically potent coalition of the overemployed, unemployed and underemployed.[49] Moreover, reduced work time without the loss of base pay challenges important aspects of capital's control over the exploitation of the labour force.

There are, however, limitations and dangers in this political agenda. In and of itself working time reform cannot solve the jobs crisis. It must be part of a larger policy package which will stimulate domestic growth and offer strong social security and labour standards protections. If pursued in isolation, work time reform will inevitably fail to create sufficient employment opportunities and will likely result in declining incomes for many. Such a scenario would prove politically fatal for work time reform advocates. Moreover, working time reform must also address the issue of 'global capitalism'. For example, substantive legislative reductions of working hours 'without simultaneously addressing the issue of capital flight is unthinkable'.[50]

Conclusion

In a more globalized and deregulated economy, national governments, especially those that have embraced a strong neo-liberal policy path, are increasingly limited in their capacities to positively influence employment creation through interventionist policies. None the less, governments still enjoy a range of policy options which are often discounted by neo-liberal critics of activist government. Europe has been more open to experimentation with work time reforms, enjoying some limited success. The European Union's Social Charter and labour standards directives, while far from ideal, do represent a more state interventionist approach to meeting the challenges of neo-liberal globalization. It is an approach which has resisted both the full-scale dismantling of social security systems and an activist labour market policy designed to stimulate job growth. Neo-liberalism has made significant inroads in Europe, but is certainly not as advanced as in the Anglo-American political economies.

Ironically, the evidence to date indicates that legislated reductions in the work week are likely to produce their most substantive employment generation effects in a time of sustained economic growth. However, the less visible but no less beneficial effects on job retention should be noted. Contemporary high rates of unemployment, even during periods of sustained expansion, suggest that governments will need to remain proactive with respect to job creation since markets, left to themselves, appear incapable of producing sufficient employment opportunities. A significant problem is that new job creation will also be highly uneven in its quality as employers replace large proportions of their core standard workforce with contingent workers suited to the demands of the new flexible economy and lean production. Of course, the movement away from 'good jobs' to 'bad jobs' is a more generic problem of the contemporary employment market.

An additional challenge is the problem of increased levels of income polarization. Many workers have only been able to sustain their standards of living by expanding their hours of work. Moreover, the threat of job loss has driven many workers to accumulate as many hours of work as possible in preparation for leaner times. In this context the sharing of work time entails potential losses of income through hours of work restrictions. This problem is particularly acute in North America because of greater levels of polarization, more volatile labour markets, and the lack of strong political advocates for this policy option.

Many studies have focused on a shorter work week. However, fundamental changes in the global economy and labour market suggest that we consider work time in its broadest terms – annual or lifetime working hours. There is some evidence that the encouragement of shorter working lives and more annual leisure time produce greater employment. Reduced work time should, consequently, be recast in broader terms. In any event, the potential for modest job gains and significant job retention effects through reduced work time does exist. While work time reform is not a panacea, it can play a supporting role in a policy package designed to manage high unemployment.

The political demand for a shorter work week (the 35-hour week) with no loss of pay has the potential to become a cross-national movement which could begin to pose an alternative agenda to the neo-liberal globalization framework. This radical initiative challenges capital's control over the labour process itself. However, if the demand for a reduced work week is cast in a less encompassing and a more economistic manner, it runs a greater risk of political failure. If work time reductions are accompanied by wage cuts they are unlikely to win broad worker support given the political economy of austerity faced by so many. Work week reform will not by itself solve the jobs crisis, and if sold this way the policy will be branded by its critics as a failure. Broad-based support for policies of work time reductions will only occur when it is 'tied to a much broader set of policies aimed at improving material living standards along with more leisure time'.[51]

Notes

1   M. Barlow and H. Robertson, *Class Warfare: the Assault on Canada's Schools* (Toronto: Key Porter Books, 1994), p. 63.
2   OECD, *The OECD Jobs Study: Facts, Analysis, Strategies* (Paris: OECD, 1994), pp. 9, 10; and Commission for Labor Cooperation, *North American Labor Markets: a Comparative Profile* (Dallar: Commission for Labor Cooperation, 1997), p. 8.
3   G. Betcherman, 'Globalization, Labour Markets and Public Policy', in R. Boyer and D. Drache, eds, *States Against Markets: the Limits of Globalization* (London: Routledge, 1996), p. 252.

4   S. McBride, 'The Political Economy of Economic Restructuring: Implications for the Labour Force', Paper presented to the International Workshop Conference on Human Resources Development, Work Organization and Learning in a Changing Economy, Green College, University of British Columbia, August 19–21, 1996.

5   Human Resources Development Canada, Report of the Advisory Group on Working Time and the Distribution (Ottawa: Ministry of Supply and Services, December 1994), p. 21; and Commission for Labor Cooperation, p. 73.

6   W. Riddell and A. Sharpe, 'The Canada–US Unemployment Rate Gap: an Introduction and Overview', *Canadian Public Policy*, 24, Supplement (Feb. 1998), pp. S9–10.

7   C. Offe, 'Towards a New Equilibrium of Citizens' Rights and Economic Resources?', in OECD, *Societal Cohesion and the Globalising Economy: What Does the Future Hold?* (Paris: OECD, 1997), p. 86.

8   B.M. Evans, S. McBride and J. Shields, 'National Governance Versus Globalization: Canadian Democracy in Question', *Socialist Studies Bulletin*, 54 (Oct.–Dec. 1998).

9   A. Donner, 'Redistribution of Working Hours: an Approach to Dealing with High Unemployment in Canada', in D. Drache and A. Ranachan, eds, *Warm Heart, Cold Country: Fiscal and Social Policy Reform in Canada* (Ottawa: The Caledon Institute of Social Policy, 1995), p. 140.

10   Commission for Labor Cooperation, p. 43.

11   D. Galarneau, 'The Redistribution of Overtime Hours', *Perspectives on Labour and Income*, 9, no. 4 (Winter 1997), p. 25.

12   R. Morissette, J. Myles and G. Picot, 'What is Happening to Earnings Inequality in Canada?', Business and Labour Market Analysis Group, Analytical Studies Branch, Statistics Canada, no. 60 (1993).

13   OECD, *Employment Outlook: 1996* (Paris: OECD, 1996).

14   Morissette et al., op. cit. 7.

15   Commission for Labor Cooperation, op.cit. p. 79.

16   See Morissette et al.

17   M. Drolet and R. Morissette, 'Working More? Less? What do Workers Prefer?', *Perspectives on Labour and Income*, 9, no. 4 (Winter 1997), p. 35.

18   B. Bluestone and S. Rose, 'Overworked and Underemployed: Unravelling an Economic Enigma', *The American Prospect* (March–April 1997).

19   A. Jackson as cited in: 'The New Work Order: a Round Table on the Future of Work', *This Magazine* (July/Aug. 1998), p. 16.

20   'Working Time in Europe: Part One', *European Industrial Relations Review* (March 1997), p. 4.

21   Ibid., p. 14.

22   G. Bosch, 'From 40 to 35 Hours – Reduction and Flexibilisation of the Work Week in the Federal Republic of Germany', *International Labour Review*, 129, no. 5 (1990).

23   'Working Time in Europe: Part One', p. 20.

24   *Fiet* (online journal), 23 Oct. 1997.

25   'Working Time in Europe: Part One', p. 20.

26   EIRO (info website), 'Working Hours and Equal Opportunities in Recent Company Level Bargaining' (Oct. 1997), pp. 1, 3.

27   EIRO, '35 Hour Working Week Adopted' (Nov. 1997), p. 1.

28 E. Leary, 'Shorter Work Time', Boston Forum on Shorter Work Time (Nov. 1996), p. 3.

29 B. Cross, 'Deal Could Mean 1,000 New Jobs', *The Windsor Star* (15 Sept. 1993).

30 Human Resources Development Canada, *Reduced Hours at Bell Canada: an Experiment That's Working* (Ottawa: Human Resources Development Canada, April 1998), p. 2.

31 J. White and D. Goulet, 'Contemplating the Four-Day Week: Lessons from Bell Canada', *Policy Options*, 19, no. 3 (April 1998), pp. 31–2.

32 R. White, 'A Global New Deal to Create Jobs', *The Globe and Mail* (14 March 1994).

33 A. Jackson, 'Employment Creation', in Canadian Centre for Policy Alternatives and Choices: a Coalition for Social Justice, *Alternative Federal Budget Papers 1997* (Ottawa: Canadian Centre for Policy Alternatives, 1997), pp. 309–11.

34 V. Galt, 'CLC Asks for Laws to Curb Overtime', *The Globe and Mail* (17 May 1994); and V. Galt, 'Union Says Overtime Talking People's Jobs', *The Globe and Mail* (11 Dec. 1993).

35 Leary, 'Shorter Work Time', p. 3.

36 S. Cohen and K. Moody, 'Unions, Strikes and Class Consciousness Today', in L. Panitch and C. Leys, eds, *The Communist Manifesto Now: Socialist Register 1998* (Suffolk: The Merlin Press, 1998), pp. 115, 113.

37 S. Rosenberg, 'More Work for Some, Less Work for Others: Working Hours, Collective Bargaining and Government Policy in the United States, France and Germany', *Changes in Working Time in Canada and the United States* (Ottawa: Canadian Employment Research Forum, June 1996), p. 4.

38 See A. Molloy and J. Shields, 'Tackling Unemployment through Working Time Reductions: a Cautionary Tale', *Window on Work*, 2 (July 1998).

39 G. Watson, 'Hours of Work in Great Britain and Europe: Evidence from the UK and European Labour Force Surveys', *Employment Gazette* (Nov. 1992).

40 Nando Net et Agence France Presse, 'Battle Lines Drawn in France over 35 Hour Week' (26 Jan. 1998).

41 J. Bastian, K. Hinrichs and K. van Kevelaer, 'Problems of Employment-Effective Working Time Policies – Theoretical Considerations and Lessons from France, the Netherlands and West Germany', *Work, Employment & Society*, 3, no. 3 (1989).

42 J. Mangan and J. Steinke, 'Working-Time Reductions: a Survey of the Australian Experience', *Industrial Relations Journal*, 2 (1987).

43 Ibid.

44 G.R. Steele, 'Legal and Trade Union Limitations Upon Hours of Work: the Problem of Overtime', *Economic and Industrial Democracy*, 7 (1986).

45 Ontario Task Force on Hours of Work and Overtime, *Report of Ontario Task Force on Hours of Work and Overtime* (Toronto: Queen's Printer, 1987).

46 Human Resources Development Canada, p. 25.

47 J. Blyton, 'The Working Time Debate in Western Europe', *Industrial Relations* (Spring 1987).

48 J. White as cited in 'The New Work Order', *This Magazine*, p. 18.

49 A. Gorz, *Capitalism, Socialism, Ecology* (London: Verso, 1994).

50 Stanley Aronowitz and William DiFazio, *The Jobless Future: Sci-Tech and the Dogma of Work* (Minneapolis: University of Minnesota Press, 1994).

51 Bluestone and Rose, p. 69.

13
The Dilemma of Organizing: Trade Union Strategy in International Perspective

Carla Lipsig-Mummé

Introduction[1]

Writing in 1972 on the emergence of the multinational corporation and its impact on unionism, Charles Levinson, then Secretary-General of the International Federation of Chemical and General Workers' Unions, observed: '[P]erhaps the most critical challenge to the trade union movement in accommodating to the rapidly changing environment... is to break out of its social confinement and isolation in order to intervene directly in the primary area of economic decision-making. Nothing is going to stop [the] transfer of real power from the nation-state to the international corporation. The requirement is for international organizations with policies and power to confront and redirect these influences.'[2]

This chapter deals with the renewal of organizing strategy in several developed countries, and its relationship to crafting effective international labour action. Over the past decade, trade unions in Australia, the UK, the US and to a lesser extent Canada, have turned to organizing new members as their principal strategy for redressing declining authority and power. They have also shared tactics internationally.

Union leaders in all the developed economies stress the need for new, effective international union action to cope with new forms of international corporate integration. But international union strategy is slow in developing. Nor is there acknowledgement that new organizing within developed countries is linked to the effectiveness of international union response to corporate globalization. Levinson's 1972 statement identifies the central issues defining today's trade union choices: how can unions recapture representation of the new, but still domestically anchored, working classes, at the same time as they transcend competition amongst unions in different countries, in order to confront and contain capital internationally?

Context

The rapid and profound economic transformations in the high-wage, Western capitalist countries have been experienced by the union movements as a three-pronged dissolution of post-war welfare state relationships.

By the early 1990s in Canada, the United Kingdom, France and elsewhere, the *centrifugal pressures* pushing the nation into supranational political and economic links with other countries catalysed longstanding *centripetal pressures*, expressed as regional or national separatisms. Combined with the reduction of protectionism, the development of free trade zones, common currencies, and more open labour and product markets, these pressures resulted in the evisceration of many states' ability or willingness to maintain standards for their citizens, responsibilities that had long been associated with welfare statism. They also put unbearable pressure on classic trade union political strategies, which had been based on the nation state as the pivotal arena for exercising influence and power.

In addition, by accelerating the integration of continental labour and product markets between unequal national partners, the trading blocs contributed to the re-emergence of metropolis–hinterland economic relations *within* regions, and possibly to a renaissance of trade union imperialism as well. As the locus of decision-making migrates to the metropolis, how realistic is it for unions to target the junior-partner state, such as the Canadian, if it no longer serves as the principal arena for defining social priorities and economic policies?

Internationally, union movements are being forced to reexamine their relationship to the (largely unorganized) working class in the light of these developments. In the high-wage countries, a double polarization is occurring. The welfare state's deepening and broadening of worker security created a certain convergence between organized and unorganized workers. This began to break apart in the 1980s. Now, however, unemployment and a weakened safety net have intensified tensions between unionized and unorganized populations, with the latter looking at the former as a labour aristocracy. In addition, the differential impact of neo-liberalism on employment in the manufacturing and primary sectors, the public sector and the private service industries, has driven a wedge among unions representing workers in these three groups, whose priorities and relation to the state are diverging. At the same time as workers in a particular sector in several countries *within* the North American trading bloc are being made to compete with each other for migrating manufacturing jobs, the need for effective, cross-border union alliances on the basis of industry is both greater than ever and more threatening to multi-sector, *national* union solidarities. How do these pressures relate to large-scale organizing of the domestic working classes?

In many developed countries, union movements, faced with important membership decline since the 1980s, have turned to organizing as the strategy of choice for renewal and survival. The language of the organizing renaissance is omnipresent but it does not, directly, speak to the issues of international solidarity. Two tensions define the language of the return to organizing: between transformative and instrumental organizing; and between unions and other organizations and movements which represent workers' interests. The term 'organizing model' has been coined to describe the new approach to organizing.

The organizing model: transformative vs instrumental approaches

The organizing model has come to symbolize the way in which activist unions view themselves. It was coined in the US, and spread to Australia, the UK and Canada. The minimal international consensus on definition is that the organizing model is an attitude and a world-view. It represents a union's will to place recruitment at the top of its list of priorities. It signals that the union is on the move and wants to be seen as a militant and democratic organization, and that the union is willing to make changes in the way it allocates resources and assigns staff.

Beyond the minimal shared definition, there is an important distinction to be made between instrumental and transformative approaches. *The instrumental approach* knows that new union recruitment is essential, but it sees organizing as saving the union by adding to its numbers, only. Unions which seek primarily to increase membership numbers tend to think in terms of union survival and market share rather than the survival of the labour movement. Recruitment is not viewed as a source of union transformation. Rather, organizing is the union's 'core business'. In the UK and Australia, instrumental organizing is likely to focus on infill recruitment: signing up workers in work sites where the union is already present. In Canada and the US, the instrumental organizers may also focus on greenfield sites and define organizing as a campaign.

From *the transformative perspective* on the other hand, organizing is synonymous with union renewal which can only occur through democratization and rank and file militancy, not simply through adding to the numbers. A distinction is made between recruitment, which is seen as instrumental and opportunistic, related to individual unions protecting their 'market share'; and organizing, which is seen as revolutionary and transformative. In practice, of course, recruitment is a necessary condition for organizing. But too often it has been seen as the end of the member – union relationship rather than as the beginning. Recruitment should be part of *an organizing cycle* which begins with recruitment and moves to integrating the new member into an activist role within the union. As members, recruits become part of the internal life of the union. Ideally, newly recruited members can become activists within the union's own ranks, so that recruits become recruiters at the same time as they become educators, counsellors and negotiators. Organizing unions reduce the money and staff allocated to servicing, and redirect it to organizing. Everything the union does revolves around bringing in more members, and staff who do not learn the new culture are often marginalized.[3]

There are some real similarities in the population these unions seek to organize: women are the majority, and most operate predominantly or partly in the service sector. In other cases, like the Canadian Autoworkers or UNITE, either the union is ideologically committed to organizing that will transform the power of labour, or its core population comes from traditionally exploited and self-aware groups.

What these diverse unions share is the insistence that organizing is a way of transforming every aspect of trade unionism, to turn it into a social movement. Thus, transformative organizing will have a considerable impact on the internal operations of unions, far more than instrumental organizing might suppose.

One potential impact is on servicing. Particularly in the US, it has been quite common to oppose organizing to servicing – for the past generation, 98 per cent of union budgets have been going to servicing, and just 2 per cent to organizing. Servicing has come to be seen as focusing on the minutiae of grievances and arbitration that have bogged down trade unionism. In this view, servicing stands in the way of organizing, and has come to symbolize the do-nothing unionism of the 1970s and 1980s. But servicing members is not a shabby, despicable task.

Responding to members' needs is what unions are all about. In fact, organizing and servicing are the two faces of what every union needs to do and do well.

If unions redirect their resources massively to recruiting, and if recruiting is a radical, transformative and inclusive activity – how will the union service its already-recruited members? The answer seems to lie in unions renegotiating priorities, training and responsibilities within the organization, particularly between staff and membership, and drawing more upon union activists.

Internal organizing: salting, seeding and educating

Intimately linked to the debate between servicing and organizing is the idea of internal organizing, which while having various meanings, has a common base which comprises two basic ideas: a union needs to engage members in the work of the union on a regular and inclusive basis; and organizing should manifest itself in all the work a union does. Both these ideas imply making the union more *permeable* to members and community groups.

In both Canada and the US, internal organizing means the continued education and mobilization of people who are already members: organizing the organized. The Canadian Union of Public Employees, with 460,000 members Canada's largest union, focuses on internal education and mobilization. The union is deeply concerned that the down-sizing and privatization of its work sites has made the traditional separation between 'the union' and 'the members' no longer useful: 'We know from first-hand and bitter experience that recruiting and organizing workers into a union doesn't by itself necessarily advance the interests of the workers. Once organized, workers must fight for a collective agreement, fight to keep that collective agreement, fight for their jobs, fight for their rights forever after.'[4] Internal organizing thus becomes a lever to transform all aspects of union life, not merely a tool for increasing membership numbers.[5]

Internal organizing can mean signing up unorganized workers in unionized workplaces which have departments or occupational categories that have been left unorganized, or in workplaces that have no provisions for automatic union membership for all who work there. This is infill organizing and currently figures very importantly in Australia and the UK.[6]

It can mean also 'salting' and 'seeding'. In salting, unions 'sprinkle' rank and file (rather than staff) organizers in unorganized workplaces, where they obtain employment. They become the base for a new recruitment campaign. In seeding, students and young workers who also attend school are the activists. They are 'cultivated' both as future organizers and as young workers who can carry the seeds of union membership with them to future employment. In Australia, some unions have associate memberships on university campuses for students who have been members during summer jobs, or part-time during the academic year. They keep their membership when they return to school. In the US, participants in Union Summer have formed Associates Clubs on a number of campuses to keep them in touch with the union they organized for, when back at school.[7]

In Canada, seeding is beginning to be discussed differently. Most students at university have part-time jobs (off campus) while they study. Because the average number of workers employed at work sites has been dropping, most workplaces are more difficult to organize. Since university and high school campuses are where the largest numbers of young workers gather together, there is growing discussion of trying out union organizing drives which begin on the campuses and recruit students-as-workers (wherever they work). Unionizing campaigns carried out on campuses by a collaboration between student organizations and unions would organize students-as-workers from every industry and sector. The newly unionized student worker then carries her membership back to her workplace.[8] For Canadian unions, this campus organizing will raise the question of membership status for workers who are in workplaces without a bargaining unit.

It is possible to identify a final form of seeding. Faced with massive privatization and contracting out, public sector unions in health, telecommunications and education are asking their (former) members to carry the seed of the union into their new, non-union employment. The hope is that they will become the 'salt' of a future organizing campaign in these workplaces. This is the basis of the Organized Personnel Placement initiative created by the Communications, Electrical and Plumbing Union in Victoria, Australia.[9]

Thus organizing is a key union strategy for maintaining relevance in the global era. First, unions need to reach out to the next working class whose identity is multiple, fragmented and often based on gender, age, language, ethnicity. Are unions developing new ways to work with the community and community organizations in order to create new anchorage in civil society? Second, how does domestic union strategy in coordinating organizing and developing community unionism, link to international union solidarity?

Community unionism and new identities: Canadian patterns

In most developed countries, two parallel agents for the organization of workers are emerging: *recruitment for membership* by existing unions, and *representation* by other workers' organizations – ethnic and community associations, inner-city renewal groups, workers' centres representing foreign workers, young immigrants, women's organizations, injured workers' groups – which defend workers against violation of their rights, but which may not serve as a first step to joining a union.

'Community unionism' is the North American term used to describe a range of new links between unions and community groups. It represents a profound shift for unions away from the historic assumption of union hegemony in worker organization and representation.[10] A core definition of community unionism would include: a self-redefinition by a union so as to see itself as a part of the community; a new approach to union definition of goals and strategies which considers alliances with the community essential; the definition of the union as a type of community organization; recognition that community organizations which work on work-related issues are legitimate players in the field.

The questions of representation and identity are crucial here. In the late twentieth century, the labour movements of developed countries no longer reflect the demographic composition of the working class. In Canada, young workers represent 17 per cent of the workforce, but only 5.7 per cent of the labour movement.[11] In most of these countries, women, workers of colour, workers whose first language is neither English nor French, new migrants, are over-represented in the under-unionised, bad jobs, and under-represented in union leadership. As young workers recently said at a large conference bringing them into contact with the leadership of the English Canadian labour movement: 'The labour movement is not structured in the ways we work.'[12]

For trade unions, this continued reliance on membership from the former working class threatens the reconstruction of community links. Historically, unions were always community-based. Community was defined historically by class, occupation and residence. Over the past 50 years, however, class and place of residence have receded as primary sources of labour identity and union engagement. This has much to do with urbanization and the proliferation of occupations 'between labour and capital', but it also has to do with the post-war welfare state.

In the 1990s newly defined community linkages are becoming important. The new communities of identity have complex roots, and they point to a relationship between work and life which differs profoundly from both pre- and post-war models. In the contemporary fragmented labour market, unions are seeking to organize workers whose identification with employment is partial, negative, anxious, precarious, instrumental and mediated through ethnic, educational age, gender or linguistic identity.

Identity, however, implies a variable degree of awareness of community of interest. Feminist organizing with and within unions represents the most important model of the past 25 years, but it is far from uniform.[13] In some places young workers are just now beginning to crystallize their sense of identity both as workers and as students. They link education and work in a complex ebb and flow of participation and marginality which may force unions to appeal to them on terms different from – and more complex than – those through which they appealed to their parents. And as employment of the garage-and-basement variety in the service sector flourishes anew, prematurely elderly workers returning to the labour market after down-sizing, and trapped in those pre-welfare state working conditions, may form their own communities of identity. These may be organizing tools, certainly, but they are also ways of life and ways of relating to an anomic civil society.

The danger of these new identities is that they isolate labour movements further and expose them to claims that they represent a labour aristocracy and are no more than a special interest group.[14]

Individual unions and national labour movements have dealt with the promise and threat of the newly fragmented, otherly-identified working class in a range of ways, from the instrumental to the inclusive. They have sought out representatives of the 'new communities' to train as organizers and elected leaders; set aside seats on governing bodies for their representatives; modernized and diversified the historic linguistic and ethnic caucuses, adding gender, age and sometimes sexual preference to foster involvement by under-represented groups; linked with particular communities over particular strikes; sought to develop union–community coalitions over the dismantling of the welfare state and moved towards 'like recruits like' strategies. They have been less comfortable with autonomous organizing among particular identity groups, and the linking of identity group caucuses within the union to external, larger social movements. Here, workers' centres may reflect the needs of particular communities.

One interesting Canadian innovation in community unionism is the International Ladies' Garment Workers Union in Ontario, which merged with other textile and clothing unions to form UNITE, the Union of Needle Trades Employees, in 1995. The ILGWU, a US-based union, was famous prior to 1950 as a visionary, creative organizer of women workers in sweatshop situations. It has been the immigrant union *par excellence*, and the women's industrial union *par excellence*. In Canada it was not, until the 1990s, a women's union led by women.

By 1990, its membership had dwindled dramatically, to less than 2,000 in Ontario because of manufacturing restructuring, the rise of homeworking, the use of non-union contractors, and the shift of production to Mexico and the Pacific Rim. Facing imminent extinction, its young and creative feminist leadership consulted widely and then refashioned the union's whole way of working. First, it commissioned sophisticated studies of the changing structure of corporate ownership and responsibility in women's clothing, and then applied legislative pressure to modify employment standards so as to protect homeworkers who had been defined as self-employed. Second, the union developed joint campaigns with the smaller Canadian designers and obtained government funding for garment production to stay at home. Third, it reached out into the ethnic communities of garment workers – the South-east Asian, Chinese, Indian subcontinent and Caribbean communities – and, by hiring organizers who spoke the requisite languages, organized an Association of Homeworkers whose members became associate members of the union. These members staged public demonstrations which exposed the ultimate responsibility of the big retailers for sweatshop conditions. Fourth, through its parent US union, Canadian ILGWU made links to garment workers in Mexico and Honduras working for the same retailers. Finally, the union moved to organizing the outlets for the clothing its traditional core membership produced – the salespersons in the clothing boutiques.

But there is a postscript. By 1997, the union had transformed its entire internal structure into an instrument for organizing. But it also realized that organizing small groups of home workers could not, alone, be a long-term proposition because it was not viable in terms of the resources of a small, over-stretched union. It therefore turned its attention to more traditional, blitz campaigns in larger workplaces and a much wider range of industries. The blitz campaigns, which were quite successful in recruiting new union members, both support the smaller, slower, more difficult organizing of the invisible homeworkers in Toronto's Third World garment industry, and raise the union's fortunes and credibility.

The blitz campaigns created a forceful internal debate about gender and contrasting strategies for organizing within the union. Is the US organizing model – reaching out aggressively to visible workers in factories, labs and stores – suitable to organizing women workers, and particularly women workers from new immigrant communities? Is the community union approach to organizing – ready to work with vulnerable and largely invisible workers, so respectful of diversity and difference, patient with small groups, willing to struggle for even small-scale gains in respect – more suitable to these women, in this industry, in these times? Or does this rejection of the organizing Model assume you cannot do both at one time?

Community unionism and workers' centres

The history of union relations to 'the community' has too often been short-term and instrumental: we need help with this strike, and your interests and ours coincide. In the US, long-term frustration and marginality led to the formation of a range of Workers' Centres: 'Much of the most innovative organizing prefigures new union structures; linking workplaces and communities; revolving around "worker centers"'.[15]

But do these workers' centres become unions? Do they recruit workers to unions? Or do their frustrating experiences with inactive or instrumental unions lead them to become parallel union formations?

In Canada, there are fewer workers' centres than in the US. They fall into three categories. Long-established groups like Au bas de l'Echelle (Montreal) and WIACT (Toronto) are supported by government and private funding, and see themselves as pre-union formations: first-stage sources of information and referral for workers whom they hope will unionize. Groups like Intercede (representing immigrant domestic workers) and the Parkdale Legal Clinic defend workers when their rights are violated. They see themselves neither as alternatives to unions nor as pre-union formations. Finally, there is the new workers' centre formed by the Canadian Union of Postalworkers with local community action groups in Winnipeg, as a place for trade union and community activists to mobilize over a range of community issues.

The US is different: 'Workers centers fall into several categories. Some centers work closely with unions and see unionization as an ultimate goal. Others want nothing to do with the labor movement ... While they don't represent workers in collective bargaining, some centers support workers engaged in bargaining struggles, but only as part of a larger strategy to address the broader concerns of workers in the workplace and community. Centers who do this kind of work view unionization as a tactic; not the end of workplace struggles.'[16]

One such ambivalent experiment is the 9 to 5 Association in Cincinnati. It traces its origins to the early 1970s, when 9 to 5 started in Boston as an independent clerical workers' association.[17] By the late 1970s the association began collaborating with the Service Employees International Union, and in 1981 it became the National District 925 of the SEIU, its national clerical workers' union organization. It is one of the rare occupational or sectoral unions in the US. But an independent 9 to 5 association continued to exist, in free-form relationship to SEIU and to SEIU District 925.[18]

In mid-1994, SEIU funded the 9 to 5 Association in Cincinnati to establish a workers' centre for clerical workers. The idea was to test out the possibilities of city-wide sectoral organizing of clerical workers. From the union's perspective, it was to be a new way to get into the workplace: not to target particular employers, but to aim to unionise 1 per cent of all clerical employees in Cincinnati, then 10 per cent, then 30 per cent.

One year later, from the union's perspective, it was all moving too slowly. From the perspective of the dozen or so staff and activists who work for the Association, however, only slow movement was possible. Respect for the diversity of clerical workers, their fear of losing their jobs, consciousness-raising, in other words – meant slow but creative movement. One activist said: 'The 9 to 5 Association is more innovative than most unions allow.' And the 'Dignity Dollars' which they distributed throughout the financial district, or the 'Rate Your Job' leaflets with which they papered downtown Cincinnati, attest to their creativity and ability to speak to non-union workers about their issues.

SEIU, on the other hand, paying a number of salaries, office rent and costs for more than a year, wanted to see at least one union local formed, or even a pre-union formation emerge. It began to rethink its relation to the Association, while the Association was considering diversifying its funding base.

The dual anchorage of worker centres – in the community and in the union – allows them the potential for creativity. Their provocative existence and credibility within the immigrant communities of developed countries also leads us to ask: can workers' centres provide a new form for linking union action in developed and underdeveloping economies?

From organizing to international action

The portrait painted above is of trade unions in four developed countries articulating new organizing strategies to respond to perceived new domestic realities. These strategies entail change of union practices, innovation on links to external groups, a willingness to consider ceding hegemony in worker organization. All this adds up to strategic innovation – necessary but not sufficient in the face of employment shifts, continentalization and globalization.

Enter Charles Levinson, still relevant after 25 years. His questions go to the heart of the contemporary union dilemma. If the nation-state continues to be viable as an instrument for regulating national economies and national labour markets, then labour's primary focus must remain the national arena. Union strategy will focus on nationally-coordinated organizing, or at the very least, a separation between strategy for national union organizing and strategy for international labour rights. Not much faith is put in the creation of international 'governments' here.

If, however, as Levinson believed, the nation-state is no longer a viable arena for economic regulation, TNCs have emerged as the institution of power in the post-national world. Labour needs economic and political leverage over capital through internationally coordinated collective bargaining, and transnational unions organized by sector and by world company council. This 'new internationalist' argument foresees an internationalizing working class confronting internationalized capital. Minimally, national trade union centres will decline in relevance.

Following Levinson's formulation, two routes emerge. *The coalition route* is international labour solidarity from the bottom up. It brings together unionists and community activists within a developed country, and links them to similar coalitions in underdeveloped countries and other developed countries, over issues of human rights, labour rights violations, trade union rights and social justice. These campaigns have strong moral content. They weave together alliances that traditional unionism has not, and are issue-based and internationalist in outlook. But their strength has usually been in their local anchorage. And they have not given priority to the establishment of ongoing institutions of coordinated labour, or labour–community action.[19] There is about them a kind of guerrilla mentality, which contrasts significantly with the second route, the one Levinson espoused.

The second route creates *international structures for the coordination of trade union action*. It is sectorally based, grouping workers in food production around the globe with each other, or teachers, public servants, metalworkers, chemical workers, etc. It is based on international information sharing leading to coordinated collective bargaining, by TNC or even by industrial sector. Some international trade secretariats (ITSs) are active on this road, and it is meant to inform union action in particular countries, rather than to integrate it.

Coordinated collective bargaining works to set up the structures, the alliances and the arena to constrain the international mobility that makes TNCs so difficult to confront. This is where Charles Levinson put his hopes. *Continental sectoral secretariats* are regroupings of all unions in a given sector, like telecommunications or hydro-electric power, on a given continent. These should be information-sharing devices, which allow the unions to link with each other and with the social movements working in the same area. *World Company Councils* already in existence include all unions which bargain with a particular TNC, like General Motors, Rio Tinto, Nestlé. Coordinated collective bargaining among all the unions in one WCC would allow the unions to coordinate demands, coordinate expiry dates and strike support and bargain for influence over investment, research and corporate development policy.

Is synthesis between the two roads possible? It depends on the arena of struggle. Marjorie Griffin Cohen's argument in 1998 for moving beyond the purist versus revisionist debate on NAFTA is relevant here.[20] Griffin Cohen made the case for creating international regulatory institutions and arenas in which labour and community forces and national governments can struggle to set the rules by which footloose multinational capital can be confronted and constrained.

In these potential supranational arenas, international collective bargaining, coordinated by a WCC or by ITS, would confront capital according to international rules. But in member countries, local and international union–community coalitions would continue to confront violations by TNCs and complaisant governments in the street, at the factory, in the community.

Conclusions and the questions they raise

Internationally labour is at a turning point. The late 1990s were, like the 1920s, a time in which capital almost unilaterally reshaped the world for workers and their communities, while governments were complicit, compliant or incompetent. Then, perhaps as now, unions found it difficult to move beyond their natural constituency, the *former* working class. Now, as then, unions are at centre stage of the working-class crisis: responsible for their future and for the future of working-class defence. The question becomes: can existing unions move beyond their current strategic anachronism and transform themselves sufficiently, creating a new internationalism, integrating it with new organizing and anchoring it in the new communities of identity? Or do new points of solidarity have to be created?

Notes

1 The author wishes to thank Kate Laxer for her work in creating the bibliography, and SSHRC for its financial support.
2 C. Levinson, *International Trade Unionism* (London: Allen and Unwin: 1972), p. 2.
3 D. Schneidermann (Vice-President, Service Employees International Union), interview, Cincinnati, Ohio, Dec. 1995.
4 M. Ballantyne (Assistant to the President, Canadian Union of Public Employees), letter to author, Feb. 1999.
5 CUPE, *Organizing: a Renewed Commitment*. Policy Statement adopted at the 1993 National Convention; *Organizing the Organized*, adopted at the 1995 National Convention.
6 Interviews with L. Connor (Manager, ACTU Trust), Melbourne, Dec. 1998; P. Slape (Secretary, Australian Services Union), Melbourne, March 1996; J. Roe (Assistant Secretary, Victorian Branch, Australian Manufacturing Workers Union), Melbourne, Feb. 1998.
7 In Australia the Australian Services Unions has created clubs of associate membership in Victoria. In the US, UNITE has created university clubs of Union Summer trainees who worked on UNITE campaigns and then returned to school.
8 'The Next Working Class Speaks Out', *Our Times*, 18, no. 1 (1999), pp. 39–42.
9 L. Cooper, interview, Melbourne, Feb. 1999.
10 A. Bank, 'The Power and Promise of Community Unionism', *Labor Research Review*, 18 (Winter 1991), pp. 17–31.
11 C. Lipsig-Mummé and K. Laxer, *Organising and Union Membership: a Canadian Profile*, CRWS Working Paper Series, Jan. 1998.
12 'The Next Working Class', a special edition of *Our Times Magazine*, Jan.–Feb. 1999.
13 L. Briskin, 'Equity and Economic Restructuring in the Canadian Labour Movement', *Economic and Industrial Democracy*, 15 (1990), pp. 89–112. D.S. Cobble, *Women and Unions: Forging a Partnership* (Ithaca: ILR Press, 1993); A.H. Cook, V. Lorwin and A.K. Daniels, *The Most Difficult Revolution* (Ithaca: ILR Press, 1992); M. Cornish and L. Spink, *Organizing Unions*, 2nd edn (Toronto: Second Story Press, 1998).
14 L.M. Ching, 'It's A Respect thing: Organizing Immigrant Women', *Equal Means* (Fall 1993), pp. 21–3.
15 P. Rachleff, 'Worker's Centers', *The Nation* (21 Feb. 1994), p. 227.
16 M. Hollens, *Labor Notes* (Sept. 1994), p. 8.
17 D. Schneidermann (International Vice President, Service Employees International Union), interview, Cincinnati, Ohio, Dec. 1995.
18 C. Cameron, 'High Noon at 9 to 5: Reflections on a Decade of Organizing', *Labor Research Review*, 8 (1996), pp. 103–9.
19 K. Moody, *Workers in a Lean World* (London: Verso Press, 1997).
20 M. Griffin Cohen, 'What to do about Globalization', Canadian Centre for Policy Alternatives, 1997.

14
Here to Stay? The 1998 Australian Waterfront Dispute and its Implications

John Wiseman

Australian waterfront disputes have a long and bloody history. In 1890 striking maritime workers seeking the right to be union members were shot and beaten as police and troops broke the strike.[1] In 1919 maritime unionists picketing against scabs in Fremantle were violently attacked by a force personally led by the Western Australian Premier. In 1928 more wharfies were shot and one was killed in another attack on pickets at Melbourne's Station Pier. The bitter 1998 Australian waterfront battle was part of a long history of concerted attempts by employers and the state to break unionism on the Australian waterfront.[2]

However, the 1998 waterfront battle also signals a new context for Australian industrial relations. While maritime trade has always been crucial for this island nation, the globalizing strategies of both Labor and Liberal governments intensified pressure on Australian employers to maintain international competitiveness by cutting costs and increasing productivity. The industrial relations policies of the Howard Liberal government represent a particularly brutal attempt to crush unionism in Australia and bring about a historic shift in the balance of power from labour to capital.

Here, the 1998 Australian waterfront dispute is used to demonstrate the dilemmas facing unions in resisting corporate and state assaults in an age of globalisation. The core lesson is that it is truer than ever that local and national struggles between labour and capital are fought on a global stage and require transnational resistance and solidarity.

Full circle? The historical context of the 1998 waterfront battle

The central demand of the striking seamen, backed by waterside workers, coal miners and shearers, in 1890 was the right to union membership. The failure of the strike led Australian workers to conclude that effective industrial strategy had to be based on a combination of legal and political power. It was the catalyst which led to the creation both of the Australian Labor Party and the uniquely Australian system of centralized industrial courts for wage fixing and dispute resolution.

By the 1980s significant numbers of Australian employers had come to the conclusion that centralized wage fixing should be broken. They began to publicly canvas strategies for breaking the Australian union movement and turning the clock back to pre-union individual contracts between employers and workers.[3]

The overall strategic direction of the Hawke and Keating Labor governments can be described as 'progressive competitiveness' in which radical restructuring and globalization of the Australian economy was accompanied by attempts to soften the impact on vulnerable groups.[4] Government enthusiasm for free trade and international competitiveness increased the pressure on importers and exporters to raise productivity; transport infrastructure was identified as a prime target.

The close connection between the Australian Labor Party and the ACTU meant that the Labor governments could not pursue full labour market deregulation as quickly as the business community would have liked. None the less the various 'Accords' negotiated between the Labor government and the ACTU led to a fundamental shift away from arbitration and the award system towards decentralized enterprise bargaining. The 1980s also saw a steady decline in union membership which further weakened the industrial power of the labour movement.

The Howard Liberal government came to power in 1996 determined to pursue an even faster and more savage programme of free-market, neo-liberal economic policies with a particular emphasis on labour market deregulation. The cornerstone of their industrial relations strategy was the introduction of the 1996 Workplace Relations Act.[5]

The Act ended the centralized industrial relations system, undermining the role of unions, and moved many Australians onto individual employment contracts. Closed shops were banned and severe fines were introduced for strike action taken during the life of an enterprise agreement. Employers were given the capacity to pursue massive damages claims against unions taking 'secondary boycott' strike action to support other unions.

The government immediately signalled that waterfront workers would be prime targets for the full range of weapons provided by the Workplace Relations Act. The Waterside Worker's Federation (WWF) and the Seamen's Union have long had a well-deserved reputation for being two of the most militant unions in Australia. This militant tradition had its roots in the bitter struggles of the 1920s and 1930s against the low pay and often lethal working conditions which were endemic in a system of non-unionized and casualized labour hire practices involving daily 'auctions' of workers. Unionization was the key to decent working conditions, job security and a more equal bargaining position with the stevedoring companies.

The combination of a strong Communist Party presence in the union leadership and a key strategic position in relation to an island nation's shipping lanes led the WWF and the Seamen's Union to become powerful players in domestic and international industrial disputes as well as broader political conflicts. Over the last 60 years the Australian maritime unions have often acted as the 'shock troops' of the Australian union movement, often in solidarity with unionists in other countries. They campaigned to improve working conditions on non-unionized ships operating under 'flags of convenience'.

Australian maritime unions have taken a wide range of boycott, strike and fund-raising measures to support many international civil rights struggles and political conflicts in settings as diverse as Indonesia, South Africa, Vietnam and the United States. This record of domestic and international solidarity has triggered the obsessive determination of Australian employers and conservative governments to destroy their power. However, the history of international solidarity has provided these unions with a powerful international support base.

Throughout the 1980s and early 1990s the maritime unions (now merged and renamed the Maritime Union of Australia or MUA) came under constant pressure to improve productivity and reduce manning numbers. However, as the truth about the Howard government's real intentions in provoking the waterfront dispute has emerged it has become clear that the real agenda was far broader. The aim of the government and key employer groups was to use the conflict with the MUA as part of an overall strategy to rewrite the industrial relations rules in Australia so as to move unions to the margins and institutionalize direct bargaining between employers, individuals and non-unionized groups of workers.[6]

'An activist approach to waterfront reform': the Howard government's battle plan

Once the Workplace Relations Act was passed in October 1996 the government was able to begin the implementation of its assault on the Australian trade union movement – all in the name of improving waterfront productivity.[7]

In July 1997, Industrial Relations Minister Peter Reith presented a confidential strategy paper on waterfront 'reform' to the Cabinet.[8] The objectives of the strategy were listed as:

- 'Increased economic growth and employment opportunities, through the establishment of a reliable and cost efficient waterfront;
- Removal of MUA/ACTU control over the waterfront and therefore its use a political/industrial weapon;
- To demonstrate the effectiveness of the Government's industrial relations and transport reforms which will have a flow on effect into other sectors of industry.'

The option of an 'evolutionary' approach to waterfront reform was rejected in favour of an 'activist' approach involving the provocation of industrial action which 'would provide stevedores with the option of dismissing their employees and rehiring new people under different arrangements'. Of the two existing stevedoring companies (P&O and Patrick), Patrick was chosen because of its greater willingness to confront the MUA.

The Cabinet briefing paper argued that the key to the success of the strategy was 'to get the main ports going as soon as possible and then to establish a national pattern of growing movement on a daily basis until the strike collapses or becomes irrelevant'.[9] The government would need to be prepared to actively assist Patrick with a wide range of supportive actions including:

- The provision of strategic advice, legal assistance and physical security services;
- Managing public and business opinion;
- Chartering overseas tugs;
- The employment of foreign skilled labour including the arrangement of visas and accommodation;
- Substantial public expenditure including (in a later decision) up to A$250 million to fund redundancies.

The road to Dubai

Removing MUA members from Patrick's operations involved setting up a new company to train a non-unionized workforce which would be ready to move straight on to the wharves to replace the MUA workers.[10] Container Management Services (a Hong Kong registered company) was established as part of the front for the recruitment and training operation. Patrick contracted a former army commando officer, Mike Wells, to recruit and train the non-union stevedoring workforce. Wells established another new company, Fynwest, and advertised in *The Army* newspaper in late October 1997 for 'trade specialists'. The advertisement suggested it was looking for soldiers who were considering leaving the army, although in the end servicemen on leave were also recruited.

To secretly train the new workforce for instant readiness to take over from the MUA members, Patrick hired a section of the docks in Dubai for A\$800,000. It was calculated that about 260 workers would be hired with a core group of about 70 trained in Dubai. The plan was for them to leave Australia quietly in early December and be ready to commence Australian operations by late March 1998. There is substantial evidence that the government actively supported the Dubai operation at the highest levels and assisted in fast-tracking passports and visas.[11]

The plan involved establishing a mechanism for facilitating the swift and complete removal of the existing workforce. The trick here involved restructuring Patrick so that four new companies were set up to supply labour to run Patrick's stevedoring operations.[12] These companies were then asset stripped so that their only assets were the labour supply contracts.

The labour hire contracts included tight productivity targets and the capacity to hire non-union labour. The idea was that the companies would be unable to meet their targets. They would then become insolvent and the union workforce could be removed. The workers would not be sacked. They would simply be the victims of being employed by insolvent companies. The government would facilitate the process by providing up to \$250 million in redundancy payouts. Then Fynwest would be contracted to supply its Dubai-trained non-union workers who would be able to take over the docks instantly. It was an ingenious plan but it did have some serious flaws.

On 3 December 1997 as the Fynwest recruits prepared to leave Melbourne airport they were ambushed by journalists and camera crews who had been tipped off by the National Secretary of the MUA, John Coombs. Coombs in turn was being regularly briefed by a senior public servant (known as 'Number One Friend') with excellent access to information about the whole covert operation. The trainees still left for Dubai but, hounded by the media and with the port of Dubai facing the threat of international union action against ships using its ports, they returned ten days later.

Plan B: provocation and demonization

The response to the failure of the Fynwest/Dubai strategy was another closely related plan to break the MUA under the direction of the head of the National Farmers Federation (NFF), Don McGauchie.[13] McGauchie's plan was to set up more new companies known as Producers and Consumers (P&C) to train stevedores and run stevedoring operations. The P&C employees were a motley crew of farmers and unemployed contractors as well as some of the Dubai mercenaries who were still angry that their employment had not continued.[14]

Early in 1998 the NFF struck a deal to take over some of Patrick's operations at Melbourne's Webb Dock with the support of both State and Commonwealth governments. On 28 January 1998 armed security guards overran a small union picket, changed all the locks and took over 5 Webb Dock, allowing non-union workers to begin training with the clear intent of being available to work on other docks in the near future.[15]

The aim of both Chris Corrigan, Managing Director of Patrick, and the government from this point was to provoke the MUA into industrial action which would provide a pretext for sacking the MUA workforce, suing the union for damages and commencing deregistration procedures.[16] While the union was generally careful to avoid being provoked, industrial action taken at the Brisbane and Sydney (Port Botany) docks in February finally provided the excuse Corrigan was waiting for.

Throughout the six months leading up to the April mass sackings Corrigan and the government attempted to demonize the MUA and its leadership by hammering home a simple message about lazy wharfies.[17] They argued that the MUA workforce was grossly inefficient by world standards and that they were implementing a strategy for increasing waterfront productivity and therefore international competitiveness by breaking the MUA's monopoly over the waterfront labour market.

Debates about the relative efficiency of the Australian waterfront are complicated by problems of comparison.[18] It is hard, for example, to easily compare crane rates at a vast port like Singapore where all containers are being taken off at once, with rates in ports like Melbourne or Sydney where only some containers are being taken off at each port, requiring considerable shifting of containers. Along with a number of independent analysts the MUA also noted that productivity improvements are at least as likely to be achieved through improved management as by mass redundancies.[19] A range of commentators also noted that container movement costs represent only a tiny fraction of total shipping costs.[20] However the real aim of the government's strategy was to break the MUA and put the rest of the Australian union movement on notice by demonstrating that even the strongest of unions could be destroyed.

Dogs and thugs: 'A defining moment' in Australian industrial relations

At 11 p.m. on 7 April 1998 armed guards, some in black balaclavas and with dogs, moved on Patrick's operations across Australia, securing gates and changing locks. All 1,400 of Patrick's MUA workers were informed that they had been sacked, although this was done under the cover of the message that the labour hire companies they worked for had become insolvent.[21] Prime Minister Howard described the sackings as a 'defining moment' in the history of Australian industrial relations.[22]

The Reith/Corrigan strategy had always been based on the need to move swiftly to get the docks operating again with non-union labour. Their perception was that public opinion would be against the MUA and that union opposition would be quickly overcome.[23] Industrial action by other unions would be easily dealt with by secondary boycott laws. Again the plot did not work out quite as the plotters had hoped.

'MUA: Here to Stay': The battle to save unionized jobs

Mass pickets rapidly deployed at the gates of all Patrick's operations preventing trucks getting in or out. To evade legal action the MUA made sure the pickets were not called 'pickets' but rather 'Peaceful Community Assemblies'. Importantly the MUA strongly encouraged the general public to support the union and join the blockades. Patrick and the government had assumed that pickets would be quickly and easily swept aside by police action. While there certainly were attempts by police to move on the pickets they were unsuccessful in opening up Patrick's operations for a number of reasons.

The first was the sheer numbers of people involved.[24] On one famous cold autumn night in Melbourne early in the dispute, thousands of people converged on the docks in response to evidence of imminent police action. The next morning when the police began to move in, they withdrew in the face of another thousand building workers marched off building sites to the wharves. The combination of physical barricades and the constant presence of hundreds of people made it difficult to implement an effective strategy for breaking the picket lines, many of which became small communities complete with soup kitchens, toilet blocks and entertainment.[25] The dispute's signature slogan, 'MUA Here to Stay', became a common sight on car stickers and posters in many cities.

A second factor may well have been ambivalent police views about the dispute. Police forces in many Australian states were themselves being threatened by regressive industrial relations policies and the MUA made concerted attempts to build a rapport with police unions. The Australian Federal Police made it clear very early in the dispute that they would refuse to act as strike breakers.[26] When picketers shouted to the state police on the other side of the barricades 'join us – you'll be next', there is no doubt that they were heard.

The longer the lockout went on the more public opinion moved away from the government and Patrick. While the general public continued to view the MUA with suspicion there was also considerable dislike of the tactics of sacking an entire workforce simply because they were union members and of using armed guards and dogs to do it. Emerging evidence about the close links between the security guards involved and former senior police officers as well as the apparent use of riot gear from privatized prisons did nothing to improve public support for Patrick.[27]

While the MUA suffered a short term public relations set-back when children were shown being caught up in police actions to clear picket lines, the overall management of the media was relatively effective, with an emphasis on humanizing union members and their families to overcome the government's demonizing propaganda.[28] The MUA also ensured that it would not block the movement of cargo such as perishable goods and racehorses which might have had damaging public relations implications.[29] By mid-April public opinion had turned to the extent that, while most people still wanted waterfront reform, the majority were also sharply critical of the way which the dispute had been handled by the government.[30]

On 16 April Patrick gained an apparent victory when the Victoria Supreme Court granted an injunction preventing any member of the public from protesting at Melbourne's Swanston dock.[31] The Australian Council of Trade Unions Executive, which was meeting in Melbourne, responded by marching *en masse* to Swanston dock. The absurdity of a ban on all members of the public had the effect of adding a human rights dimension to the dispute, bringing a broader range of new supporters for the MUA cause.

The prospects for a rapid Patrick victory were further reduced by the actions taken by international unions. The International Transport Workers Federation quickly promised to black-ban ships loaded by Patrick's non-union labour, as did waterfront unions in the United States, Japan, South Africa and Europe.[32] Members of the International Longshore and Warehouse Union in the United States also began a series of noisy public demonstrations and pickets in Californian ports in support of the MUA.[33]

The Australian government blustered about the illegality of international solidarity campaigns and unsuccessful attempts were made to attack the ITWF actions in British courts.[34] In Australia the MUA was threatened with legal action by the Australian Consumer and Competition Commission (ACCC) for encouraging international boycotts. Whether this can actually be proved remains questionable.[35]

The threat of international action provided powerful moral and practical support to the MUA and the Australian union movement. The impact of international union actions and the dispute as a whole seriously concerned a range of major Australian exporters and importers who in turn expressed their concerns to the government.[36] By mid-April there was mounting evidence that the dispute had the potential to cause major problems for wool and mining exporters already concerned about the impact of the Asian financial crisis.[37]

On 11 April the MUA asked the Federal Court to grant an order reinstating the MUA workers on the grounds that their sacking had been illegal. On 21 April the Federal Court brought down a judgment indicating that there was indeed a plausible case that Patrick had acted illegally in sacking all its MUA workers and that all workers should be reinstated pending the hearing of the full conspiracy proceedings.[38] On 4 May 1998 the full bench of the High Court rejected Patrick's appeal against the Federal Court decision. The High Court did, however, vary the orders, giving greater discretion to the administrators of the four Patrick labour hire companies in relation to their financial viability.[39]

The immediate outcome was that the operations of the Patrick labour hire companies were handed over to administrators charged with seeing whether the companies could be made viable.[40] On 7 May MUA workers began returning to work. In early June a final settlement was reached involving almost 600 workers taking redundancy packages agreed on by the union. Crucially the settlement also maintained MUA coverage for all Patrick workers.

Outcomes and implications

Unsurprisingly all players tried to put the best possible spin on the outcome of the dispute. Twelve months after the resolution of the dispute a partial victory for the MUA is perhaps the fairest verdict, although both sides can claim some success as well as suffering some damage.[41]

Reith and Corrigan plausibly argued that they had substantially reduced the size of Patrick's workforce.[42] Yet while the government has certainly not abandoned its long-term plans to de-unionize the Australian waterfront, this was clearly a major set-back.[43] The MUA remains an effective presence on the docks.

Estimates of the financial losses suffered by Patrick varied between $30 and $100 million, although this will be offset by a wages bill reduced by up to $50 million per year.[44] The NFF companies were wound up in June with ominous noises from some of the workers about suing the NFF and Patrick for breach of contract.[45]

The outcome temporarily halted the full force of the assault on the Australian labour movement, but the opposing forces will regroup quickly and will learn from their mistakes. The failure of the Reith/Corrigan strategy was partly due to self-inflicted wounds. The decision to sack all MUA members from all ports, even the most efficient ones, was a severe tactical error as it exposed the exercise as primarily one focused on union busting rather than productivity. The government and Patrick also underestimated the strategic ability of the MUA leadership and the degree of support which would be mobilized from other Australian and international unions and from the general community.

For its part the MUA suffered a further 600 redundancies but maintained a fully unionized workforce at Patrick. In the longer term some of the broader implications of the dispute may be the most significant.

The Federal Court decision helped to clarify the way in which the Workplace Relations Act still protects freedom of association for union members in that it prohibits the dismissal of employees because of their union – or indeed non-union membership.[46] Another important victory was the exposure and defeat, at least in the short term, of Patrick's tactic of setting up dummy labour-hire companies as a means of getting rid of union workers.[47] Borrowed from United States, this will be harder to employ in Australia. As eminent lawyer and former Tax Avoidance

Royal Commissioner Frank Costigan noted, 'it is in my view as unacceptable for a company to shift assets around between subsidiaries and to strip assets from those particular subsidiaries which are likely to be faced with claims from employees and creditors as it was for companies to bury their assets in the harbour to avoid the payment of tax... It is almost beyond belief that such endeavours attracted the applause of the Government.'[48]

The dispute also united the Australian labour movement in an unprecedented way as well as forging important new alliances between the labour movement, community organizations and religious groups.[49] One of the ironic consequences of the 1998 dispute is that, like the 1890 maritime dispute, and for the same reasons, it may lead to a greater focus on parliamentary and legislative change. In doing so it will be important to remember that it was a Labor government which laid much of the ground for the Howard/Reith strategy. This is true not only because of the moves under Labor towards enterprise bargaining but also because of the Hawke and Keating governments' obsession with international free market competitiveness.

But the most important lessons from the 1998 waterfront dispute are to do with the broader challenge of building new kinds of social movement unionism at local, national and transnational levels. Important bonds developed between community organizations and the labour movement during this dispute. It is vital that these be built on and extend beyond calls for help with demonstrations or picket lines at times of crisis. A spirit of mutual respect and reciprocity will be essential, as will concerted efforts to explore other ways of working together both on campaigns and in building new kinds of financial and service provision – organizational forms which can explore alternatives to the dominance of deregulated markets and 'share-owning democracies'.

New forms of transnational social movement unionism will need to become a central focus of labour movement and emancipatory social movements. Again this is not just a matter of defensive tactics at critical moments, although the kinds of international solidarity actions demonstrated in this dispute will become increasingly important in dealing with globalized corporations. The longer-term task is to begin to bring together labour movement and social movement organizations in ways which provide alternative global and regional forums for democratic decision-making and non-capitalist relations of production and consumption.[50]

Rumours of the death of the trade union movement continue to be premature. It is still not clear for just how long the MUA is 'here to stay'. The Howard government and its corporate allies will of course be back. In some ways the game is the same as ever. Solidarity matters. But in other crucial ways the game is different: with no legal constraints and more complex, globalized arenas. A nostalgic reliance on old forms of union solidarity will be fatal. But the partial victory of the MUA and the Australian trade union movement in coalition with a wide range of community organizations and concerned citizens has at least provided some breathing space in which to explore new forms of resistance and political transformation.

Notes

1 An earlier version of this chapter including many additional references appeared in *Labour and Industry*, 9, no. 1 (1998), pp. 1–17. I would like to thank Nick Halfpenny for his invaluable work as research assistant on this project.
2 S. Carney, 'Crushing the Wharfies Fulfills a Liberal Dream', *The Age*, 11 April 1998, p. 8, and S. Macintyre, 'The Maritime Dispute Then and Now', Evatt Victoria Centre, Melbourne, April 1998.
3 See C. Fox, W. Howard and M. Pittard, *Industrial Relations in Australia* (Melbourne: Longman, 1995).
4 J. Wiseman, 'A Kinder Road to Hell: Labor and the Politics of Progressive Competitiveness in Australia', *The Socialist Register*, 1995.
5 G. Singleton, 'Industrial Relations: Pragmatic Change', in S. Prasser and G. Starr, eds, *Policy and Change: The Howard Mandate* (Melbourne: Hale and Ironmonger, 1997).
6 N. Way, 'The Right to Join a Union is the Real Issue', *The Australian*, 29 April 1998, p. 13.
7 See C. Kermond, 'The Story So Far on the Waterfront', *The Age*, 30 March 1998, p. 8; M. Steketee, 'Watershed', *The Weekend Australian*, 11–12 April 1998, p. 17.
8 E. Hannan, 'Docks Battle Plan', *The Age*, 5 June 1998, p. 1.
9 Ibid.
10 E. Hannan and C. Kermond, 'Docks Chief Admits Dubai Link', *The Age*, 4 Feb. 1998, p. 1.
11 J. Walker, 'Dubai Transcripts Raise More Doubt', *The Weekend Australian*, 9–10 May 1998, p. 9.
12 S. Marris, 'Creative Restructuring Highlights Opportunity for Firing Power', *The Weekend Australian*, 11–12 April 1998, p. 5.
13 N. Way, 'Dubai Fiasco Provided a Smoke Screen for Docks Coup', *The Weekend Australian*, Jan. 31–Feb. 1 1998, p. 1.
14 S. Rintoul, 'Howard's Army: a Soldier, a Farmer, a Bloke Off the Dole', *The Weekend Australian*, 11–12 April 1998, p. 1.
15 E. Hannan and C. Kermond, 'Rebel Dock Firm in Trade Row', *The Age*, 11 Feb. 1998, p. 2.
16 E. Hannan, 'Union Busting Laws Force Rethink on Dock Action', *The Age*, 26 Feb. 1998, p. 6.

17 P. Reith, 'Union Inhibits Efficient Port Culture', *The Age*, 30 Jan. 1998, p. 13; C. Corrigan, 'Rocking the Boat to Reform the Docks', *The Age*, 12 March 1998, p. 13.

18 M. Steketee, 'World's Best Practice? We're Almost There Already', *The Weekend Australian*, 25–26 April 1998, p. 6.

19 M. Steketee, 'The Shipping News: Who's Telling the Truth', *The Weekend Australian*, 11–12 April 1998, p. 15.

20 J. Quiggan, 'Perils of Waterfront Reform', *The AFR*, 29 Jan. 1998, p. 10; T. Colebatch, 'In the Dock: Just How Bad are our Ports?', *The Age*, 29 April 1998, p. 6.

21 J. Hughes, 'Axe Falls on 1400 Wharf Jobs', *The Australian*, 8 April 1998, pp. 1–2.

22 S. Carney, 'Crushing the Wharfies Fulfills a Liberal Dream', *The Age*, 11 April 1998, p. 8.

23 E. Hannan, 'Dock Workers Struggle in the Face of Waning Public Sympathy', *The Age*, 20 Feb. 1998, p. 15.

24 R. Gibson, 'The Human Wall Prepares for a Test of its Strength', *The Age*, 21 April 1998, p. 4.

25 M. Bachelard, 'On the Picket Line, Uneasy Calm before Industrial Storm', *The Australian*, 30 Jan. 1998, p. 2.

26 J. MacDonald, 'Police Won't Act on Docks', *The Age*, 9 April 1998, p. 6.

27 B. Haslem and S. Marris, 'State Will Investigate the Source of Riot Gear', *The Australian*, 2 Feb. 1998, p. 2.

28 C. Kermond, 'Children Warned Off Waterfront', *The Age*, 16 April 1998, p. 4.

29 T. Sutherland 'Deal for Farmer Produce', *The Australian*, 23 April 1998, p. 4.

30 E. Hannan 'Docks Fight Mishandled, Poll Finds', *The Age*, 21 April 1998, p. 4.

31 P. Gregory, 'Picketers have Caused Mayhem, Says Judge', *The Age*, 21 April 1998, p. 4.

32 R. Skelton and Agencies, 'Patrick Faces Bans in Japan, Europe', *The Age*, 18 April 1998, p. 5; C. Stewart and Agencies, 'Japanese, Africans put Bans on Cargo', *The Australian*, 23 April 1998, p. 4; P. Wilmoth, J. Silvester and L. Johnson, 'World Ban Threat', *The Sunday Age*, 1 Feb. 1998, pp. 1–2.

33 R. Gibson, 'Union Forces Cargo About Turn', *The Age*, 28 May 1998, p. 2.

34 F. Brenchley, 'Union May Have to Quit Britain', *The AFR*, 14 April 1998, p. 4.

35 K. Murphy, 'Fels Keeps an Eye on Melbourne Waterfront', *The AFR*, 2 Feb. 1998, p. 3.

36 I. Porter and K. Murphy, 'Toyota and Car Makers Fear Freeze', *The AFR*, 30 Jan. 1998, p. 9.

37 M. Skulley, 'Wool and Mining Exports Miss Ships in Stand-off', *The AFR*, 18–19 April 1998, p. 4.

38 Federal Court of Australia, *Maritime Union of Australia* vs. *Patrick Stevedores No. 1 Pty Ltd & Others*; M. Gordon, 'PM's Dock Strategy Dealt a Heavy Blow', *The Age*, 22 April 1998, p. 1.

39 E. Hannan, 'Back to Work – For Some', *The Age*, 5 May 1998, p. 1.

40 L. Taylor, 'Administrators Treading Water in Peace Deal Bid', *The AFR*, 2–3 May 1998, p. 4.

41 See M. Davis, 'Reform Tide Yet to Turn', *Australian Financial Review*, 6 April 1999, p. 14.

42 See J. Hughes, S. Rintoul and N. Way, 'Waterfront War: The Wash Up', *The Weekend Australian*, 27–28 June 1998, pp. 22–3.

43 D. McKenzie and J. Ellicott, 'Reith Solicits NFF Shopping List for Next Wave of Reforms', *The Australian*, 18 Feb. 1998, p. 1.

44 J. Hughes, S. Rintoul and N. Way, 'Waterfront War: The Wash Up', *The Weekend Australian*, 27–28 June 1998, pp. 22–3.

45 E. Hannan, 'NFF Plan for Docks Abandoned', *The Age*, 12 June 1998, p. 3.

46 T. MacDermott, 'Tug of Law Haunts Docks', *The Australian*, 22 April 1998, p. 15.

47 S. Long, 'Outsourcing: the Hidden Way Business is Beating the Unions', *The AFR*, 18–19 April 1998, pp. 26–7.

48 F. Costigan, 'How Dare Howard Applaud Patrick', *The Age*, 23 April 1998, p. 17.

49 L. Martin, 'Religious Leaders Criticise Coalition on Docks', *The Age*, 14 April 1998, p. 4.

50 See, for example, R. Moody, *Workers in a Lean World: Unions in the International Economy* (London: Zed Books, 1998).

Index

Note: Authors of multiauthored texts are listed with the name of the first author in brackets.